Archives of American Time

Archives
of American Time

Literature and Modernity in the Nineteenth Century

Lloyd Pratt

PENN

University of Pennsylvania Press

Philadelphia

Published by
University of Pennsylvania Press
Philadelphia, Pennsylvania 19104-4112

Printed in the United States of America on acid-free paper

10   9   8   7   6   5   4   3   2   1

A Cataloging-in-Publication record is available from the Library of Congress
ISBN 978-0-8122-4208-9

For Karl

Contents

Introduction
Written to the Future

[I]t is the present's responsibility for its own self-definition of its own mission that makes it into a historical period in its own right and that requires the relationship to the future fully as much as it involves the taking of a position on the past.

—*Fredric Jameson,* A Singular Modernity

Nostalgia is not always about the past; it can be retrospective but also prospective. Fantasies of the past determined by needs of the present have a direct impact on realities of the future.

—*Svetlana Boym,* The Future of Nostalgia

In the winter of 1829, a handful of young women and men on the island of Nantucket began gathering the first Thursday of every month to write the history of the future. Before their meetings, each member of the group composed a short piece of writing. Upon arrival, they deposited their anonymous contributions in a small bag, or "budget," that gave the group its name: the Budget Society. One by one, each piece was drawn from the bag; one by one, each piece was subjected to friendly critique. The Budget Society wrote on many topics and in several genres. Their compositions included lyric accounts of baked beans, a caustic satire in dialect of an imagined inauguration speech by Andrew Jackson, and at least one barbed poem criticizing a member unable to endure even the mildest criticism of her writing.

The Budget Society's most telling artifact is a fictional epistle with the heading "Mouth of the Columbia River, NW Coast, February 3 AD 2000." This composition is an exercise in proleptic historiography. Its author adopts the persona of a letter writer in the future corresponding with a contemporary about the customs of nineteenth-century Nantucketers. From the imagined vantage point of the year 2000, this fictional descendant of the island and amateur historian recounts the peculiar mores of his nineteenth-century ancestors. In a dizzying and illuminating moment of self-reference, he also explains how his knowledge of his ancestors' ways derives from some "old manuscripts" of the Budget Society.[1] Detailing the conduct of the society's meetings and its goals, he impugns the women's taste for novels and applauds the ancient writings of the "chaste" Benjamin Franklin and William Ellery Channing. This dispatch notes as well the predictive savvy of the members of the society, who anticipate(d) the ability of twenty-first-century Americans to fly from one end to the other of America's transcontinental geography in steam-powered vessels.

This 1829 letter typifies the way many American writers came to manage their self-representation in anticipation of the future during the first half of the nineteenth century. That period's amateur and professional writers alike staged dialogues with the future undertaken less for reasons of vanity than out of a desire to influence how their descendants would understand their relationship to the past and in turn come to know themselves. As Anthony Giddens has written of utopian discourse, such letters to the future constitute "prescriptions or anticipations" that "set a baseline for future states of affairs."[2] In the early national and antebellum United States, these letters to the future were encoded as familiar literary genres, and they were organized around shaping how later generations would think of their descent from their ancestors, thus influencing how ensuing generations would conceptualize their own present tense. Like the Budget Society epistolarian's correspondence, such writing effectively set the parameters of "life to come" by passing down teleological and eschatological narrative structures designed to realize the nation's future history. Its authors occupied the future—our present—by captioning their own and earlier periods as the origin of an inevitable national fate and by bequeathing to us certain familiar narrative genres organized around imagining that fate. Over the past two centuries, their resilient narrative structures have often led those who study early and nineteenth-century American writing to imagine that the future these authors predicted actually came to pass—that to live on U.S. soil during this time has inevitably been to experience oneself as an "American" or one kin to Americans. Generations of literary critics and historians have argued that their own moment was finally fulfilling—for better or for worse—the future first figured in such writing. In important ways we live even now in the house these writers built.

In this book, I attempt to push back against these early efforts to populate the horizon with Americans. I do this by focusing on the often ignored disaggregating potential of the period's literature and its peculiar account of time. In this effort, I take up the increasingly accepted view that the early national and antebellum United States was the site of a conflicted experience of time characteristic of modernity. Svetlana Boym has argued that modernity allows "for multiple conceptions of time."[3] In this context, American temporality can be understood "not as a teleology of progress or transcendence but as a superimposition and coexistence of heterogeneous times."[4] I also emphasize that this particular temporal conjuncture was deeply inhospitable to the consolidation of national and racial identity. I seek to understand the nineteenth century as something other than a conflict to be overcome or a moment of transition that is interesting primarily for what it tells us about the origins of our current seemingly calcified categories of nation and race. I am more interested in the fact that, at this moment, when American writers began self-consciously to quest after a future in which national and racial identity would reign triumphant over all, the end result was that time was restructured in such a way as to begin foreclosing on that particular future. I argue that this writing's characteristic formal features—the outlines of its genres as well as its literary tropes—trace the intermittent interest of American authors in the extraliterary conflicts between different modalities of time that forbid the homogeneously linear time whose emergence has sometimes been associated with early American nationalism. In addition to suggesting that this literature gives us a measure of access to the temporalities that defined such conflicts, and thus the context of this literature's composition, I also argue that this literature superadded certain specifically literary temporalities to those already circulating in the extraliterary settings of nineteenth-century America. If the interest of American authors in the everyday lives of North Americans, the political commitments of those authors, and their intellectual inclinations led them to archive and rearticulate the conflicting experiences and understandings of time that defined life in this America, then their resort to the conventions of ancient, classical, and emergent literary genres meant that they also exposed literate Americans to antecedent and nascent orders of time in addition to those already informing their experience of daily life. In other words, I argue that their writing both documented and compounded a conflict of times that inhibited the consolidation of U.S. national and racial identity. I adopt from recent social theory and from postcolonial studies the view that modern time is internally differentiated in unprecedented ways that are only now coming to be understood. I also propose that the expansion of print and transportation technologies magnified this pluralization of time when it made literature's various printed avatars increasingly commonplace. In this sense, I claim that the print and reading revolutions that distinguish this period did not come close to achieving the homogenization of time with which they have sometimes been associated in American literature, American literary studies, and U.S. history. I describe this period's literature as instead having helped to stimulate the near collapse of processes of national and racial formation at a conjuncture that the literature itself (and later scholarship) routinely associates with the opposite event.

For reasons that I will explore in more detail later, this internal failure of nationalism and race in the United States has received less attention than it warrants. This period's writing has bequeathed to us a way of thinking in terms of social inevitabilities that has often controlled literary critical and historiographical approaches to time in the colonial American and U.S. national environments. Such approaches have, in turn, supported a particular portrait of the social fortunes of nineteenth-century America. As I indicate later, commentators on both sides of the Atlantic began to argue as early as the late eighteenth century that the emerging national print culture of the United States would Americanize its readers by homogenizing time. National literature, national newspapers, and other nation-based print media would function as the nation's temporal infrastructure. In the nineteenth-century United States, thinkers as seemingly dissimilar as Nathaniel Hawthorne and Frederick Douglass, as well as other authors I study here, would contribute to thinking in this vein (when they were not countervailing it). They implied that new modes of industrial printing, emerging models of professional authorship, and a revivified cultural nationalism would hasten the full-scale emergence of a soon-to-be-secured American national identity. In polemics and asides, they suggested that print culture's specific contribution to this emerging American national identity would be to supply U.S. citizens with a virtual experience of time as linear progress that they all could share. These authors often contradict themselves and each other; there can be no absolute uniformity of opinion across such a wide range of writing. The combined effect is nevertheless to suggest in an overarching way that progress would quickly emerge as America's common time and as the basis of a renewed sense of national belonging. In an exceedingly diverse nation, this collective temporality, which would later be identified as "homogeneous empty time," would be a crucial unifying resource. The emergence of a homogeneous empty time associated with progress and delivered via the medium of print culture would produce a future dominated not just by America but also by Americans.

It will surprise no one familiar with nineteenth-century American writing to learn that the vision that pervades this period's writing is of a United States inclined uniformly toward a single glorious destiny. The strong counterevidence of form suggesting that this period and its literature articulate a conflicted experience of time working against this notion of destiny is less well known. The early national and antebellum United States did give us the Young Americans, the benevolent kingdom, and the Transcendentalists, all of whom were indebted at some level to an ideology of linear progress. Yet, however much this period's writing may seem to anticipate a uniform national destiny emerging from the narrowing down of future possibility that the American ideology of progress envisions, the very same literature articulates at the level of form a modernity defined by not one but several distinct temporal dispositions. This literature also deepens the period's temporal repertoire; it supplements the orders of time that emerged from industrial manufacture, slave economies, and the like with the anachronistic temporalities that any literary genre (re)introduces into the present. Stuart Sherman has argued that a "given narrative will inevitably, by the particulars of its form, absorb and register some of the temporalities at work in the world that surrounds its making."[5] If literature not only "absorb[s] and register[s]" but also superadds to the temporal landscape it inhabits, then it only makes sense to say that when this literature speaks of an inevitable future emerging from a uniformly structured present tense, it speaks against evidence that it routinely manifests to the contrary. There might be a plurality of futures implicit in this literature, but it offers no reliable prediction of the nation's singular destiny. Despite its often well-articulated wish that the nation share a consistent experience of time around which its members might unite, the available evidence contradicts the idea that this experience of national simultaneity actually came to pass. This literature combined the temporalities of everyday life with the untimely chronotypes that its conventions of genre demanded and then redistributed both of them to Anglophone readers.[6] This literature pluralized time. It did not purify it.

This book therefore deflects the overtures of this earlier period's letter to the future by attending to certain aspects of time's articulation—in this period and through its literature—that have been downplayed or ignored. Chapter 1 explains how the classic American literature of roughly the first half of the nineteenth century cites and revises certain late eighteenth- and early nineteenth-century European ideas about historical time, progress, and destiny to support specific U.S. national ideologies of historical time and the future. Here I give an account of what we might call early American modernization theory, and I indicate the extent to which something called "print culture" was figured—in fact, figured itself—as a uniquely homogenizing and nationalizing force. I identify certain "figures of print" that emerge early in the nineteenth century and persist in later historiographic and theoretical accounts of the advent of modernity. These figures of print helped to suppress the complex industrial history of printing, authorship, distribution, and copyright currently being recovered by the history of the book, while at the same time they encouraged the reduction of literature's many avatars to a uniform fetish called print culture lacking in both form and content.

In the next three chapters I offer a counterhistory of time in this period's literature that focuses on recapturing at a reasonably detailed level something of that form and content.[7] I demonstrate how three of this period's more influential genres have been repeatedly linked to the work of consolidating "social totalities" (nation, region, and race), while at the same time I show how they seek to diagnose certain pivotal aspects of the conjuncture called modernity. This is a literature of modernity in that it is "contradictory, critical, ambivalent, and reflective on the nature of time."[8] I also propose that these genres, as well as literary tropes such as dialect writing and ekphrasis, register and compound a pluralization of time—a splitting of time into temporalities—characteristic of modernity. This literature archives the extraliterary emergence of linear progressive time, a laboring time that is a compound of repetitive and static temporalities, and a politicized revolutionary messianic time—each one of which is associated with one or more of modernity's signal economic and societal features. Yet I focus just as much (or more) on how this literature also overlays these temporalities with literary ones pulled from the past and the near future into the present by virtue of the fact that every author must inhabit at least some of the conventions of literary genre. This literature's characteristic formal features track and compound, I suggest, an experience of time that precipitated superlocal experiences of belonging and encouraged detachment from broader supralocal identity categories. As various theories of modernity, global capitalism, and postcolonialism explain, the spread of market capitalism, now called globalization, does not homogenize the globe but rather involves the tactical "production of locality."[9] This production of locality proceeds, I contend, more in temporal than in spatial terms, and it confounds the broader identifications typically associated with nation, region, and race in conditions of modernity by encouraging identification across and within these naturalized categories of modern selfhood. Literature played a significant role in the production of locality, and its role is irreducible to the movements of global capitalism.

In this book, therefore, the self-nominations associated with nation, region, and race turn out to matter somewhat less than and much differently from what has been imagined when it comes to the cultural work of the literature of the first half of the nineteenth century. Literate Americans spent their laboring days, and their hours of leisure reading, negotiating a conflicting experience of time that made internally consistent collective selfhood(s) largely impracticable. In this respect, I elicit through a reading of literary form a modern subjectivity rendered increasingly invisible over the course of the last two centuries. I do not locate in the past only Americans, whites, and other figures of abstract identity, a gesture that allows nationalism and race to colonize both the past and the present. I recount a reading subject faced with a relationship to the future in which that future is a disconcertingly undefined vector made so by virtue of the fact that any given present is felt to incline toward several different futures (and pasts) at once. I also suggest that some of this reading subject's most significant political tendencies can be traced to an encounter with literature. This subject resembles, for reasons outlined later, the "torn divided monster" that D. H. Lawrence once characterized as America's peculiar offering to the world. However, this subject is not immune to or insulated from his environment, as the literary modernist Lawrence might have had it:[10] he is instead made "monstrous" by it.

In telling the story of American modernity and American literature in this way, without the emergence of social identity as a structuring entelechy, I seek as much to reanimate our own present tense as I do to reorient our knowledge of the past. One consequence of reading the past as this literature would (sometimes) have us do is a shutting down of our own present as a site of possibility. The inevitability thesis that is one of this period's enduring contributions to world literature seeks to claim the present—our present, any present—as a direct lineal descendent whose (in)hospitableness to individual political and subjective self-realization has been, as it were, genetically predetermined.[11] In its most programmatically future-oriented moments, which are in a counterintuitive sense also its most conservative ones, this literature takes up the conventions of progressive historiography and discourages us from understanding the past as defined by a series of breaks and ruptures; it also discounts the view that any given present (or past) portends a variety of different futures. It asks us to lose sight of our own moment as the potential site of origin for many possible future presents and so forbids the sort of "utopian realism" Anthony Giddens has encouraged.[12] It encourages us to ignore the disaggregating force of literature in modernity and recommends instead the sense of "false necessity" that Roberto Unger has described.[13]

I pursue my interest in this literature's unclosed openings onto the future by way of extended engagements with the novels known as historical romances, the regional writing called Southwestern humor, and the (auto)-biographies categorized as African American life writing. As my second, third, and fourth chapters outline in more detail, it is a curious and significant fact of American literary history that these (and other) categories of genre have been so firmly and so often tied to the project of nationalism and to racial formation. Most of the credit for the recent resurgence of a paradigmatic approach linking genre to nation and race, as well as for the limited view of literature's relationship to time that this approach reflects, goes to Benedict Anderson's work on what he calls print capitalism—a category he associates specifically with the realist novel and the daily newspaper. In particular, his account of the realist novel's production of an experience of simultaneity and homogenous empty time continues to be taken for granted in many quarters. Yet early and more recent responses to Anderson's imagined communities thesis, as well as Anderson's more recent writings, have indicated the extent to which correlating genre with temporal or social homogeneity ignores one of the most salient facts about the history of literary form, and in particular the theory of genre.[14] As genres take shape over the course of one or several centuries, they cannibalize and adapt previous genres. Along the way, they accrete a range of different and competing temporalities. As Wai Chee Dimock has recently argued, this trait not only defines the novel, as Bakhtin suggested, but also applies equally to any genre. All genres are "[b]orn of the local circumstances that shape them," but they also "ech[o] other forms shaped by circumstances more or less alike."[15] For this and other reasons, postcolonial literary studies early on redirected our understanding of time in the realist novel away from the Andersonian account of simultaneity. Homi Bhabha and Partha Chatterjee, in particular, identified Anderson's seemingly social scientific account of nation formation as resting on the bedrock of an imperfect theory of genre, and they reversed Anderson's account of nationalism by way of a refigured account of the realist novel. Where Anderson proposed that the novel articulates homogeneous empty time, <u>postcolonial studies showed how the realist novel articulates competing orders of time</u>. Dimock has summarized, for example, the challenge that Bhabha's work posed to the Andersonian account of the novel: "For Bhabha, then, the breakdown of a single, enforceable chronology stands as one of the most powerful challenges to the sovereignty of the state. It directly contradicts the regime of 'simultaneity' adduced by Benedict Anderson as the hallmark of the nation. Against that regime—against Anderson's account of national time as 'homogeneous empty time . . . measured by clock and calendar'—Bhabha calls attention to many alternate temporalities: 'disjunctive' narratives, written at the margins of the nation and challenging its ability to standardize, to impose an official ordering of events."[16] By reinhabiting the literary genre of the novel in the way that Dimock describes, postcolonial theory effectively rewrote our understanding of the sociopolitical genre called the nation. When it destabilized standing accounts of the temporality of the realist novel, postcolonial theory also destabilized received notions about the nation across a range of intellectual fields. It dissolved the coherence of the nation as a category of belonging by dissolving the coherence of one of the nation's most recognizable imputed sources: the genre of the novel. And it made analysis of literary form a full partner in the interdisciplinary enterprise of postcolonial studies.

This revised account of the temporality of the novel genre, and of genre more generally, broke with an intellectual tradition dating to late eighteenth- and early nineteenth-century Germany, a tradition that viewed literature and its genres as expressive of what Bhabha calls "social totalities." We see this view of literature as socially expressive represented in the influential nineteenth-century editor Rufus Griswold's introduction to *The Prose Writers of America* of 1845: "Literature, the condensed and clearly expressed thought of the country, will keep pace with its civilization; and without any straining after originality, without any tricks of diction, without any aim but to press the truth directly, earnestly and courageously upon the popular heart, under the inspiration of an enlightened love of country, and the guidance of a high cultivation, our authors will be sufficiently distinctive and national, in both manner and matter."[17] Hegel had earlier extended this view of national literatures specifically to the issue of genre. For him and for others, the three "natural" genres—epic, lyric, and drama—track the progressive development of individuals and of nations. Similarly, as George Dekker explains in his discussion of the American historical romance, "the Enlightenment philosophical historians who shaped the social thought of Goethe, Scott, and Cooper believed that peoples with the same basic mode of subsistence were bound to have the same or at least very similar political institutions, military practices, and artistic forms."[18] As Pascale Casanova has recently argued, and as the contributors to recent *PMLA* (2007) and *New Literary History* (2003) special issues on genre and world literature confirm, Hegel and other influential thinkers from this and later periods reformulated classical genre theory, laboring to align particular genres with social totalities such as the nation.[19] Stephen Owen demonstrates, for example, how a "nineteenth-century evolutionary account of genres seems to have been so thoroughly internalized that it survives as unreflective assumptions by scholars who would reject such claims on a theoretical level."[20] According to Owen, moreover, "Hegel's genre scheme, popularized, has been so well digested that it has become the very tissue of the educated mind."[21] As this recent scholarship on genre indicates, modern genre criticism emerged alongside and in collaboration with the nation form. This kind of criticism has often provided the nation with an air of coherence in the era of modernity by introducing abstract aesthetic categories that appear to unify unruly literatures and, in turn, the peoples that produced them. Of course, Anderson and those who followed him reversed this model's order of determination. If for Hegel (and later for Lukács) genres express historical change, then for the Andersonians they produce it. However, neither Anderson nor the school of criticism he inspired broke the mutually occlusive bind linking genre to nation.

Extending the postcolonial critique into the current critical conjuncture, Casanova, Dimock, and Gayatri Spivak, among others, have soundly rejected this habituated assertion of the coherence of social totalities vis-à-vis literary genres and their imputed organization of time. These critics dispute the idea that either genres or the social totalities they have been said to "express" (or to create) are clearly bounded, internally coherent, or temporally homogeneous. They argue instead for a renewed attention to the category of genre that (implicitly) reworks postcolonial theory for the broadest possible context. For these critics, reexamining the category of genre in general, specific genres in particular, and the temporalities of both, dissolves the boundary separating the formerly national literatures from one another and from the world, past and present. This renewed interest in genre's relationship to time recalls how postcolonial critique led British literary and cultural studies to acknowledge the presence of the colony in the imperial center and its literature. In Chapter 1, I address in more detail the objection that the nineteenth-century United States was not, properly speaking, a postcolonial nation and that therefore the extension of the post-colonial critique to the U.S. context is inapt. For now, it is enough to recall Edward Said's classic account of the contrapuntal nature of empire, as well as Amy Kaplan's " 'Left Alone with America,' " which together indicate the extent to which the postcolonial critique of nation was not simply, or even primarily, an argument about the postcolonial nations of the second half of the twentieth century.[22] This critique aimed to change our view of the imperial metropole as much as it attended to the experience of the former colonies. The world literature critique calls for a similar refashioning of literary study in part through the lens of genre. It asks us to acknowledge how any individual genre, as well as any individual instance of a genre, imports the formal, thematic, and chronotypical concerns of several different national contexts and chronological moments into what can only heuristically be called the present tense of a single national tradition. As even Rufus Griswold acknowledged in 1845, "[T]here never was and never can be an exclusively national literature. All nations are indebted to each other and to preceding ages for the means of advancement; and our own, which from our various origins may be said to be at the confluence of the rivers of time which have swept through every country, can with less justice than any other be looked to for mere novelties in art and fancy."[23] What seems to be exceptional about America here is its utter lack of exceptionality. Like any national literature, American writing has no single time to call its own. Instead, it stands at the conjunction of the rivers—plural—of time.

Yet the literary genres that this book attends to have in fact been characterized as either expressively or productively "American" ones. These genres are also distinctly concerned with documenting and commenting upon the new orders of time that modernity introduced. My attention to genre here will therefore attempt to participate in the broader effort just described of questioning how certain implicit notions of literary genre function to stabilize against all odds the national literary studies model. Over the past two decades, the field of American literary studies has increasingly turned away from the nation as an organizing principle. Indeed, most critics now working in this field would instinctively reject an unselfconsciously nation-based account of American literature. As early as 2001, Bruce Burgett titled an *American Literary History* review essay "American Nationalism—R.I.P."[24] Clearly the idea that literature self-evidently relates to an internally coherent national culture has receded in significance. To name just two of the more influential examples of how this critique has flowered, the recent spatial turn in literary studies has reframed American literature as a hemispheric, transnational, global, diasporic, and oceanic enterprise. Although I contend in my epilogue that certain versions of the spatial turn have the potential to elide a temporal logic that reproduces the nation form in code, the spatial turn has in a practical sense effectively redirected literary and cultural studies toward thinking in new ways about humanistic scholarship. Its focus on contact zones, extranational territories, and supralocal systems has given us an "American" literary studies designed to trouble that comfortable designation. The most compelling recent contributions to the history of the book, such as Meredith McGill's *American Literature and the Culture of Reprinting, 1834–1853*; Matthew P. Brown's *The Pilgrim and the Bee*; Leon Jackson's *The Business of Letters*; and *A History of the Book in America*, volume 3, *The Industrial Book, 1840–80*, also reshape our view of how industrial bookmaking, the book trades, periodical culture, authorship, copyright, and reading actually worked during this period. Rather than describing a single national literary culture or print capitalism writ large, these and other studies recount a fractured literary marketplace that is articulated at the global and the local scales but that does not begin to look distinctively national until at least the middle of the nineteenth century—and perhaps not even then. As the history of the book increasingly tells the story, early national and antebellum American literature was not unified in any obvious way, nor was it self-evidently unifying.

I propose here that in order to realize the full transformative potential of the postcolonial critique, the spatial turn, and the history of the book— all in relation to the long history of American literary study—[Americanists will need to reinhabit and trouble the distinctions of genre and the attendant arguments about time that have helped to organize American literary practice, American literary studies, and the teaching of American literature since their inception.] With the notable exception of the sentimental novel and perhaps the lyric, the productive scrutiny that postcolonial studies brought to bear on the stabilizing influence of an implicit idea of literary genre—its organization of time, its relationship to nationalism—has not been present in the field of nineteenth-century American literary studies.[25] This absence is noteworthy in the context of a period preoccupied, as I endeavor to show later, with reorganizing time so as to service the expansionist designs of what John L. O'Sullivan called "the great nation of futurity" while developing a distinctively national literature. As I have suggested, the strength of the postcolonial critique of genre followed from the fact that it collapsed the idea of a nationally expressive or nationally productive (European or postcolonial) literature from within by addressing that idea's oversimplification of time in the realist novel. This critique first reinhabited the suppositions about genre that had given life and form to current dogma about the relationship between genre, time, and nation; then rejected those suppositions; and finally rewrote our understanding of the novel genre, time, and the nation. The fact that Americanists have done somewhat less to contest how calcified ideas about genre and its relationship to time have organized writing and instruction in this field means that genre is one of this field's few remaining stabilizing touchstones. This relative indifference to rethinking genre as a mechanism of time means that genre classification's proven capacity to overwrite nuance and the unresolved—its power to co-alesce the fantasy of a stable present tense, an internally coherent nation form, or a consolidated social identity of some other kind—has gone largely unaddressed. The recent *Cambridge Introduction to the Nineteenth-Century American Novel* opens, "Defining the novel is easy."[26] Gregg Crane goes on to provide a careful and well-researched account of the nineteenth-century American novel that belies this opening statement—a statement admittedly made in the context of an introduction to the nineteenth-century novel rather than a close analysis of it. However, the initial ease of definition here recalls the extent to which genre can emerge as the totem where the nation once stood. One might also point to the proliferation of new undergraduate curricula designed to acknowledge the perceived bankruptcy of the national literatures model, but that do so by turning to categories of genre for a new sense of coherency.

In this context, my usage of the categories of genre will be unfamiliar. If American literary criticism has sometimes displayed a taste for neat taxo-nomies of genre traceable to the nineteenth century, I focus more on the internal *in*coherencies of genres than on cleanly divisible categories.[27] I use genre primarily as a heuristic principle that allows us to see both how the field of nineteenth-century American literary studies has come to be orga-nized and how close attention to conventionally exemplary as well as mar-ginalized instances of a given genre speak to the layered temporalities of American modernity. In this latter respect, I follow Wai Chee Dimock's suggestive prospect for a new model of genre criticism in *Through Other Continents*. In her chapter on "genre as world system," Dimock begins by acknowledging those critiques, from Benedetto Croce to Jacques Derrida, that suggest the inability of any account of genre to provide a full measure of the thing it claims to describe. These critiques lead Dimock to "invoke genre less as a law, a rigid taxonomic landscape, and more as a self-obsolet-ing system, a provisional set that will always be bent and pulled and stretched by its many subsets."[28] By a "self-obsoleting system," Dimock means one whose constituent components are always in motion. Where John Frow emphasizes that in order to make meaning one must inhabit a recognizable genre, Dimock charges us to recognize more of what any individual genre has to offer by way of habitation and meaning making.[29] For Dimock, genres are dissolving and constantly reassembling conjunctures of literary forms drawn from the *longue durée* of literary history. In taking this position, Dimock adverts to a view articulated in Fredric Jameson's classic discussion of the romance genre in *The Political Unconscious*: "[P]roperly used, genre theory must always in one way or another project a model of the coexistence or tension between several generic modes or strands: and with this methodological axiom the typologizing abuses of traditional genre criticism are definitely laid to rest."[30] For Dimock, this "scattering and mixing of genres [makes] literary history an exemplary instance of human history, which is to say, multipath, multiloci, multilingual."[31] If Dimock is right, moreover, then literary history does not exemplify what it has often been made out to signify: the selfsame integrity of a single people.

With Dimock's provocative outline in mind, I reframe the literary genres I address as complex archival forms and as actors in the realization of America's modernity. In *The Consequences of Modernity*, Anthony Giddens has convincingly argued that modernity is intensively self-reflexive. I suggest that nineteenth-century American literature was a crucial part of this self-reflexivity. Focusing on the social sciences, Giddens rejects the notion that modern knowledge-work provides a cumulative empirical account of a stable object called society. Instead, the social scientist participates in a feedback loop that destabilizes the object of study. The knowledge of society produced by social scientists provides members of modern society with a mode of self-understanding that restructures society itself. We can think of nineteenth-century literature in similar terms, especially regarding its relationship to time. This literature routinely positions itself as providing a diagnostic account of the society it describes, and it takes particular care to diagram the temporal conditions that obtain in that society. What Stuart Sherman says of eighteenth-century British literature applies here too: this literature provides a "reading" of the temporalities of modern life.[32] In so doing, it refracts its readers' understanding of time. In this respect, this period's literature participates in the mutually constituting double hermeneutic that Giddens identifies as a primary characteristic of modernity. Although Giddens associates that double hermeneutic specifically with sociological knowledge, it should not be too much of a stretch for those familiar with nineteenth-century American literature—especially the historical romances, Southwestern humor, and African American life writing examined here—to accept that this literature also aims to produce a diagnostic account of modernity and modern time. Importantly, however, this literature not only archives (in the transitive sense) the temporalities of its era, comments on them, and feeds them back to its readers—reconstituting those readers' understanding of time in the process. The anachronistic formal precedents that inhere in any genre guarantee that this literature also functions as an archive of temporalities drawn from moments other than its own—temporalities that it returns to the present. In other words, this literature's reflexivity works not only to reflect and comment upon the moment of its composition. This literature comprises a strangely reflexive archive of times drawn not strictly from its own present tense and that are in no way conducive to the constitution of a selfsame "American" subject. [This literature restructures its readers' understanding of time, as Anderson has argued, but it does so in more ways than one. The temporality of modernity that this literature articulates is cross-cut with different orders of time, and not all of them "belong" to the present tense of its composition.]

Considering nineteenth-century American writing in terms of its recourse to and deformation of particular literary genres, as well as its diagnostic interest in modern time, reveals the extent to which nineteenth-century American literature, notwithstanding the desire of many writers and editors to create a national literature, is more properly thought of as a literature of modernity. Its concerns are those that distinguish the era of modernity—the distanciation of time-space relationships, in particular, but also the reordering of social relations more generally. By attending to issues of literary genre and literary figures—by attending to this literature as such rather than as, say, a more generalized form of print culture—we gain a more refined sense of the exact role that these materials played in constituting modernity. When Anderson focused on one particular aspect of modernity, the emergence of the nation form, his approach proved particularly attractive to a field long interested in the specifically national qualities of this period's writing. His argument also brought questions of literary form to bear in the context of a broadening interest in the wider social significance and socially constituting force of literature. Yet I demonstrate later that an even closer attention to issues of literary form yields a different sense of this literature and, consequently, a different sense of American modernity. To be sure, literature played a role in the making of American modernity, but that role included the drawing of improper temporalities from other historical moments into the present tense. In that sense, this literature articulates a modernity of unequal but coeval orders of time that encourage simultaneous identifications across and within the naturalized boundaries separating colony from postcolonial nation, south from north, future from past.

For a specific example of the approach to literature, genre, and modernity I propose here we can return to the Budget Society epistolarian's letter to the future—that peculiar instance of nineteenth-century nostalgia for the present.[33] This letter opens with a problem of genre. As I have indicated, its conceit is that of a twentieth-century descendant of Nantucket who lives at the mouth of the Columbia River and who is corresponding with a contemporary about the customs of his ancestors. This correspondent begins, "Dear Madam, In looking over some old manuscripts in my possession a few evenings since, I came to a detached piece of writing, which, in these days, I know not how to class. The author is one unknown, and as no allusions are made to him by contemporary writers, which throw any light upon the subject, I must leave you, as I am myself in conjecture. This much, however is certain, that up to the time of his writing the piece above alluded to, no production of his excepting a small piece of poetry, had been published."[34] The letter continues, "By the old manuscript above mentioned, it appears that our ancestors were possessed of means and devices by which they blended amusement with instruction." Over the course of the letter, the author details the "conduct" of the Budget Society. However, the problem the author introduces in the first line—"I know not how to class" this writing—is never resolved. The source of the writer's knowledge of his ancestors is first described as a "detached piece of writing" and an "old manuscript"; the author shifts halfway through the letter by referring to "these manuscripts" and "compositions." At the conclusion of the letter, its author refers to "compositions, humorous and nondescript, in rhyme and in prose, which were contributed by the members male and female."

If we think of this society in terms of the culture of emulation that Leon Jackson has identified with this period, the letter writer's interrupted desire to classify this "detached piece of writing" is both significant and unsurprising. As Jackson explains, "Between the 1780s . . . and the 1850s, literary competitions flourished in America."[35] These widely advertised and influential competitions encouraged aspiring writers to complete compositions that met the requirements of specific literary forms.[36] They "offered premiums for genres as different as poems, plays, prologues, essays, articles, analyses, disputations, dissertations, tracts, treatises, short stories, novels, and even conundrums."[37] Although Jackson does not pursue this point, it is worth acknowledging that these contests and the emulation they sought to engender were organized around the reproduction of literary genres. Although originality had its place in the increasingly Romantic aesthetic of nineteenth-century America, the real imperative was to demonstrate knowledge of and facility with the conventions of known and admired forms. At this early stage of American literary history, in other words, convention as much as a capacity for novelty set expectations for what qualified as literature. Such expectations were also clearly at play in the activities of the Budget Society. The compositions recorded in the society's logbook were original only in the moderate sense that any particular iteration of a genre differs from those that precede it. With the possible exception of the letter itself (an issue I will turn to in just a moment), these compositions obey the precedents of genre set for (among others) the lyric, the inaugural address, and the it-narrative—this last witnessed in a composition titled "Diary of a Quill."

Of all the genres Jackson names, however, the novel seems to have played an especially significant role in the lives, if not the labors, of the Budget Society's members. Here is the letter's description of a typical Budget Society meeting:

The society appears to have been established by women. They met one evening out of seven during the winter season, and were usually all convened by 7 o'clock. Each one of them brought a kind of work called "knitting work" that is to say, a slow and mechanical physical method of making stockings by hand! Why I should have as soon thought of making coats and pantaloons by hand! These women were employed a fortnight in making a single pair of stockings, and no doubt would have pronounced any one crazy who should assert that in the year 2000 a little girl would make a hundred pair of long hose daily. . . . It was customary in the aforesaid "Budget Society" for some of the women to read from some book, for the benefit of the whole, until the men (generally their husbands) arrived, which was commonly from half past eight to nine o'clock. Concerning the books they read we have no knowledge further than that they were usually novels which are now extinct, with a few exceptions.[38]

In this account, the society operates like clockwork. The punctual regularity of their practice recalls the advent of modern regimes of the clock and the calendar. A first reading discloses a community participating in the rituals of homogeneous empty time associated with modernity and with the novels that they read aloud. They "met one evening out of seven" at a regularly established time. When they arrived, the firstcomers (i.e., the women) participated in a knitting circle. Although the letter writer comments on the "now"-anachronistic nature of their knitting, its proximity to the reading of novels encourages us to think of the novel genre not only as a women's form but also as a genre tied to the punctual regularity of the "knitting work" undertaken at these meetings. The regularity of the stitch recalls the page-by-page unfolding of linear time that we have been taught to expect from the realist novel. Moreover, this image is first and foremost that of a community brought together through a shared sense of time facilitated by the popularity of the novel.

However, the full story of this letter is more complex than this initial reading would allow, and it runs against conventional accounts of genre's relationship to time and its socializing force. To produce this more complex story, one would want first to focus on how the specific practice of reading described in this letter complicates the assumption that literature works to articulate social totalities. It is obvious but no less important for being so that the society's novel reading is gendered. Whatever collectivizing force is at play here, that force impacts only a portion of the society's members. The women and the men of the Budget Society do not experience time in common: the rhythms of the stitch and of the page collaborate to exclude the society's male members. Yet this focus on gender aggregation can end up distracting from a more profoundly disaggregating force revealed in this short letter to the future. That force begins to appear when we return to the anxious question in the letter's first line: How is one to "class" the writing that provides our epistolarian with his knowledge of the past, especially given that this letter functions as its own source? We can first class this letter in relationship to the novel. Literary historians have long argued for the epistolary form's centrality to the novel genre.[39] Here the letter writer's description of the reading of novels at the Budget Society confirms some standard assumptions about the novel's contribution to the time consciousness of modernity. The inscription at the top of the letter suggests that in the context of the Budget Society, the letter articulates a sense of synchronic simultaneity often associated with the advent of modernity and routinely identified with the realist novel. However, the writer of this letter also achieves a kind of diachronic simultaneity—or a simultaneity-along-time—usually reserved for premodern societies in relationship to ancestors.[40] He does so by figuring a coeval relationship not only between "Madam," the letter's addressee, and "Any name but the right one," its signatory, but also between the Budget Society writer and his or her descendants. The difficulty of determining the genre of this "detached piece of writing" stems at least in part from the tension it sustains between diachronic and synchronic simultaneity. The future-oriented simultaneity of the letter does not trump or displace the synchronic simultaneity implied in the letter form—or vice versa. Instead, the two are constant adjuncts.

A restrictive approach to genre might alternatively classify this letter as protonovelistic writing, utopia, epistle, or progressive historiography, but this letter in fact includes features of all four of these genres. In particular, it draws the temporalities customarily identified as the exclusive property of one or the other of these genres into a single framework. Obeying epistolary conventions, this letter imagines a shared sense of time linking addressee to signatory, while implicitly acknowledging the lag time separating these two. (If the epistolary genre assumes that sender and receiver inhabit the same global nexus of time, it also acknowledges any letter's latecomer status. Epistolary form aspires to the coeval while never really participating in it.) As epistolary form finds its way into the novel, it is stripped of some of its commonsense associations with delay and disjuncture. Through the artifice of the novelistic universe, the letter is refigured to signify the simultaneity of characters living at a geographic distance—the "meanwhile." But the letter never completely sheds its association with delay—indeed, plots often turn on epistolary delay—and so the epistolary novel is much less about simultaneity than would first appear to be the case: think *Clarissa* and *Charlotte Temple*. This particular letter is also a form of utopian writing in that its author adopts a mode of anticipatory consciousness that projects the author and the Budget Society's members into the future. Finally, in its synoptic view of the past as directly related to the present as figure to the later period's fulfillment, this letter adopts the new conventions of progressive historiography. The competing relationships between past, present, and future entailed in these several genres might appear to be mutually exclusive, but this letter provides a concentrated example of their capacity to coexist. This modest composition includes a utopian impulse inherited from Francis Bacon sharing the page with the epistolary time consciousness of Samuel Richardson. The conventions of nineteenth-century progressive historiography can also be glimpsed in the early stages of their formation.

My claim is that an equally complex universe of time defines any individual work of writing if we are willing to recognize it there. The majority of this book is therefore devoted to focused discussions of the genres of the historical romance, Southwestern humor, and African American life writing. Outlining the fine details of a given genre's internal overlays (as I have just done with the Budget Society letter) will concern me sometimes more and sometimes less in my discussion of these forms of writing. However, the fundamental approach to genre just outlined constitutes the enabling background of the entire study. Why these three genres in particular? The answer concerns their relationship to what Jürgen Habermas calls the "philosophical discourse of modernity," as well as to the foundational assumptions of nineteenth-century American literary studies. Each one of these forms assigns itself the task of narrating some of the key shifts in social organization that social theorists and historians identify with modernity: the emergence of market culture, the depopulation of the rural backwoods, the imperial European colonization of North America, the economic entrenchment of racial slavery, and the construction of national communication and transportation networks. They are also acutely interested in the apparent reorganization of time taking place in America as a result of these key shifts. In this respect, each of these genres anticipates the way that later social theory and historiography would narrate this moment. The historical romance addresses the evolution of the nation form, Southwestern humor recounts the death of local culture and the emergence of the region, and African American life writing describes the formation of modern categories of race. [In other words, each of these genres offers an account of modernity that focuses on its restructuring of time and how that restructuring relates to the consolidation of national, regional, and racial identity in turn. If these genres identify and diagnose the condition(s) of modernity, however, they also operate as literary genres not strictly mimetic in nature. They contribute to modernity by engaging readers in conceptualizations and formal enactments of time that are not exclusively "modern" in cast but that go into the making of an American modernity rather different from that which has been imagined.]

Beyond the issues of how this literature narrates the character of modernity, these genres have also had a particularly important role to play in the discipline of American literary studies. Indeed, work on this writing can be said to constitute the disciplinary unconscious of nineteenth-century American literary studies. As the following chapters demonstrate, these genres have had a peculiar staying power in the long history of intellectual work on American literature. In the early nineteenth century, as the sentimental novel was being castigated for (among other things) its transatlantic origins, the historical romance seemed, to some critics at least, to be one of the few novel forms worth reading.[41] Its interest in the fortunes of early white settlers and its attempt to reconcile the destruction of Indians with the progress of the nation secured it a seat at the table of acceptably Ameri-

can forms of writing. Although the genre's debts to Scott did not go unacknowledged, it managed to transcend these suspect origins even among ardent cultural nationalists. Not only in the United States but also abroad,
Southwestern humor was one of several species of literary regionalism
deemed worthy of the designation "American." In the earliest anthologies
of American literature, Southwestern humor was classed as "humor of the
backwoods" or as "comedy" aboriginal to its site of origin. From early descriptions of the slave narrative as the first (and only) truly American form,
such as those of Theodore Parker, African American life writing has persistently claimed the right to be classed as a national production. The early
views of these three genres as "the condensed and clearly expressed thought
of the country," to borrow from Rufus Griswold, found confirmation in
the work of Cold War Americanists; in more recent decades, this body of
literature has been scrutinized for its role in America's virulent racial ideology. In important ways, these genres have been central stabilizing influences
and touchstones of this field in moments of transition and consolidation.
If they are not the keystone in the arch of American literature, then they
are among its most important voussoirs.

In my first chapter, "Figures of Print, Orders of Time, and the Character of American Modernity," I identify this period's notion of a national
common time as one articulation of a broader transatlantic discourse about
modernity. The familiar contours of Washington Irving's "Rip Van Winkle" serve here to exemplify the way in which eighteenth- and nineteenth-
century thinkers on both sides of the Atlantic came to identify modernity
with a new experience of time as rapid change and linear unfolding that
they named progress—a modern time destined to supplant all local temporalities. In addition to sketching the history of this transatlantic approach
to thinking about time, this chapter also identifies the especially viral millennial variant of it that characterized writing in the United States through
a discussion of the journalism of Manifest Destiny. This first chapter closes
with a reading of period paintings based on "Rip Van Winkle" and of Irving's turn to the formal figure of ekphrasis. This discussion reconceives
the history of American modernity as the story of modernity's failure to
produce the generic individual—a failure tied to the appearance of literature as a modern incarnation of the premodern storyteller.

Chapter 2, "'A Magnificent Fragment': Dialects of Time and the
American Historical Romance," addresses a literary genre often identified
as the first specifically American novelistic form of writing. From the 1820s
through the 1850s, historical romancers characterized their genre as the key-

stone of a national historical consciousness crucial to stabilizing U.S. national identity. Yet the romance also articulates at the level of form a nonsimultaneous present, one torn by competing temporalities and unsuited to function in the way that many of its authors envisioned. The figure of dialect writing, which unexpectedly characterizes this genre, captures precisely its quality of a divided present tense. In the romance, moreover, characters have as much in common with their ancestors and descendents as they do with their contemporaries. In that sense, the genre traces the copresence of synchronic and diachronic simultaneity. This genre also encourages identification across political divides that are customarily marked as chronological ones—colony versus postcolonial nation; premodern versus modern culture; European versus (North) American; slavocracy versus democracy—when it recounts a revolutionary messianic temporality that draws past, present, and future into the same tense moment. Here there is no uniform and empty present tense that the nation can share.

Chapter 3, "Local Time: Southwestern Humor and Nineteenth-Century Literary Regionalism," turns to literary regionalists writing retrospectively in the 1830s, 1840s, and 1850s about the early nineteenth-century Southwestern frontier. Southwestern humor offers nostalgic portraits of rough-and-ready, dialect-speaking poor whites supposedly drawn from memories of a time before these people were assimilated to national cultural norms. This genre also differentiates its largely middle-class, white male readership from the poor country folks it describes by suggesting that, in the Old Southwest, time worked differently from the way it did elsewhere in the nation. This gesture appears to acknowledge the local character of time. In practice, however, such binary comparisons of local time to a national standard temporality always figure local time as an anachronistic remnant of a premodern past that has been or will be overcome. This chapter attempts to disable that binary by demonstrating how Southwestern humor registers not one but several deeply localized temporalities developing out of new travel technologies such as the steam engine. Although travel technology is typically thought to dissolve local time, Southwestern humor shows how it can fissure time into acutely circumscribed temporal microclimates. Southwestern humor also reintroduces the storytelling figure from Irving's "Rip Van Winkle," suggesting that he too is a force for deep locality.

Chapter 4, "The Deprivation of Time in African American Life Writing," investigates fictionalized biographies, spiritual autobiographies, and fugitive slave narratives from African America, which characteristically argue that European Americans dehumanized and disenfranchised African Americans by manipulating time. The classic example of this argument is the slave narrative's opening line, "I was born," and its attendant condemnation of the way slaveholders refused to record the birth and death dates of their slaves. African American literature and its critics describe the European American manipulation of birth and death records as a strategic withholding of time. Yet the very same scenes associated with that deprivation of time actually disclose and reproduce more than one temporality. Laboring time and revolutionary messianic time frequently overlap here; often they must compete with linear progress. Although this conflict of time foreclosed any holistic experience of African American belonging, it also produced a radically sustaining relationship to the future that European America often sought to prohibit.

I close with an epilogue on Gilded Age artist William Lamson Henry's historical genre paintings and the recent spatial turn among Americanists. Known for their nostalgic backward glances at scenes of eighteenth- and early nineteenth-century U.S. history, Henry's late nineteenth-century paintings long for a moment when the arrow of time flew in only one direction. Yet those paintings fail to convincingly represent that moment as having ever occurred, especially when they turn to iconic American images such as those of the nation's early trains. Instead these paintings articulate in visually spatialized terms the nature of the temporal conjuncture. If Henry's approach to the past demonstrates how a rhetoric of American modernity permeates late nineteenth-century culture, the recent spatial turn in American literary studies signals its migration into the present moment. Here I suggest how an undertheorized embrace of global and transatlantic studies can mask the spread of nineteenth-century America's manifest destinarian impulses into the present.

If my arguments in the following chapters depart from some of the historicist protocols that currently dominate American literary study, this is because to adhere to those protocols too closely would be to betray this book's central claim. The historicism that currently predominates in this field tends to follow the principle that a unified present tense organizes the past, present, and future.[42] I take a different view of things. I also adopt the standpoint that a reconstructed literary criticism has something significant to offer to interdisciplinarity. As others have before me, I endeavor to imagine what it would mean to include the study of literature—its forms, its problems—as a full voting member in the congress of scholarly opinion.

Chapter 1
Figures of Print, Orders of Time, and the Character of American Modernity

> There was, as usual, a crowd of folk about the door [of the village inn], but none that Rip recollected. The very character of the people seemed changed. There was a busy, bustling, disputatious tone about it, instead of the accustomed phlegm and drowsy tranquility. He looked in vain for the sage Nicholas Vedder, with his broad face, double chin, and fair long pipe, uttering clouds of tobacco-smoke instead of idle speeches; or Van Bummel, the schoolmaster, doling forth the contents of an ancient newspaper. In place of these, a lean, bilious-looking fellow, with his pockets full of hand-bills, was haranguing vehemently about rights of citizens—elections—members of congress—liberty—Bunker's Hill—heroes of seventy-six—and other words, which were a perfect Babylonish jargon to the bewildered Van Winkle.
>
> —Washington Irving, "Rip Van Winkle"

The figure of print epitomizes a certain theory of American literature. As in Washington Irving's "Rip Van Winkle," nineteenth-century American writing often features images of invasive handbills, newspapers, and other forms of print culture assaulting the integrity of local people and their places. Delivered by strangers who resemble Irving's "bilious-looking fellow," these figures of print signify a new way of being in time and a recalibration of the scale of social life.[1] In the epigraph to this chapter, for example, Irving asks his reader to date the Hudson Valley's nationalization to the intrusion of printed matter into bucolic scenes of local life. The implication is that an emerging national culture of print will use America's new roads, trains, and waterways to penetrate the nation's farther reaches. Its periphery and backwoods will be provided with an experience of reading that echoes the heady currents of progress coursing through America's urban centers. And they will be provided with this experience whether they want it or not.

A viral national culture of print is implicated, then, in the temporality of progress's becoming the nation's single common denominator. It is also credited with the newly discovered American ability to imagine the nation as what the nineteenth-century railroad magnate Mark Hopkins called "a single body, pervaded by one sympathetic nerve, and capable of being simultaneously moved by the same electric flash of thought."[2] If the citizens of the United States are finally coming to know themselves as subjects of a national common time, then the figure of print demands print culture's fair share of credit for this swift and far-reaching change.

The figure of print's account of modernity anticipates the great social theories that begin to emerge later in the nineteenth century. As in Tönnies, Durkheim, Weber, and Marx, Irving's modernity initially appears to involve a radical rupture with the past. This rupture's implications are both wide and deep: a destruction of locality follows the loosening of ties to kith and kin, local folk are reembedded into broader translocal networks (i.e., nations, regions, and races), and a countervailing bourgeois antimodernism becomes the dominant mode of social critique. In classic and more recent theories of modernity, these radical changes follow from a fundamental severing of the traditional relationship between time and space. The increasing sophistication of travel technologies figures large in this narrative because it compresses space and brings geographically distant people closer together. Yet these new travel technologies are just one component of a process that permanently unhinges the measurement of time from the contingencies of space. In this critical narrative of time-space distanciation and supralocal social reaffiliation, there is no more important actor than the rise of mass communication symbolized by industrial technologies of print.

In this chapter, I examine the contribution of the figure of print to an account of American modernity with roots in the nineteenth century. I also propose a reconceived role for literature in modernity's disarticulated time and space. In the period in question, which is roughly the first half of the nineteenth century, two important theories of literature predominated in the United States. The first is the cultural nationalist model identified with editors such as the Duyckinck brothers, with Emerson, and with Whitman's uptake of Emerson's charge. In this first familiar model, literature expresses the feeling of the nation, systematizes its thought, and allows nascent Americans to identify with their distant countrymen. Although the second approach is related to the first, it has not been recognized as a theory of literature as such. This second theory, which is encapsulated in the figure of print, positions literature as just one more instance of a generalized print culture; here the figure of print metonymically substitutes for modernization's congeries of signature forces: "the formation of capital and the mobilization of resources[;] the development of the forces of production and the increase in productivity of labor[;] the establishment of centralized political power and the formation of national identities[;] the proliferation of rights of political participation, of urban forms of life, and of formal schooling[;] the secularization of values and norms; and so on."[3] By way of implication, the highly abstracted figure of print reduces modern literature to a further example of modernization's many aggressive instruments. Literature is the "and so on" in this formulation. According to Irving, moreover, in America it has special force: "Over no nation does the press hold a more absolute control than over the people of America; for the universal education of the poorest classes makes every individual a reader."[4] The figure of print reveals precious little about the formal qualities of any particular instance of print culture. There is no sense that these qualities matter to the texture of daily life. This is because the figure of print's main purpose is to confirm that an ever-expanding scale of social affiliation looms on the horizon.

I offer a critique of this capsule theory of literature contained in the figure of print through a reading of "Rip Van Winkle." This story has several significant things to say about the character of American modernity. For one, Irving will end up criticizing as bankrupt the idea that modernity involves a revolutionary rupture with the premodern past. He has little patience for the proposition that "the modes of life brought into being by modernity have swept us away from *all* traditional types of social order, in quite unprecedented fashion,"[5] and he rejects the notion of a "dramatic and unprecedented break between past and present."[6] This idea of radical rupture is, for Irving, at the very least incomplete. In the post-Revolutionary world that he would have his reader acknowledge, traditional and modern forms of time overlay each other with disjointing and disaggregating effects. [Bruno Latour's sense of the relationship between the time of progress and that of tradition is germane: "[T]he modern time of progress and the antimodern time of 'tradition' are twins who failed to recognize one another: The idea of an identical repetition of the past and that of a radical rupture with any past are two symmetrical results of a single conception of time."[7]] In the story that Irving's "Rip Van Winkle" tells, modernity superadds to existing modalities of time. It is not a winnowing or a process of replacement; it involves "superimposition" and the "coexistence of heterogeneous times."[8] The repetitive temporality of tradition is supplemented here with the linear time of progress. ⟦According to "Rip Van Winkle," in other words, it is perhaps best to think of modernity as a peculiar new arrangement of time orchestrated in a disharmonized minor key.⟧Although Irving's sleepy Hudson Valley village at first appears to have been transformed by the American Revolution into a place where a "busy, bustling" environment of progress has completely replaced the temporality of tradition, Irving offers a challenge to this view of modernity in his enigmatic description of a portrait-bearing sign hanging outside the village hotel. This figure of ekphrasis belies the more familiar story about modern time, its relationship to nationalism, and the theory of modern literature that the figure of print encapsulates. Before Rip departs for his nap in the mountains this sign features a portrait of King George, but upon his return it is markedly different: it has turned into a kind of palimpsest. Although it aims to represent George Washington, Rip notes an uncanny resemblance to the earlier portrait of King George. In nineteenth-century paintings based on Irving's story, the suggestive nature of this figure is made clear by virtue of comparison—as is the difficulty of visually paraphrasing Irving's sign. These canonical paintings often render the portrait in the simplest possible terms, editing out any evidence of the unheimlich qualities described by Irving. They tender instead straightforward internal portraits of the American general that obey recognized conventions.

This painterly tidying up of the portrait obscures a more considered account of American modernity that Irving's story suggests we would do well to entertain. In the context of his story, Irving's post-Revolutionary, portrait-bearing sign articulates the character of a modernity in which incommensurable temporalities fail to resolve into a single arrow of time. This moment of ekphrasis suggests, in other words, that what typifies this modernity is not a displacement of the past or the antiquation of former modes of inhabiting time. In this modernity, new temporal modes are coeval with old ones; long-past and present orders of time work together to undo the social ordering of the present. As Rip's post-Revolutionary role as the village storyteller and Irving's attention to the *Sketch-Book*'s form indicate, moreover, literature has a significant role to play in reintroducing certain long-lost chronotypes into the modern present tense. Walter Benjamin speaks for many when he suggests a major difference between the modern novel and premodern forms of the story and when he ties this contrast to "the invention of printing": "The earliest indication of a process whose end is the decline of storytelling is the rise of the novel at the beginning of modern times. What distinguishes the novel from the story (and from the epic in the narrower sense) is its essential dependence on the book. The dissemination of the novel became possible only with the invention of printing."[9] Yet in the *Sketch-Book*, Irving variously describes his own equally print-dependent writing as fireside gossip, document-based historiography, travel writing, and, importantly, folk legend. In this respect, he describes his contribution to America's national culture of print—that is, the *Sketch-Book*—as a palimpsest of antique and modern, foreign and domestic literary forms. By implication, Irving also suggests that the *Sketch-Book* resurrects antique and modern, foreign and domestic ways of inhabiting time. These are not the observations of an author insensitive to the actual character of his own writing. When Irving reproduces communal folk legend drawn from American and European contexts, he in fact draws the storyteller's premodern chronotypes into the modern present. In describing his contribution in this way, Irving successfully deflects the narrative of national progress that such reified figures of print as his "pocket full of handbills" endorse by way of metonymy. He does this by filling in the abstract figure with a content of various forms. Irving insists that his own work is a formal hybrid, rejecting the notion that the figure of print is a sufficient mode of description for any given instance of print culture; in other words, he refuses to understand literature as a hollow shell. In this respect, Irving's arguments suggest that actually existing examples of print culture (to which that term does descriptive injustice) often do more to retard the consolidation of identity than they do to secure it. Rather than helping to expand the social scale and facilitate modernity's dialectic of social dislocation and translocal reembedding, certain specific examples of print culture actually encumber this process. The lack of clarity in Irving's ekphrastic portrait of the world's then most recognizable American bears witness to this encumbrance. Irving's internal portrait self-consciously haunts the figure of print's tidy account of how modern print culture homogenized time to secure the emergence of American identity. It exemplifies and instances the temporal superaddition that defined this period. And in its resistance to visual paraphrase, it points to the difficulty of fully registering the conflicted nature of modern time.

Where Ian Baucom argues that a conflicted order of time signifies the approach of global capitalism, I suggest that it follows even more directly (and identifiably) from the flow of modern literature.[10] In this sense, nineteenth-century American literature did as much (or more) to disorder American identity as it did to reassemble it on an expanding scale. Indeed, this literature both describes and engenders the radically localized subjectivity signified in Irving's ekphrastic portrait. A permanent chrysalis of sorts, Irving's George has no self-evident future, nor is it entirely clear whether he belongs to the present or the past. This quality of irresolution and nonbelonging encourages Irving's reader to view with a certain skepticism any account of modernity that designates it as a radical break with the past or as the origin of new translocal social forms. George is the caveat emptor at the center of Irving's story. On the one hand, Irving's figure of print (i.e., the "pocket full of hand-bills") reifies print culture: it encourages Irving's reader to class newspapers, novels, and handbills together in a story of technological determinism. On the other hand, Irving's portrait of George is emblematic of an unresolved modernity. By filling in the figure of print with attention to the finer details of form in the *Sketch-Book*'s critical apparatus, moreover, Irving encourages his reader to discern a more vexed role for literature in the making of the modern time that results in this irresolution. And in light of this attention to issues of form, modernity itself begins to take on new characteristics. The political handbill that Irving references is one of the few genres of writing organized around a punctual temporality: the political handbill is necessarily addressed to the national "moment." When Irving frames his *Sketch-Book* writings as the product of local folk wisdom, however, he suggests that his and other forms of literary print culture did as much to draw forward antique modes of being in time as they did to introduce the "busy, bustling disputatious tone" and national punctuality that Rip at first witnesses upon his return. In this impossible modernity, Irving seems to argue, no single order of time can be said to rule the day.

Secular Time in America

When Rip Van Winkle returns from his twenty-year nap, which spans the years of the American Revolution, Irving's narrator observes, "The very character of the people seemed changed." As it turns out, changeability itself suffuses this people's new character. Time as change seems to be a rule rather than the exception in Rip's post-Revolutionary village; Rip's are a people seemingly steeped in and fashioned by linear progressive time—a new people experiencing time in a novel way. However, the specific events that produced this new experience of constant change have gone missing. In their place stands the somnolent ellipsis at the story's center. Although the events of the American Revolution are in one sense an absent cause, they are, strictly speaking, just plain absent. Instead, time is "promoted to the rank of a power in its own right."[11] Even Rip never really rises to the position of the story's protagonist; that role is given over to time. "Rip Van Winkle" in this respect reflects [what Jürgen Habermas has called the "time-consciousness of modernity," to the extent that it abstracts time from contingent local circumstances and features it as one of the story's main characters. According to Peter Osborne, one of the signatures of modernity is the abstraction of "the logical structure of the process of change" from "its concrete historical determinants."[12]

Although Rip remains the same over the course of the story, the basic features of time radically differ in this tale's first and second halves. The first half portrays Rip and his village as organized by a local experience of time as repetitive return. Rip and his peers are more than simple country folk predictably out of synch with the wider expanse of colonies surrounding them and the emerging metropoles that anchor those colonies. The issue is not so much that Rip and his village need to synchronize their watches to a national standard time. Rather, the issue is that, in colonial America, time has a hermetically absolute tenor. Rip's village is a place apart, but more important, it inhabits a time apart: Rip's village has its own temporality, one characterized more by the recursive than by linear progress. The added implication is that Rip's village fails to conform to a standard New World temporality because no such temporality exists. There can be no experience of national simultaneity and therefore no experience of national belonging, because there is no national common time. The Hudson Valley is one corner of a colonial environment strafed with nonsynchronous times; Rip's village is the norm precisely because of its temporal idiosyncrasy. Here time's measures are tied to the contingencies of the local landscape: "Every change of season, every change of weather, indeed every hour of the day, produces some change in the magical hues and shapes of these mountains, and they are regarded by all the good wives, far and near, as perfect barometers."[13] There are seasons, the diurnal cycle, and the changing same of the weather, but there is no clear sign of the linear time of progress. The leader of the "junto" that camps out before the village inn, its keeper Nicholas Vedder, moves "just . . . sufficiently" over the course of the day "to avoid the sun and keep in the shade of a large tree; so that the neighbors could tell the hour by his movements as accurately as by a sundial."[14] Rip himself notices during his sojourn in the woods that "evening was gradually advancing; the mountains began to throw their long blue shadows over the valleys; he saw that it would be dark long before he could reach the village."[15] Rip's son, Rip—not Rip Jr. or Rip II, just Rip—is an "urchin begotten in his [father's] likeness" who "promise[s] to inherit the habits, with the old clothes of his father."[16] When the dissipated elders of the village gather at the "kind of perpetual club of the sages, philosophers, and other idle personages of the village" that is their junto, they chew the cud of old gossip.[17] On occasion, an "old newspaper [falls] into their hands from some passing traveler," and at these moments this club of the venerated, if not venerable, "sagely . . . deliberate[s] upon public events some months after they had taken place."[18]

In the story's second half, however, Rip's sleepy Hudson Valley village at first seems to have morphed from being a place where a recursive local temporality dominates daily life into a site that is nationally au courant. The "bustling" flavor of progress appears to dominate all quarters of Rip's newly up-to-date village, and everywhere he turns Rip notices change. The colonial immersion in local time we saw before Rip's nap has apparently evaporated in the face of linear progressive time. In concert with this new experience of time, Rip's fellow villagers have changed from provincials identified with colonial icons, such as an old Flemish painting Rip remembers, into national subjects identified with the nation that emerged in Rip's absence. One of the first questions Rip must parse upon his return to the village is "'Whether he was Federal or Democrat?'"[19] This is a newly nationalized community sharing time, notwithstanding the increasing partisanship of America's national elections. Those out-of-date newspapers that defined the background of the first half of the story have been replaced by a form of print culture completely dependent on its tie to a single and nationally shared moment of election: the political handbills spilling from the stumper's pockets. Missing from Irving's story is a considered account of what the Revolution was and what it did. Instead of that account we find a portrait of what time is and what time does, as well as a figure of print associated with delivering this new order of time to the Catskills. Here linear progressive time would appear to function as this story's subject matter, context, and protagonist all at once. Upon Rip's return, the inevitability of change looks at first to be a transparent fact, and Rip notes the ubiquity of a generalized experience of unfolding difference in his lamenting list of the transformations confronting him: "'I'm not myself—I'm somebody else—that's me yonder—no—that's somebody else got into my shoes—I was myself last night, but I fell asleep on the mountain, and they've changed my gun, and every thing's changed, and I'm changed, and I can't tell what's my name, or who I am!'"[20] The repetitive invocation of these several instances of difference does not foreground the specific events that have produced the changes Rip names but rather suggests an environment defined by a general aura of progress. This new experience of time as change coordinates, moreover, with a national standard: the lazy sages with their out-of-date newspapers have disappeared, and Rip discovers instead "a lean, bilious-looking fellow, with his pockets full of hand-bills, . . . haranguing vehemently about rights of citizens—elections—members of congress—liberty—Bunker's Hill—heroes of seventy-six."[21] Rip reenters an America about to participate in the ultimate ritual of national simultaneity and coordinated time, the national election—an America where newspapers must be current in order to serve a public united in its exercise of the franchise.

In the context of American political history, Irving's account allegorizes the anxieties of life in and after the Age of Revolution, and it rehearses certain Whiggish imagery of the *ricorso*.[22] Yet Irving's description of the distinction between British North American and U.S. national culture also participates in a broader transatlantic discourse about the character of modernity and modern time that reached its apex in the late eighteenth and nineteenth centuries. According to the standard historiography on the secularization of modern time, Europeans and Britons began to conceive of time in radically new ways as early as the mid-1700s. It was then that secular models of history began fully to replace the eschatological worldview that had previously dominated the Christian West. It is generally agreed that this Anglo-European secularization of time led to the horizon of the future being radically telescoped into infinity, as the Apocalypse no longer loomed on the horizon. [Simultaneous with this opening up of the future prospect, modern science began to argue for the independent character of time, as when Newton proposed an absolute time that never repeats or doubles back upon itself. Although religious models of historical time had been said to unite only the faithful, Newton's absolute time proposed to organize all human experience equally.][23] Reinhart Koselleck explains that this epochal shift toward a new conceptualization of time followed the slow but inexorable secularization of Europe that began not long after the Renaissance. In the eschatological vision of Christianity, each seemingly new event is recuperated as part of a divine plan determined in advance with the Apocalypse as its teleological endpoint. Europeans therefore generally lived "in expectation of the Last Judgment."[24] There was no sense of an open-ended future; the future was always a limited expanse, and its significance was always already known. There was literally nothing new under the sun. Moreover, because every historical episode was thought to realize an event foretold in

[handwritten marginalia: canonical acct of dawn of modern time]

the Bible, no given moment was understood to exist independent of the event that provided it with significance. There was no time separate from biblical history, no objective chronology expanding infinitely into the future and the past. Time lacked the autonomous profile it would develop in a story like "Rip Van Winkle."

In this canonical account of the shift from a premodern to a modern time consciousness, the eschatological view came under fire starting in the fifteenth century and was contained by the middle of the eighteenth century. The Anglo-European religious civil wars of the seventeenth century prompted disenchantment with eschatology: disputants on all sides had framed those wars as augurs of the Final Judgment, so when the wars concluded and the Apocalypse did not arrive, the argumentative force of eschatology was severely compromised. Astrological predictions, which were a common and respected post-Renaissance system of prognostication, tended to foresee a much longer course of history still to unfold than traditional biblical scholarship anticipated. The future that astrology envisioned reached far beyond the previously anticipated end of time. These and other developments represent what Koselleck calls the modern "containment[,] destruction, [and] channeling of millennial expectations" and allowed for a "new plane" of the future to come into being: "Neither the One Big End of the World nor the several smaller ones could apparently affect the course of human affairs. Instead of the anticipated millennium, a new and different perspective of time had opened up."[25] This revised plane of the future allowed for the very idea of the "new" to arrive. Freed of typological meaning and eschatological parameters, each event could register in its full novelty. This secularization of time meant that every occurrence was to be understood as novel to the extent that the future would remain a permanent unknown: whatever meaning an event in the present might derive from its similarity to or difference from past episodes, its ultimate significance remained unclear because its impact on the future was unforeseeable. Past events were no longer "exemplary" lessons for the present; "in [their] place" stood "the discovery of the uniqueness of historical processes and the possibility of progress."[26] This discovery marked a radical departure from even those protosecular models of history available prior to the eighteenth century. The perennially resuscitated classical notion of *historia magistra vitae est*, or history as teacher of life, applies, for instance, "only as long as the given assumptions and conditions are fundamentally the same" across the expanse of human experience.[27] After the transition to a modern time consciousness, that similitude is no longer understood to hold. This shift toward a new perspective on the future as permanently receding horizon also propelled increased attention to the shared nature of time; nowhere did this sense of a single time line occupied simultaneously by the entire globe emerge more clearly than in historiography. Before the mid-eighteenth century, there was no strong sense of history in the "collective singular." By the middle of the nineteenth century, "history (*Geschichte*)" had come to be "conceived as a system that made possible an epic unity that disclosed and established internal coherence."[28] Time came to serve as "a cosmic metric" that was "present everywhere, the same everywhere."[29]

In the classic social theories of modernity, this secularization of time and the invention of "cosmic metrics" set the stage for the disarticulation of time from space. If Newton and his peers were providing the scientific justification for a new approach to time, the rationalizing technologies of expanding capitalism were supplying the practical framework that allowed this approach to time to spread. Anthony Giddens neatly summarizes this view of the "consequences of modernity": "The dynamism of modernity derives from the *separation of time and space* and their recombination in forms which permit the precise time-space 'zoning' of social life; the *disembedding* of social systems (a phenomenon which connects closely with the factors involved in time-space separation); and the *reflexive ordering and reordering* of social relations in the light of continual inputs of knowledge affecting the actions of individuals and groups."[30] We will return to the issue of the "reflexive ordering and reordering of social relations" in just a moment. For now, the material point is that in classical social theory, as Giddens describes it, modernity denatures time. This is to say that, in the modern era, time is disconnected from the features of the natural world around us; time becomes a noncontingent measure. This freeing up of time from space facilitates an expansion of the social scale and reorientation away from the local toward the supralocal. The disjoining of time's measure from specific natural locales and the invention of "cosmic metric[s]" permits, in other words, the rise of what Giddens calls "disembedded institutions": "The separating of time and space and their formation into standardised, 'empty' dimensions cut through the connections between social activity and its 'embedding' in the particularities of contexts of presence. Disembedded institutions greatly extend the scope of time-space distanciation and, to have this effect, depend upon coordination across time and space. This phenomenon serves to open up manifold possibilities of change by breaking free from the restraints of local habits and practices."[31] The invention of universal measures of time underwrites supralocal social forms. The disembedded institutions that we now encounter daily (i.e., global media, nonstate actors, international tribunals) descend from the trade cartels, credit instruments, and nation-states associated with modernity and that depend on cosmic metrics. These disembedded institutions engender processes of social dislocation—"the 'lifting out' of social relations from local contexts of interaction and their restructuring across indefinite spans of time-space."[32] The secularization of time that historians describe is the condition of possibility for new social forms stretched across "indefinite spans of time-space": the distanciation of time and space underlies the nation's claim to represent people living at distant removes from one another as well as from their ancestors and descendants.

Although the history and social theory of modern time have tended to focus on European contexts, John Demos has suggested that a similar reorientation took place in and around the years of the American Revolution. According to Demos, the life of the colonial British followed the repetitive circular patterns defined by the diurnal cycle, the life cycle, and other instances of natural rhythm tied to the locale—until, that is, the American Revolution, industrial manufacturing, and urbanization landed on North America's shores. Even early America's models of history conceptualized time as circular: for colonials, "the past generally prefigured and predicted both present and future. . . . [T]hose who pondered history in a more systematic way saw cyclical movement as its underlying principle."[33] Demos's colonial Americans resemble Irving's pre-Revolutionary Rip and Koselleck's early Europeans: they know time only as an experience of recursion, and they think of it as involving a repetition of the known. Yet from the mid to the late eighteenth century, Demos argues, the line supplanted the circle in America: "The circles-to-lines transformation flowed out from its eighteenth-century sources, strengthened more and more by all the social currents we now describe as 'modernization.' Its initially distinctive American stamp, produced by indigenous (and unprecedented) Revolution, gradually blurred as history at large began to follow a similar track. The forces promoting linearity were as broad as urbanization and capitalism . . . and as specific as the invention of the electric light bulb."[34] Demos envisions a transfer from the circle to the line, from one experience of time to another. "[F]or the first time" after the Revolution, Demos explains, "was newness embraced, and celebrated, in quite unequivocal terms."[35] In what is a significant point, he observes that this was not always an easy transition, for "the vast majority of eighteenth-century Americans retained their conservative and cyclical mentality, even as their experience began to move in fresher, more linear, channels."[36]

It is important to acknowledge, however, that in the American context a distinctly eschatological tone extended into modernity. In the early nineteenth century, for example, American writers began to revise and redeploy more traditional eschatological models of historical time, as well as their secular offshoots, to service the nation's expansionist designs. Their efforts resulted in that potent synthesis of Christian millennialism and nationalism: Manifest Destiny.[37] Not only the obvious candidates such as John L. O'Sullivan but also more popular and canonized nineteenth-century writers emphasized that a determinate future loomed on the horizon. Where European accounts of modernity were (ostensibly) organized around the utopian open-endedness of a constantly receding future horizon brought into view by secularization, in the United States the future was turned into a site of imperial projection.[38] The musings of committed manifest destinarians, for instance, indicate a pressing discomfort with the notion of an indeterminate future; in its place they offer America and Americans, or what O'Sullivan would call the "Great Nation of Futurity." This sense of the United States as what Ernest Tuveson once called a "redeemer nation" strongly inflects the way nineteenth-century American writers conceptualize the course of historical time and especially the future. Although Tuveson's insights are constrained by his narrow focus on New England and mid-Atlantic culture, his account of Manifest Destiny is useful to the extent that it both confirms and corrects Koselleck. Tuveson's observations suggest that modernity has to do with a new relationship to eschatological thinking, but he also argues that the decisive move in America was not from a religious to a secular model of historical time. It was instead a reorientation away from an Augustinian model to one favored by English Protestants.[39] Where Koselleck identifies the wars emerging out of the Reformation as the source of a secularism strictly disenchanted with eschatology, Tuveson points to the staying power of an American "millennialist" doctrine that envisions transformation in the world as the Second Coming's precondition. For its adherents in the eighteenth and nineteenth centuries, it seemed "almost as if the 'finger of prophecy'" were pointing to America, "the last, the best child of the Reformation," as the nation designated to bring about that earthly redemption.[40]

On October 13, 1845, John L. O'Sullivan turned his attention to producing a concrete statement of this view. Writing in New York's *Morning*

News, which, along with the *United States Magazine and Democratic Review*, he famously edited, O'Sullivan claimed the following:

The records of the past, teeming as they are with instructive lessons, fail to convey an adequate idea of what will be the history of this Republic. We are not merely to possess and occupy an unequalled extent of territory, or to extend our laws and institutions over a countless population, for the territory, though vast, will be compact, and what is of still greater value, the population will be homogeneous. This latter element of power and stability has heretofore been wanting to all great empires. Those which have passed away, were all, without great exception, composed of dissimilar and hostile materials, and the same may be said of the great European monarchies of the present day. The glittering diadem of England must fade, the colossus of Russia must crumble, but who can foresee the decline of American freedom.[41]

The first line of O'Sullivan's editorial indicates his certainty that the United States faces an absolutely novel situation. His moment and his nation are indisputably distinct from the past, so much so that the history of the American Republic still to be written will have to find its own coordinates: the past will provide no exemplars, and the traditional republican emphasis on national decline comes in for some sharp criticism. This particular passage reflects the sense of novelty that Koselleck associates with Anglo-European modernity. Even opponents of the Mexican American War, which O'Sullivan supported and which prompted much ardent theorizing around Manifest Destiny, formulated their arguments in similar terms. Writing against the war but in favor of the acquisition of western territories extending to the Pacific, John C. Calhoun would opine, "There is only one means by which it can be done: but that, fortunately, is the most powerful of all— time. Time is acting for us; and, if we shall have the wisdom to trust its operation, it will assert and maintain our right with resistless force, without costing a cent of money, or a drop of blood. There is often, in the affairs of government, more efficiency and wisdom in nonaction than in action. All we want to effect our object in this cause, is a 'wise and masterly inactivity.' Our population is rolling toward the shores of the Pacific with an impetus greater than what we realize."[42] For Calhoun, time is an agent in its own right, motoring America toward its destiny: his recommendation of "masterly inactivity" applies only in a circumstance where a greater agent of change—time itself—is at work. Like their European counterparts, Manifest Destiny's advocates associated this new agential time with the recent technological innovations that would come to be known as modernization. These writers focus in particular on the way that innovations in printing and communication technology were uniting the nation in an unprecedented experience of national simultaneity. O'Sullivan wrote in 1845 that "[t]he magnetic telegraph will enable the editors of the 'San Francisco Union,' the 'Astoria Evening Post,' or the 'Nootka Morning News' to set up in type the first half of the President's Inaugural before the echoes of the latter half shall have died away beneath the lofty porch of the Capital, as spoken from his lips."[43] Here the telegraph and the press join to fulfill the precondition for a homogeneous national identity. This figure of print describes a technologically enabled national common time that is crucial to the consolidation of America: it describes the work of reembedding people into a broad supralocal network that is identified with the modern era and taken to be the logical outcome of mass communication.[44]

In this regard, the writings of Manifest Destiny proponents argue that a determinate future looms on the horizon. As O'Sullivan's editorial on "The Great Nation of Futurity" makes clear, many nineteenth-century Americans anticipated a very specific form of supralocal social reembedding. In a characteristic moment of cultural nationalism, O'Sullivan bemoans the "tendency to imitativeness, prevailing amongst our professional and literary men, subversive of originality of thought, and wholly unfavorable to progress."[45] He takes this lack of originality, and the prevailing unwillingness among America's writers to explore its "native" splendors, to be one of several "untoward circumstances" threatening "to retard our good," where the "our" signifies not only Americans but also the entire "human race." This tendency to imitativeness is especially objectionable in the United States, a nation whose "unparalleled glory" obtains in the fact that it has "no reminiscences of battle fields, but in defence of humanity, of the oppressed of all nations, of the rights of conscience, the rights of personal enfranchisement."[46] Echoing Irving's claim in "The Author's Account of Himself," his *Sketch-Book* manifesto, that America lacks "storied and poetical association,"[47] O'Sullivan declaims, "We have no interest in the scenes of antiquity, only as lessons of avoidance of nearly all their examples. The expansive future is our arena, and for our history."[48] Where some might perceive lack, O'Sullivan sees instead the enabling ontology of America: no American should need a past once he realizes that his rightful patrimony is not the past but the future. For O'Sullivan, America *is* the future. He ends "The Great Nation of Futurity" with a biblically inspired injunction outlining America's specifically eschatological attractions: "All this will be our future history, to establish on earth the moral dignity and salvation of man— the immutable truth and beneficence of God. For this blessed mission to the nations of the world, which are shut out from the life-giving light of truth, has America been chosen; and her high example shall smite unto death the tyranny of kings, hierarchs, and oligarchs, and carry the glad tidings of peace and good will where myriads now endure an existence scarcely more enviable than that of beasts of the field. Who, then, can doubt that our country is destined to be *the great nation* of futurity?"[49] Here O'Sullivan projects into the future the constant unfolding of America's destiny. "America" is both the national future looming on the horizon and a global future meant to encompass all beings. What will this future look like? O'Sullivan's *Morning News* editorial provides the answer: "We are not merely to possess and occupy an unequalled extent of territory, or to extend our laws and institutions over a countless population, for the territory, though vast, will be compact, and what is of still greater value, the population will be homogeneous."[50] The future that Manifest Destiny envisions is millennial in this specific sense: it is a moment when the heterogeneity of difference—from oneself, from others, and from God—dissolves into the homogeneity of eternity. As Lauren Berlant has it, "This is the American utopian promise: by disrupting the subject's local affiliations and self-centeredness, national identity confers on the collective subject an indivisible and immortal body, and vice versa."[51] Adapting traditional eschatology, the goal is a future in which to be American is to escape the contingency of local life.[52] In a deeply antidemocratic gesture, O'Sullivan seeks to clear the future—our present—of intralocal democratic contest and to conjure in its stead a homogeneous population. The related desire to expand the United States to the Pacific seems tame by comparison.

Archives of the Invisible

The conventional idea that modernity involves a radical rupture with the past, and with past modes of inhabiting time, has been subject to increased scrutiny in recent decades. As historians interested in time consciousness shift their attention away from broad intellectual history and toward specific industrial or national formations, social theorists are also questioning how nineteenth-century theories of modernity were translated into the idiom of "social-scientific functionalism."[53] As Mark Smith indicates, the "coexistence of sacred, natural, and clock time in societies has been well documented by historians."[54] The new conversations initiated by historians regarding the coexistence of competing orders of time have often turned on a reconstructed sense of the parameters and possibilities of an archive of time. Mary Ann Doane points out that for Freud, as for many others, "[t]ime is antithetical to the notions of storage and retention of traces."[55] If one follows Freud, then a seemingly irresolvable paradox emerges: If "time disallows its own record" and "temporality eschews . . . representation," then what will comprise the archives of American time?[56] Historians have sought to circumvent this issue by focusing on mechanisms of time measurement and by constructing what we might call a historical epistemology of time. In a roundabout way, this redirected approach to modern time has confirmed one of social theory's most compelling recent claims: both Giddens and Habermas have argued that objectivist social theory fatally ignores how the "time-consciousness" that emerged after the seventeenth century changed the very phenomenology of modern time. According to Peter Osborne, moreover, "Two fundamental assumptions underlie, and vitiate, most of the writing about 'modernity' in recent debates about historical periodizations and cultural change. One is that the term can be used unproblematically to refer to some chronologically distinct span of historical time, marked out by epochal changes in the structure of European societies— whatever the precise limits of such a time-span are taken to be. The other is that the question of the forms of time consciousness produced within European societies during this period can be separated off from the question of the temporality of periodizations itself."[57] Here "most of the writing about 'modernity'" unselfconsciously employs a language and conceptual framework that is specific to the modernity this writing seeks objectively to describe. In other words, this writing claims to offer unmediated access to modernity's new time consciousness. However, the very idea that modernity involves a radical reorganization of time and an abrupt break with the past is in fact one of modernity's ideological formations. This theoretical insight regarding the "time-consciousness of modernity" endorses the entirely compelling view that modern time may be best thought of as the sum of its many measures. There is no unmediated experience of time in modernity, because modernity itself involves a heightened and self-conscious awareness of time. The point would be to access those measurements and conceptualizations of time that comprise the time consciousness of modernity. As Giddens argues in another context, the central issue here "is not that there is no stable social world to know, but that knowledge of that world contributes to its unstable or mutable character."[58] It turns out that the introduction of new timekeeping devices and new discourses about time produces an "unstable" and "mutable" modern time. And as the social sciences have increasingly acknowledged the acute time consciousness of modernity, a revised sense of the nineteenth century has emerged: it is more and more taken for granted that competing orders of time overlapped to define this period.

In recent studies of clock time, industrial labor, and other features of market capitalism, for example, historians start from the premise that the ticking of a clock or a stopwatch has no existential relationship to time itself. As Marx argued in *Capital*, these measures of time are techniques for extracting potential and actualized labor; they are mechanisms of regulation and surplus value extraction more than they are traces of prediscursive time.[59] The discourse of time-work discipline associated with modernization sought to rationalize power relations by attaching its practices of labor extraction to a reified time, but the time it creates is an ideological projection. Of course, it is both naïve and unproductive to think of ideology as (only) false consciousness, and so Michael O'Malley demonstrates in *Keeping Watch: The History of American Time* how the "commodification of time" that came to dominate nineteenth-century America contributed to determining its experience of time. The swift decline of traditional measures of time based on nature or the Bible was matched in this century by the spread of watches, industrial timekeeping, and telegraphed time signals. Until the late nineteenth century, O'Malley explains, rural communities relied on the local position of the sun for their sense of time, and even urban centers relied on clock towers coordinated with the sun's local position at noon. By century's end, a national common time coordinated to the scientific fetish of a telegraphed sidereal time had redefined life in every quarter of the nation. Importantly, however, this period also saw "a sense of time rooted in nature confron[t] a seemingly arbitrary time based on commerce, revealing itself in machine movements and the linear progress of invention."[60] In other words, the penetration of American life by standardized linear clock time did not all at once supplant earlier systems of timekeeping: "No precise point of transition from 'traditional' to 'modern' understandings of time can be fixed," O'Malley explains, and "different conceptions of time often co-exist simultaneously in the same society."[61] Mark Smith's *Mastered by the Clock: Time, Slavery, and Freedom in the American South* tells a similar story. Historians have conventionally argued that the antebellum South adopted a precapitalist and premodern understanding of time, because the close ties between agricultural slave labor and traditional patterns of temporal order based on diurnal and celestial cycles prevented linear industrial clock time from penetrating the South. Yet Smith shows that plantation economies actually married these two orders of time to each other. Industrial clock time and agricultural time systems colluded to perpetuate and even to strengthen the rule of the master.[62] Examining the link between proto-Taylorist time-based models of labor efficiency and the power of the overseer and master, Smith makes a strong case for the collaboration between different orders of time: "[T]he point needs to be stressed," Smith writes, "that the presence or even predominance of natural time in a society does not necessarily preclude the existence of a potent and powerful mechanical conception of time. The South was, without doubt, a society born in nature's diurnal womb and suckled on her agricultural and crop-producing climate and geography. But clock time and natural time were never mutually exclusive in the South."[63] More broadly, he argues, "[i]n every postfeudal society, [linear] clock time conjoins and mates with natural time."[64] These two histories mirror Fredric Jameson's recent challenge to standard accounts of modernity that posit a late eighteenth- and nineteenth-century transition from mercantile, rural, and premodern time systems to market, industrial, and modern forms of time. Discussing the artistic, political, and philosophical revolutions of the nineteenth century, Jameson writes: "I want to conjecture that the protagonists of those aesthetic and philosophical revolutions were people who still lived in two distinct worlds simultaneously; born in those agricultural villages we still sometimes characterize as medieval or premodern, they developed their vocations in the new urban agglomerations with their radically distinct and 'modern' spaces and temporalities. The sensitivity to deep time in the moderns then registers this comparatist perception of the two socioeconomic temporalities, which the first modernists had to negotiate in their own lived experience."[65] For Jameson, here the modern is precisely the lived contrast between two different orders of time. In modernity, the experience of an "alternate temporality" is retained, and this comparatist perspective on time persists into the twentieth century.

These recent histories of modern time are significant not only for what they confirm about the temporally conflicted nature of American modernity but also because they implicate the United States in a global experience of (postcolonial) modernity. In his influential account of modern nationalism, "DisemmiNation," Homi Bhabha identifies a bifurcated experience of time at modernity's very core. In Bhabha's estimation, both colonial and postcolonial nations rely on two different temporalities to pursue the fantasy of a coherent nation. On the one hand, they employ what Bhabha calls a "continuist, accumulative temporality of the pedagogical" that we might associate with linear time; on the other hand, national culture mobilizes the "repetitious, recursive strategy of the performative."[66] For Bhabha, national culture is subject to a double bind. It must validate itself by claiming to speak for an already existing national people; this claim to represent a people and their history is the source of national culture's "pedagogical" authority. Yet national culture must also deny the existence of this originary, autochthonous people if it is to fulfill its "performative" function and continually create the nation anew by embracing those novice citizens who come to it via birth and immigration. Nationalist discourse therefore simultaneously constructs and gives the lie to the idea of a natural national community, and it demands that the nation retain these two competing orders of time.[67] For Bhabha, moreover, these "disjunctive temporalities" amount to an opening that allows for the undoing of the narrative of nationalism. Yet this undoing will never take the form of one "social totality" directly opposing another. "[T]here can be no question of a simple negation or sublation of the contradictory or oppositional instance," Bhabha writes, suggesting that the character of modern time disallows a dialectical approach.[68] Where O'Malley, Smith, and Jameson argue that modernity involves the eventual overcoming of a "comparatist perspective on time," Bhabha proposes that (postcolonial) modernity forbids the process of dialectal overcoming. It also frustrates the reembedding of local subjects into larger "social totalities." In this sense, the revised history of modern time that O'Malley and Smith offer conforms to the broad outlines of Bhabha's analysis, while Bhabha's observations suggest the need to resist a dialectical impulse that obscures the most interesting findings of these studies. These analyses indicate that the "progressive metaphor of modern social cohesion—*the many as one*—shared by organic theories of the holism of culture and community, and by theorists who treat gender, class, or race as radically 'expressive' social totalities," and that relies on the idea of a single common time, applies no more to nineteenth-century America than it does to later or different contexts.[69] On the evidence of these histories alone, in other words, the nineteenth-century United States belongs to the same modernity that Bhabha describes. This is the case despite the fact that Smith and O'Malley end up surrendering their most incisive observations to the dialectic by suggesting that at the end of the nineteenth century time had finally been homogenized.

In its broad outlines, Bhabha's account represents an engagement with the theory of modern time outlined in Louis Althusser's "The Errors of Classical Economics: Outline for a Concept of Historical Time," an essay that strikes at the heart of this issue of the dialectic and its place in critical narratives of the past. In this essay, Althusser proposes the temporal "conjuncture" as a figure for the simultaneous presence of several nonsynchronous temporalities. He also suggests that the conjuncture is the defining condition of capitalist modernity. According to Althusser, Hegel's writings on the philosophy of history propose that homogeneous continuity and contemporaneity define historical time. For Hegel and his followers, "[t]he structure of historical existence is such that all the elements of the whole always co-exist in one and the same time, one and the same present, and are therefore contemporaneous with one another in one and the same present. This means that the structure of the historical existence of the Hegelian social totality allows what I propose to call an '*essential section*' (*coupe d'essence*), i.e., an intellectual operation in which a *vertical break* is made at any moment in historical time, a break in the present such that all the elements of the whole revealed by this section are in an immediate relationship with one another, a relationship that immediately expresses their internal essence."[70] Althusser later calls this Hegelian conception of historical time "the ideology of a homogeneous-continuous/self-contemporaneous time."[71] Hence time is an infinite sequence of evenly spaced "moments" lining up one after another, with each new moment differing absolutely from those preceding it. The world is ruled by the passage of only homogeneous-continuous/self-contemporaneous time: this kind of time preexists and preforms the world; everyone everywhere has the same time in common. Consequently, this notion of time suggests that one can represent the totality of a given historical moment via a cross-section, as all the constituent components of totality are both defined and restricted by their shared participation in the same interval of time. No one can get ahead of or fall behind time, because homogeneous-continuous/self-contemporaneous time, as the medium of our existence, restricts and subordinates the world to its even and linear unfolding. Thus time resembles a series of regularly spaced paving stones rising up to meet the world and, in rising to meet it, allowing the world to unfold. Time is composed of an infinite sequence of these paving stones, not one of which precisely resembles its predecessors.

Drawing upon Marx's "The Poverty of Philosophy," Althusser argues against this model, contending instead that several radically discontinuous and socially regulated temporalities articulate any community conceived by and through capitalism. He proposes the conjuncture to be the proper concept for addressing this phenomenon.[72] For Althusser, society must be conceived as temporally heterogeneous and as immeasurable according to a

[margin handwritten note:] Hegel homogeneous continuous time

single reference time; social totality is a conjuncture of incommensurable temporalities. He moreover observes that "we cannot restrict ourselves to reflecting the existence of *visible* and measurable times . . . ; we must, of absolute necessity, pose the question of . . . *invisible* times, of the invisible rhythms and punctuations concealed beneath the surface of each visible time."[73] Capitalism makes time's variety "invisible" and "essentially illegible": "This time, as a complex 'intersection' of the different times, rhythms, turnovers, etc. [required by capitalism] is only accessible in *its concept*, which, like every concept is never immediately 'given,' never *legible* in visible reality: like every concept this concept must be *produced, constructed*."[74] Althusser establishes a goal of making the temporal conjuncture legible through a critical reading of the past. He concludes his observations with the assertion that any reading of time should eventually return to the question of how the different temporalities comprising a conjuncture work together and in coordination. Describing the potential dangers of reading for temporal conjunctures, he contends, "It is not enough . . . to say . . . that *there are* different periodizations for different times, that each time has its own rhythms, some short, some long; we must also think these differences in rhythm and punctuation in their foundation, in the type of articulation, displacement and torsion which harmonizes these different times with one another."[75] According to Althusser, the final effort of any analysis should be to understand how a conjuncture's temporalities "harmonize" in the service of capitalism. The imperative is to understand the nature of a given mode of production.

In an important modification of Althusser's statements, Bhabha suggests that the conjuncture of different temporalities does not involve harmony of any sort. It is this perspective that I pursue in the context of nineteenth-century literature. According to Bhabha and Partha Chatterjee, the idea of harmonic emergence or dialectical overcoming profoundly misapprehends the character of modernity. To reconcile the conjuncture into a single logic of development—whether of the nation or of race or of capital—would be both to ignore the incommensurable temporalities of any given conjuncture and to project into the past a logic of social inevitability.[76] Stated differently, forgoing the move to see harmony in distension avoids the deeply interested intellectual operation of producing a fait accompli account of nationalism.[77] The conjuncture as concept holds out the possibility of a discussion of the American past that does not involve the specter of an already known social destiny. It combats the inclination to view modernity as entailing a single inevitable future—the inclination to

:lose off the future as a *source* of disruption" in the present and the past.[78] And it defends against the politically deadening notion of inevitability.

Across the Great Divide

When Rip returns to his village after his nap in the mountains, a tatty hotel catering to the transitory humanity engendered by the post-Revolutionary economy has replaced the "quiet Dutch inn of yore." That "quiet Dutch inn" was associated more with the locals lingering outside than it was with strangers, but something curious has occurred in Rip's absence:

> [Rip] now hurried forth, and hastened to his old resort, the village inn—but it too was gone. A large rickety wooden building stood in its place, with great gaping windows, some of them broken and mended with old hats and petticoats, and over the door was painted, "The Union Hotel, by Jonathan Doolittle." Instead of the great tree that used to shelter the quiet little Dutch inn of yore, there now was reared a tall naked pole, with something on the top that looked like a red night-cap, and from it was fluttering a flag, on which was a singular assemblage of stars and stripes—all this was strange and incomprehensible. He recognized on the sign, however, the ruby face of King George, under which he had smoked so many a peaceful pipe; but even this was singularly metamorphosed. The red coat was changed for one of blue and buff, a sword was held in the hand instead of a sceptre, the head was decorated with a cocked hat, and underneath was painted in large characters, GENERAL WASHINGTON.[79]

This new hotel and its accoutrements at first seem to confirm Rip's sense that omnipresent change has overtaken his village: the old inn has disappeared, and in its place stands a haphazard and ephemeral structure. Where the old inn was associated with the colonial Dutch, the new building is linked to the national project that is the United States: the linear "naked" flagpole has replaced the great branching tree of history in this "strange and incomprehensible" new world. Yet on a second reading, this scenario does just as much to question the idea of radical rupture and change. In addition to the portrait of George, whose ambivalences are clear, there is that Phrygian cap topping the Liberty Pole: it recalls the classical Roman practice by which liberated slaves signified their new status as citizens of the republic—a republic that would eventually suffer and decline. And despite the fact that "the character of the people seemed changed," we learn that "[t]here was, as usual, a crowd of folk about the door."[80] The tension between change and the "usual" that dominates this image has led Bruce Bur-

gett to describe it as Irving's reference to the "dialectical" relationship between change and historical persistence.[81] However, I want to introduce
another context for this image, one focused on reading Irving's George as a
compelling figure for the conjuncture.

According to Mary Ann Doane, a number of nineteenth-century
thinkers set out to understand why and how certain strong visual figures
persist as outlines or profiles after their physical disappearance from our
field of vision. In the classic example, Goethe recalls having stared long and
hard at an attractive woman in a pub. When she departs, he sees a negative
image of her against the white wall where she had stood. As in Irving's
image of George, the past persists into the present in Goethe's story. This
interest in what would come to be termed "persistence of vision" motivated
the production of optical toys, medical research, and philosophical speculation on the significance of the afterimage. In a description that distinctly
recalls Irving's portrait of George, Doane recounts one of these toys: "[T]he
Thaumatrope (invented by Dr. J. A. Paris in 1825), was based on the theory
of persistence of vision but produced an illusion of superimposition rather
than movement. It was a circular card with a design on the front and one
on the back (a bird and a cage, a bald man and a wig, and so on). When
twirled by means of two attached strings, the images were superimposed so
that, for instance, the bird appeared to be in the cage."[82] Doane also points
to the disruptive implications of the persistence of vision signified in the
Thaumatrope. According to the thinking of the day, "[t]he afterimage demonstrated that the 'very organization of the human eye' was imbued with a
temporal dimension, that vision was subject to delay. . . . The human experience of perception hence pivots upon a temporal lag, a superimposition of
images, an inextricability of past and present. To that extent it is a perverse
temporality, a nonlinear temporality that cannot be defined as a succession
of instants."[83] What was shocking about the afterimage was the confirmation it seemed to offer that human perception did not provide access to
homogeneous-continuous/self-contemporaneous time. The afterimage
points to a present tense that is constituted out of a "superimposition of
images," and it suggests that past and present cannot be separated from
each other. The present is always accessed through the afterimage of the
past. There can be no experience of a clear and present now.

As Doane goes on to show, this understanding of vision's relationship
to time became the conventional wisdom of the later nineteenth century.
Even in its early stages, however, there had to have been something rather
obvious about the point that both Irving and the Thaumatrope make re-

garding the reappearance of the past in the present. It is not an entirely novel discovery, after all: there are precedents for this view in classical republicanism, the writings of Vico, and typology, to name just a few. In each case, the present is accessed through the template of past experience. Yet if we take the basic idea of persistence and expand it into the surround of Irving's story, then we begin to learn something new about the character of American modernity. The great interest of Irving's story, and especially his image of George, is the extent to which it insists that past modes of being in time are coeval with present ones. In Doane's account of persistence of vision, she describes "a superimposition of images, an inextricability of past and present," characterizing this as a "perverse" and "nonlinear" temporality. But Irving's story imagines not only a "superimposition of images," but also a superimposition of social temporalities. A superimposition of images alone carries the implication of registering a single mode of time: the past might intrude upon the present, but it does not also *not* intrude upon the present. In Irving's account, by contrast, it is not simply that particular perceptions, memories, or understandings of the past are carried over into the present in such a way that linear time is made perverse. Rather it is that former modes of perceiving, knowing, and structuring time intrude upon and overlay new experiences of time in the modern present tense. The peculiar character of American modernity extends from its capacity to encompass (without harmonizing) competing orders of time drawn from the past, the present, and (as we will see) the future. In Irving's story, what persists into the present is a mode of being in time that belongs to the past, but that is not to say that this older mode of being in time forestalls the advent of other more novel ones. In other words, Irving does not offer merely another figure for the *ricorso*, but neither does he celebrate the ascendance of linear time. "Rip Van Winkle" imagines a modernity in which the past and present both differ and do not.

It is at this point in the discussion that I want to reintroduce the question of the figure of print and to raise once again the issue of the role literature played in realizing this impossible present tense. According to Irving, the function of literature in modernity is a distinctly untimely one. After Rip has contended with the (welcome) loss of his wife, the presence of a grandchild, and the final departure of many friends, he assumes the role of the village storyteller. The kind of storyteller that Rip turns out to be is the kind of storyteller that Irving himself becomes. Rip "resumed his old walks and habits; he soon found many of his former cronies, though all rather the worse for the wear and tear of time; and preferred making friends among the rising generation, with whom he soon grew into great favor."[84] Despite his seeming tie to the people of the past, this storyteller finds his place among the young:

Having nothing to do at home, and being arrived at that happy age when a man can be idle with impunity, he took his place once more on the bench at the inn door, and was reverenced as one of the patriarchs of the village, and a chronicle of the old times "before the war." It was some time before he could get into the regular track of gossip, or could be made to comprehend the strange events that had taken place during his torpor. How that there had been a revolutionary war—that the country had thrown off the yoke of Old England—and that, instead of being a subject of his Majesty George the Third, he was now a free citizen of the United States.[85]

Irving is at pains to provide a series of receding personae in the *Sketch-Book,* separating himself from his reader. In what was at the time a conventional gesture of narrative framing, he introduces "Rip Van Winkle" with the specious suggestion that the story was found among the papers of one of Irving's other personae: the historian Diedrich Knickerbocker. In this sense, the reader is asked to occupy a position at some remove from Irving's storyteller. Nevertheless, it is perhaps not too much of a stretch to read Rip at this point as a fictionalized version of Irving—and even as a stand-in for the enterprise of storytelling itself in the moment of modernity. If this is true, then what role does Irving imagine for the avocation he will famously turn into a viable American vocation? At first, it would seem that Rip's new role is that of a mere "chronicle"—"mere" because the chronicle as a form is one of the least figurative, reflective, or literary modes of historical writing. Indeed, the chronicle as a classical form of writing is thought to have anticipated the emergence of the first secular historians. If the chronicle has any specific significance in the context of modernity, it is that it describes events unfolding with only minor attribution of natural or divine intervention. Although the medieval chronicles, for instance, contained certain legendary features, they were primarily "based on the local records of the annalists and listed rather than evaluated events."[86] According to the *Oxford English Dictionary,* moreover, a chronicle is "a detailed and continuous register of events in order of time; a historical record, esp. one in which the facts are narrated without philosophic treatment, or any attempt at literary style."[87] In this sense, even the medieval chronicle anticipates a secularized time consciousness to the extent that it emphasizes linear chronological succession absent "philosophic treatment" as an ordering principle. Despite its ancient origins, the chronicle is a modern form. If Rip serves a local need for an accurate chronicle of the linear unfolding of time in the past, however, he also does something more. Irving's narrator recalls, "He used to tell his story to every stranger that arrived at Mr. Doolittle's hotel. He was observed, at first, to vary on some points every time he told it, which was, doubtless owing to his having so recently awaked. It at last settled down precisely to the tale I have related, and not a man, woman, or child in the neighborhood but knew it by heart."[88] If Rip at one level functions as a mere chronicle of the past, he is equally a genuine storyteller in his own right: he is a trustworthy chronicle of the "times before the war," but he also tells the formally considered story of his disappearance. In this sense, Rip provides his village with two modes of understanding the past and two ways of being in time. If the chronicle aims at a listlike account of people and places past that is married to linear time, then the genre of the story demands that Rip's recitation contain something "useful." "[O]ne of the essential features of every real story," according to Walter Benjamin, is that it "contains, openly or covertly something useful. In one case, the usefulness may lie in a moral; in another, in some practical advice; in a third, in a proverb or maxim."[89] In this attempt to be useful, the story endorses an understanding of time very different from that of the chronicle—that is, the view that human experience is fundamentally the same across what Wai Chee Dimock calls "deep time." Proverbs, maxims, morals, and practical advice of the kind Benjamin describes do not address themselves to specific moments in the chronological unfolding of time; much like the epic, they assume that a constant character spans all of human experience. The story is in this sense a premodern form. Yet in describing Rip as a full-fledged storyteller, Irving also suggests that it is possible to carry the storyteller's understanding of time into the modern moment. Before Rip departs from his premodern village for his long nap, Irving's narrator tells us that "the children of the village . . . would shout with joy whenever he approached. He assisted at their sports, made their playthings, taught them to fly kites and shoot marbles, and told them long stories of ghosts, witches, and Indians."[90] If in his function as town chronicle Rip assumes a new (modern) capacity, then in his role as its favorite storyteller he reclaims a long-lost (premodern) role.

In the theory of literature concretized in the figure of print, the doubled role that Irving imagines for Rip is unavailable to the modern writer. The move from voice to print constitutes an insurmountable loss. In "The Storyteller," for example, Benjamin, writing from the perspective of the 1930s, proposes that "the storyteller in his living efficacy is by no means a force today."[91] Although it sounds as though there is something specific about the interwar years that makes storytelling impossible, Benjamin insists that "nothing would be more fatuous than to wish to see it as merely a 'symptom of decay,' let alone a 'modern symptom'"—where "modern" is understood to mean "now."[92] Instead, the disappearance of the storyteller "is, rather, only a concomitant of the secular productive forces of history—a symptom that has quite gradually removed narrative from the realm of living speech and at the same time is making it possible to find a new beauty in what is vanishing."[93] In addition to the general "secular productive forces of history," Benjamin dates the decline of the storyteller to the emergence of a familiar figure of print: "The earliest indication of a process whose end is the decline of storytelling is the rise of the novel at the beginning of modern times. What distinguishes the novel from the story (and from the epic in the narrower sense) is its essential dependence on the book. The dissemination of the novel became possible only with the invention of printing."[94] For Benjamin, the figure of print signifies the culmination of a host of growing trends. In the decline of epic forms and the emergence of the novel, Benjamin finds evidence of the loss of communal experience and the emergence of a perplexed modern individual. "The birthplace of the novel," Benjamin writes, "is the individual in his isolation."[95] With the coming of print, we learn, the storyteller starts to disappear: print culture has no capacity to function as a site of storytelling in its own right due to the loss of what Benjamin elsewhere calls "the aura." In this famous essay, print culture is reduced to the novel and the newspaper, and both of these in turn are represented as signs of a decisive break with the epic past in which the storyteller had a pivotal role.

Washington Irving takes a rather different view of the significance of printing and the book to modern culture. In "The Mutability of Literature: A Colloquy in Westminster Abbey," he describes an afternoon spent in the library of Westminster Abbey. Seeking refuge from the noise and bustle of a group of rambunctious schoolboys, Irving retires to the safety of the library where he takes down "a little thick quarto, curiously bound in parchment, with brass clasps."[96] After a few moments of reverie spent "thrumming [with one hand] upon the quarto," he accidentally unclasps the volume. Thereupon it begins to speak:

[T]he little book gave two or three yawns, like one awaking from a deep sleep; then a husky hem; and at length began to talk. At first its voice was very hoarse and broken, being much troubled by a cobweb which some studious spider had woven across it; and having probably contracted a cold from long exposure to the chills and damp of the abbey. In a short time, however, it became more distinct, and I soon found it an exceedingly fluent conversable little tome. Its language, to be sure, was rather quaint and obsolete, and its pronunciation, what, in the present day, would be deemed barbarous; but I shall endeavor, as far as I am able, to render it in modern parlance.[97]

The little quarto complains of its long neglect and disregard, and Irving's narrator identifies the speaking voice's quaint and antique features. A few lines later, the book inaccurately guesses at who among its peers has managed to achieve lasting renown, and Irving takes this as an occasion to meditate upon the subject of the essay's title. Significantly, however, "The Mutability of Literature" also emphasizes a certain capacity of the quarto to bring the past compellingly forward in a way typically associated with voice, presence, aura, the epic, and the premodern. Irving associates this antecedent of modern print culture with a capacity not only to memorialize the past but also to reanimate its modes of animation. In the introduction to "Rip Van Winkle," he suggests something similar by way of reverse implication. "Whenever," Irving writes, Diedrich Knickerbocker "happened upon a genuine Dutch family, snugly shut up in its low-roofed farmhouse, under a spreading sycamore, he looked upon it as a little clasped volume of blackletter, and studied it with the zeal of a book-worm."[98] Where the figures of print examined in this chapter emphasize print culture's capacity to sever our relationship with the past and antiquate its modes of being in time, Irving would here seem to argue for a much different view. In Irving, we discover a theory of literature that has print culture drawing the past—and, implicitly, its ways of being in time—across modernity's great divide. Irving places his own print-dependent writing within a continuum of book forms, and he associates his efforts with the "black-letter" that bridged the "divide" separating medieval script from early printed typefaces. Blackletter was, after all, one of Guttenberg's first typefaces, and it was based on the medieval calligraphic form known by the same name.[99] The very reference to "black-letter" questions the notion of modern print culture's break with the past.

This interest on Irving's part in the bringing forward of antiquated forms sheds new light on the long-standing question of Irving's originality. As Michael Davitt Bell explains, "Irving has often been regarded as a mere imitator, a recycler of outworn British modes and styles, a charge already being lodged against him by contemporary detractors at the height of his greatest celebrity. It is certainly true that his works promote nostalgia, whether about Britain or about old Dutch New York; such nostalgia was Irving's stock-in-trade. And he certainly drew on British models; he soon came to be known as the 'American Goldsmith.' "[100] Although Irving's detractors took issue with this borrowing, we might just as well take it as a starting point for any discussion of literature. The cultural nationalist theory of literature with which this chapter began encouraged American writers to pursue a kind of literary autogenesis in which new forms spring Athena-like, fully formed from an Americanized Zeus's head. Irving's *Sketch-Book* encourages a rather different view of literature as a form of constant borrowing that secrets the time consciousness of other places and other peoples in its very form. This might at first sound like a specious literary humanism in which the shared forms of literature endorse a common human culture, but to conclude so would be to ignore the force of that perplexing picture of George/George. In fact this image suggests that John L. O'Sullivan was right when he argued that the "tendency to imitativeness, prevailing among our literary men" is "wholly unfavourable to progress." If "progress" means the effectuation of a national community sharing time and self, then George suggests that this is clearly beyond the scope of literature's capacity. Importantly, however, the portrait also suggests that the idea of a transhistorical supralocal community of the fully human is an equally unattainable desire. What Irving seems to know (and O'Sullivan cannot admit) is that there is no purely original literary production, and in this sense there can be no absolute break with the encumbering past. It is in the nature of literary form that any specific instance of literature will entail an overlay of different modes of being in time. To the degree that this is so, literature is no friend of the nation. But neither is it the aide-de-camp of an emerging global humanism. As Irving has it, literature sticks us to our place. In a reversal of fortunes, the figure of print turns out to be a force for deep locality.

The ultimate figure for literature in Irving's story is in this sense the ekphrastic George. In the simplest terms, ekphrasis is "the verbal representation of visual representation," as in Irving's description of the portrait outside the Union Hotel.[101] In a narrower sense, however, ekphrasis is a specific genre of poetry whose locus classicus is Homer's description of Achilles' shield. Here then, in Irving's figure for literature, we see the intrusion of a classical genre and its peculiar temporal mode into the scene of "Rip Van Winkle," where it must share the stage with both the genre of the chronicle and that of the story. The classical examples of ekphrasis, moreover, encourage a heightened focus on the relationship between temporality and the verbal arts. According to Murray Krieger, the figure of ekphrasis is an attempt to realize the "aesthetic dream of [Western] culture," a desire to bring two "opposed impulses . . . together in the paradoxical immediacy" of a literary figure.[102] These two impulses are toward representing "fixity" on the one hand and "flow" on the other. In the classical context, "ekphrasis, as an extended description, was called upon to intrude upon the flow of discourse and, for its duration, to suspend the argument of the rhetor or the action of the poet. . . . It was, then, a device intended to interrupt the temporality of the discourse, to freeze it during its indulgence in spatial exploration."[103] In its modern manifestations, Krieger continues, this literary figure manages to capture in one instance of representation both fixity and flow. Although Krieger describes ekphrasis as an attempt to yoke together the spatial and the temporal, we might do better to designate it a conjunction of two different orders of time: the linear time of progress and an experience of simple duration.

Albertis del Orient Browere's painting *Rip Van Winkle* (1833; Figure 1) suggests the consequential nature of the conflicted order of time signified in Irving's figure of ekphrasis. This painting offers a detailed picture of the moment that Rip returns to his village, and in this respect, it resembles the more famous Rip Van Winkle paintings by John Quidor, such as *Rip Van Winkle and His Companions at the Inn Door of Nicholas Vedder* (1839; Figure 2) or *The Return of Rip Van Winkle* (1849; Figure 3). The main characters of the story appear in Browere's painting, as they do in Quidor's version: Rip, his new companions, his granddaughter, and her child. So, too, does Browere provide a convincingly precise image of the Union Hotel, paying close attention to the dilapidated character of the structure and its nooks and crannies. Yet Browere's George verges on a kind of blankness. The vague shadows of a figure are visible, here, but the details of his clothes and appearance are impossible to discern. In the detailed context of the larger painting, and given the portrait's centrality to the moment of Rip's return in Irving's story, the muzzy image is striking. It also differs from Quidor's paintings. Quidor's internal portrait clearly depicts King George in *Rip Van Winkle and His Companions at the Inn Door of Nicholas Vedder's* (Figure 4), which visually retells the colonial half of the story, and in *The Return of Rip Van Winkle*, it cites the stable iconography of George Washington widely known from circulating formal and informal portraits (Figure 5). I want to suggest that the very indecipherability of Browere's internal portrait signals more exactly than does Quidor's painting the suggestive nature of Irving's ekphrastic George. This reverse ekphrasis *of* ekphrasis suggests that the "be-

Figure 1. *Rip Van Winkle* (1833). Albertis del Orient Browere. Oil on canvas, 21 1/8 × 25 in. The Metropolitan Museum of Art. Gift of Mr. and Mrs. S. Richard Krown and Family, 2002 (2002.444). Image © The Metropolitan Museum of Art.

fores and afters" of linear progress and the retrievable "instant's vision" just might coexist.[104] Yet the Browere painting also suggests that in the modernity comprised of these competing orders of time, George will never quite rise to legibility. He is instead what D. H. Lawrence spoke of at the turn of the twentieth century as a "torn divided monster."

As Lawrence notes in his *Studies in Classic American Literature*, perhaps the single question organizing nineteenth-century American writing is Crèvecoeur's famous query in *Letters from an American Farmer*: "What, then, is the American, this new man?" American literary studies has moved away from this particular question to focus instead on regional, racial, hemispheric, transatlantic, and other supralocal forms of identity; it has, however, continued to emphasize that literature has a definitive role to play in the consolidation of these forms. In a peculiar way, this approach an-

Figure 2. *Rip Van Winkle and His Companions at the Inn Door of Nicholas Vedder*
(1839). John Quidor. Oil on canvas, 27 1/8 × 34 1/8 in. Museum of Fine Arts,
Boston. Bequest of Martha C. Karolik for the M. and M. Karolik Collection of
American Paintings, 1815–1865 (48.469). Photograph © 2009 Museum of Fine Arts,
Boston.

swers to rather than rebuts the terms of Crèvecoeur's question; like the
original question, this reconfigured American literary studies caters to a
focus on the emergence of new forms of supralocal social belonging as the
defining feature of American modernity. On this familiar intellectual and
political terrain, literature is interesting primarily to the extent that it confirms the dialectic of social disembedding and reembedding conventionally
associated with modernity.[105] Here the truly local always gives way to the
nation, region, or race, with literature as its able porter.

Both Irving and Lawrence insist on a rather different view of the character of American modernity and its literature. Lawrence suggests that the
white settlers of the United States "came to America for two reasons": "1.
To slough the old European consciousness completely. 2. To grow a new
skin underneath, a new form. This second is a hidden process."[106] Once

Figure 3. *The Return of Rip Van Winkle* (1849). John Quidor. Oil on canvas, 39 3/4 × 49 13/16 in. Andrew W. Mellon Collection. Image courtesy of the Board of Trustees, National Gallery of Art, Washington, D.C.

arrived, these settlers found it impossible to cleave the new from the old. Elsewhere Lawrence describes the Europeans left behind in the Old World as snakes that had shed their penultimate world-historical skins and entered their "final phase." The "true American" is very different: "a torn divided monster," he "writhes and writhes like a snake that is long in sloughing."[107] The "true American" is never fully American. For that matter, neither is he anything else. To know him is to know a "hidden" generative process. He is an "unborn homunculus" that never fully comes into being as himself.[108] Lawrence's American fails to transcend locality.[109] The language of progress and colonization hamstrings Lawrence at moments; he finds himself trapped in its cultivated desire to see the homogenization of time and abstraction of identity at play. Notwithstanding this language, however, Lawrence manages to capture the "torn divided" monstrosity of modernity. If Lawrence and Irving are right that the American never fully emerges onto

The Original by John Quidor. 1839.

Figure 4. Detail of *Rip Van Winkle and His Companions at the Inn Door of Nicholas Vedder* (1839). John Quidor. Oil on canvas, 27 1/8 × 34 1/8 in. Museum of Fine Arts, Boston. Bequest of Martha C. Karolik for the M. and M. Karolik Collection of American Paintings, 1815–1865 (48.469). Photograph © 2009 Museum of Fine Arts, Boston.

Figure 5. Detail of *The Return of Rip Van Winkle* (1849). John Quidor. Oil on canvas, 39 3/4 × 49 13/16 in. Andrew W. Mellon Collection. Image courtesy of the Board of Trustees, National Gallery of Art, Washington, D.C.

the landscape of North America, then America would remain more an intent than an actuality. In this reading, the North American landscape figures as the site of a social anomie recognizable as modernity's challenge, but also as a place still open to unpredicted futures. The attraction of Browere's internal portrait, Irving's George/George, and Lawrence's monster is the way that they foreclose foreclosure.

Yet the figure of print has had even more than nine lives, and it is precisely about seeking foreclosure. As I indicated briefly in my introduction, Benedict Anderson's now canonical study of what he calls "print capitalism" and of nationalism contends that nineteenth-century novels and newspapers represent time as "homogeneous" and "empty." This allowed the nineteenth-century reader to imagine his "simultaneity" with his fellow citizens. This reader was encouraged to picture himself united with others who shared his national affiliation, and he was asked to indulge the fantasy that he inhabited a single "moment" in common with his peers. Print capitalism makes far-flung Americans fantasize about an "immediate relationship" with one another.[110] An "American will never meet, or even know the names of more than a handful of his . . . fellow-Americans. He has no idea of what they are up to at any one time. But he has complete confidence in their steady, anonymous, simultaneous activity."[111] Although in early America, as now, the fellowship engendered by physical proximity often eluded the incipient American, print capitalism led him to believe that he inhabited the same fraction of time as those Americans who remained permanently outside of his orbit.[112] Following Anderson, Americanists have for some time now argued that print culture "engineered" the advent of the nation, regions, and races in the American context.[113] In *National Manhood: Capitalist Citizenship and the Imagined Fraternity of White Men*, for example, Dana Nelson influentially argues that the cultural history of professional white men is a history of increasingly antidemocratic and exclusionary identification.[114] Working against the very real and powerful egalitarian energies unleashed by the Revolution, the post-Revolutionary capitalization of the United States relocated professional white men's affections and identifications away from those local experiences that previously defined them. One consequence of this relocation of identity was a failure to acknowledge, and so to attend to, the demands of figures marked as local and embodied: white women, African Americans, indigenous populations. This relocation of identity also produced a class of citizens—white men—who would remain permanently at odds with themselves. Bruce Burgett has summarized the wider field's accepted view as follows: "[M]odern nationalism works in large part through the use of mass-mediated, capital-driven technologies like print in order to stage public rituals that enable politically diverse individuals to imagine themselves as simultaneously national."[115] Yet even this accepted view permits us to glimpse a past we might yet know. Nelson writes, for example, that "[i]t is important to draw out the difference between the appeal of national manhood and its actual functional cultural installation."[116]

In recent studies of American literature the accent has tended to fall on what Nelson calls nationalism's appeal; the chapters that follow in this book strike out in a different direction. "Rip Van Winkle" suggests that nineteenth-century American literature keeps time in much more sophisticated ways than the figure of print would admit, and its caveat emptor George also demands some acknowledgment of the political significance of that sophistication. In the chapters that follow, I argue that in the American historical romance the past is both securely sealed and bleeds into the present. I suggest that notwithstanding a hollow promise to send its reader into the freeing embrace of white male fraternity, Southwestern humor actually implicates its reader in competing orders of time. And I further suggest that African American life writing's emphasis on "the deprivation of time in the life of the slave" masks a temporal surfeit that is at once more destructive and more precious than any deprivation could ever be. These different modalities of time neither alternate with one another nor harmonize; they articulate a conjuncture in which more than one modality of time defines any geographic area, social enclave, or literary form. Here fugitive slave narratives articulate in their form the constraints of an economic system that required enslaved African American laborers either to repeat the same action over and again or to repeat the same cycle of labor at fixed intervals. Scenes of cyclical repetition and formal figures of the same interlace these "narratives of the life," which simultaneously attempt to tell the story of the life as a story of linear progress. This staging of a conflict between laboring time and progressive time also typifies the American historical romance, whose authors often appear to wish that they could simply represent American history as a story of uninterrupted progress. In both traditions, depictions of violence—slave revolts, settler-Indian battles, familicide, and other forms of bloodshed connected to the struggle for freedom—limn the way violence collapses the divisions separating past, present, and future. Chronologically distinct historical figures begin to resemble each other in these episodes of messianic time. Heroes from the past inhabit the present; agents from the future realign the now. In humor from the "Old Southwest," or what is now the American South, smooth narrative lines seeking to reproduce the movements of travel fold back on themselves when steamboats and stagecoaches fail to live up to their technological promise. These tall tales proceed in fits and starts, connoting the way that engine failures, natural disasters, and self-interested chicanery make for local declensions of time and forestall the emergence of a national common time. In short, neither this literature nor any corner of the world from which it emerged could boast a common denominator of time. Laboring time and revolutionary messianic time feature in Nathaniel Hawthorne's *The House of the Seven Gables*, but they also surface in Frederick Douglass's *Narrative*. Single genres, single texts, and even single passages consistently encompass more than one temporality. More to the point, these temporalities repeatedly overlap but do not synchronize. The chapters that follow accumulate a collection of these conjunctures. In so doing, they aim to encourage a filling in of the figure of print for American literary history and a broader sense of literature's contribution to American modernity. In this American modernity, national origin, phenotype, and region of birth do not predict the future: with more than one type of time at play, there is always more than one future on the horizon. This is not to say that the future was a matter of infinite free choice, nor is it to revive the idea that nineteenth-century Americans were transcendent masters of their own destinies. Rather it is to acknowledge how this literature articulates an American modernity that is both more confusing and more capacious than John L. O'Sullivan could ever allow. If "Rip Van Winkle" rejects the notion of social destiny that distinguishes American political rhetoric from the early nineteenth century forward, then the chapters that follow try to do the same by seeking entry to a world where the future is not known.

Chapter 2
"A Magnificent Fragment": Dialects of Time and the American Historical Romance

[T]he story has a sort of expansive quality which never wholly fructifies, and as I lately laid it down, after reading it for the third time, I had a sense of having interested myself in a magnificent fragment.

—Henry James, Hawthorne

The first half of the nineteenth century saw large numbers of Americans begin the task of writing—and reading—new histories of their young nation. Committed to the endurance of the Republic, emboldened by the patriotic aftermath of the century's first international wars, and troubled by the entropic energies of the market revolution, legions of writers set about filling in the faint lines of descent connecting the modern American nation to its colonial and premodern prototype. They ventured to write narratives of serial continuity linking the not-too-distant origins of their country to a much anticipated future that would feature a settled, secure, and permanent democratic republic.[1] The first half of this century saw national historiography take root, the founding of America's early historical societies, the consolidation of a post-Enlightenment progressive historiography exemplified in the writing and the person of George Bancroft, and the establishment of history as a legitimate subject of study for women as well as men.[2]

As history writing in all its forms came to embody the hopes and aspirations of America's most ardent cultural nationalists, its fiction writers succumbed to this national preoccupation. In addition to an explosion of belletristic historical writing, this half-century witnessed the rise to prominence of one of the most enduringly popular of American literary forms:

the national historical romance. In ways that have not been fully understood, one of the most consequential contributions of this influential American genre was its attempt to consider—and its magnification of—the idiosyncratic new order of time that had come to distinguish the texture of modernity in America. This literature's diagnostic interest in preserving the feel of modern time anticipates social theory's concern for modernity's restructured time, and it offers a pointed contrast to the progressive historiography that Bancroft personified. Indeed, this interest is what distinguishes this genre (and the two others considered here) from past, future, and different literary forms.

This sensitivity to time's new character was flowering in unlikely ground. The most popular practitioners of the historical romance often appear to have been more interested in facilitating the orderly consolidation of a common national culture than they were in acknowledging impediments to it—which this new order of time most certainly appeared to be. From the standpoint of today (and as others have argued), James Fenimore Cooper, Catharine Sedgwick, and their lesser contemporaries sometimes seem to be struggling (against their own better judgment) to write nationally serviceable "from-to" stories in which the cycle of triumph and decline that classical republicanism feared, the potentially disintegrative forces of the Revolution, and the corrosive tendencies of technological modernization would rise and fall from view in orderly procession as the emergence of a national common time called progress neutralized in turn these threats to national stability.[3] As far as these writers let on, they often seem to have understood themselves to be writing nothing more and nothing less than a fictional history of the inevitable progress of progress that cast America as its lucky beneficiary. However, their interest in American history required these writers to engage a vexed conjuncture ill-suited to being depicted as the seedbed of the once and future nation. In recounting the colonization of North America, the Revolution, and more recent events, these authors found themselves compelled to contend with the experience and meaning of a perplexing new order of time that included linear progress as only one of its aspects—and not necessarily the most important one.

This experience of modern time—one feature of it, anyway—gets concisely figured in the famed preface to Nathaniel Hawthorne's *The House of the Seven Gables*.[4] In this preface, Hawthorne writes of a present tense that repeats the past while at the same time differing radically from it. He also intimates that the flexibility of the "romance" genre uniquely suits it to the task of chronicling this implausibly insistent feature of modern life—this curious bifurcation of time. The text that follows his preface is a "Romance," Hawthorne explains, and *The House of the Seven Gables* therefore has license to "attempt to connect a by-gone time with the very Present that is flitting away from us."[5] As this novel's attention to the technologies of modernity—photographic reproduction, the locomotive train, telegraphy, and the like—will later indicate, this "flitting" present is that self-transcending increment of modern time whose character is glossed in phrases such as Zygmunt Bauman's "liquid time," Anthony Giddens's "runaway world," and Marshall Berman's (or Marx and Engels's) "all that is solid melts into air." By the conventional measures of social theory, this particular species of present tenseness defines the aura of modernity. However, Hawthorne's flitting present has at least one unconventional attribute. If this present tense is self-transcending, it also (and at the same time) manages to remain continuous with certain "by-gone time[s]." This flitting present goes so far as to rearticulate those bygone times. Indeed, it is identical to them. "[T]he wrong-doing of one generation lives into the successive ones," Hawthorne explains, "and, divesting itself of every temporary advantage, becomes a pure and uncontrollable mischief."[6] The past and the present differ here, but they are also one and the same. According to Hawthorne, the romance is capable of doing justice to this discrepant—this impossible—experience of modernity.

As Hawthorne's preface discerns, the seemingly impossible happens in the historical romance. Here time takes several distinct forms that coexist in unimaginable and unanticipated ways on the same page and in the same literary figure, together producing a deep-rooted readerly awareness of this genre as a "magnificent fragment." This feature of *The House of the Seven Gables* and other works like it helps to explain why they have so often frustrated and delighted critics who arrive at their pages expecting to find the simple unfolding of a line. In the parlance of the day, and notwithstanding Hawthorne's protestations to the contrary, historical romances and novels were the closest of kissing cousins. As Nina Baym has shown, moreover, the primary criterion upon which both were judged was their capacity to maintain an orderly Aristotelian plot line.[7] It should not surprise us, then, when Susan Mizruchi notes that critics "from Hawthorne's era to the present" have objected to the "static and repetitive quality" of *The House of the Seven Gables* and complained of its "resistance to process as progress."[8] Edwin Percy Whipple's otherwise sympathetic *Graham's Magazine* review of the novel stands in for many others in its assessment that "there is some discord in the present work in the development of character and sequence of events; the dramatic unity is therefore not perfectly preserved."[9] Anthony Trollope had this to say about Hawthorne's *House*: "When Hawthorne proposed to himself to write 'The Scarlet Letter,' the plot of his story was clear to his mind. He wrote the book because he had the story strongly, lucidly manifest to his own imagination. In composing [*The House of the Seven Gables*] he was driven to search for a plot, and to make a story."[10] And Meredith McGill's recent rereading of this novel describes a "stifling convergence of sequence and repetition, declension and monotony."[11] As I detail later, this resistance to "process as progress"—this "discord" in the "sequence of events" and "stifling" absence of plot—characterizes not only Hawthorne's novel but also famous (and not so famous) examples of the historical romance in its conventional and its more experimental modes. Although I do not wish to take *The House of the Seven Gables* as typical, its long paper trail does guide us to an angle of approach we might profitably pursue vis-à-vis a consideration of the historical romance per se. Lawrence Buell observes that this most troublesome of Hawthorne's novels has difficulty "making up its mind as to whether society changes or stays the same."[12] His comment applies just as well to even more familiar examples of the historical romance. In fact, key examples in this tradition share the indecisive tendencies of Hawthorne's novel and its interest in a seemingly new order of time, two features that mark this writing as a literature of modernity. American historical romances signal their modernity exactly when they fail to choose from the limited range of options elaborated in Buell's comment. This genre's quality of resistance to easy summary and the tidiness of progress, I am suggesting, articulates an experience that is understudied, essentially important for understanding the nature of American modernity, and more or less impossible to achieve.

As the quotations from Buell and Mizruchi indicate, to observe that the American historical romance elaborates a complex experience of time is, in one respect, to rehearse a home truth of nineteenth-century literary history. Lukács's *The Historical Novel*, George Dekker's *The American Historical Romance,* and Philip Gould's *Covenant and Republic*—three of the most influential and astute studies treating nineteenth-century historical fiction—include lengthy commentaries on this complex account of historical time. For these critics, the historical romance entails political, social, and aesthetic conflicts that have everything to do with battling conceptions of historical time. In Lukács, for instance, James Fenimore Cooper's historical novels thematically and formally register a conflict between traditional societies and emerging market capitalism, as well as a struggle between reactionary and progressive views of history. For him, the successful historical novel depicts peoples defined by an experience of history as either stasis or cycle who are drawn into the future by virtue of a conflict between progressive and reactionary social forces. Dekker focuses on the intellectual heritage that influenced Cooper and the other historical romancers, rejecting Lukács's reading of the novelist as a historical symptom and his characterization of influence studies as mere antiquarianism. He traces the thick account of historical time in these novels to the impact of Sir Walter Scott and the stadialists. For Gould, early American historical fiction is shaped by competing liberal and republican ideologies and their discordant (but ultimately complementary) accounts of historical time.

I want to build on this critical foundation and occupy a dependent vantage point, but one that does more to clarify this literature's relationship to the time consciousness of American modernity. As Gould cogently explains, the generation of post–World War II liberal critics exemplified by Richard Chase influentially claimed that the "romance" genre sought to exteriorize a complex interior psychological landscape common to all human experience. In so doing, these critics severed these novels from their social milieu. Historicists such as Lukács, Dekker, and Gould advocate for a different stance, aiming to reattach the historical romance to its historical context. They take a variety of approaches to defining what constitutes a valid context for literary history—or as Gould describes it, the "historicity of the historical romance."[13] But their very different versions of historicism collectively obey the first principle that time inevitably assumes a single form in the real modernity that we all inhabit (as opposed to the fictional one this literature describes). Written with nuance and displaying a keen interest in the array of forces impacting the production of any particular work of literature, these studies also read this writing as what Lukács calls the "prehistory of the present."[14] And although their sense of the political and aesthetic legacy of the historical romance may differ, they collectively assume that we all share the same present tense—a present tense made possible by the modernization of time read as its homogenization. This placing of nineteenth-century historical fiction into what is at base a post-Enlightenment progressive historical narrative happens most explicitly in Lukács, whose Marxist historicism requires him to emphasize certain general laws of history that incline toward progress. Lukács suggests that to read the past as the necessary prehistory of the present is precisely the goal. It is inconceivable that *The Historical Novel* would describe a scenario in which the competition among different historical temporalities—clearly one concern of

his favored "classical historical novels"—is not overcome.[15] When he reads
the past as the "necessary prehistory of the present," the past always trends
toward progress. Formal difficulty of the kind we find in Hawthorne's account of time—"resistance to process as progress"—amounts to the rise of
bourgeois decadence. It is an indulgent playing with form that refuses to
acknowledge the scientifically ascertainable course of history. This historicism rejects the idea of several sustainable and competing tracks of history—not all of which are linear. It also makes it impossible to engage this
literature as the site of origin for as yet unrealized or unknown futures.

I want to shift the discussion of the historical romance by reading this
writing as a literature of the socially impossible that nevertheless goes some
way toward realizing the impossibilities it describes. In this sense, I attempt
to read this literature not as the prehistory of the present but, to whatever
degree possible, on its own terms. As the previous chapter indicated, and as
the following one will discuss in more detail, one of the primary features of
modernity is the distanciation of time and space. A natural and necessary
metric formerly predicted how the passage of time and movement through
geographic space would relate to each other, but modernity's technologies
of communication and travel dissolved this seemingly indissoluble relationship. It is easy to see how, as Benedict Anderson argues, this shift might
have permitted one to imagine a connection to people and places with
whom one has no direct face-to-face connection but with whom one shares
the same imagined present. Moreover, modernity's technologies of travel
actually did make a much wider range of people physically available to each
other, as the next chapter on Southwestern humor discusses. Lukács admits
as much, for example, when he argues that European infantrymen's experience of continental war precipitated a new historical consciousness—a
newfound sense that what happens in places to which one has no natural
ties of kith and kin might nevertheless matter at home. Yet modernity's distanciation of time-space relationships also allows literature to intervene so
that its readers are permitted to inhabit not only the present but also the
past and future in significantly unfamiliar ways. Although this belief in a
capacity to move into the past and the future might at first appear to be
fantastically supernatural, it is neither more nor less so than the belief that
one somehow has intrinsic connections to people at distances removed
from oneself who nevertheless occupy the same "present." In that sense,
this literature impinges on whether and how its readers restrict themselves
to identifying as Americans. From the perspective of the progressive historicism that first emerged during this period and that continues to dominate

historiography and literary history, the modernity that the historical romance describes—a modernity in which the past is both the same as and
different from the present—cannot sustain itself. Yet the real interest of the
historical romance is its capacity—demonstrated later—to sustain that experience as well as other impossible orientations within "historical time."
One may choose to follow Lukács and propose that this happens because
the character of the period forces its way into literary form itself. Or one
might opt instead to credit these authors with a certain underacknowledged
talent for capturing the nature of an experience that the conventions of progressive historiography have neither the inclination nor the tools to explore.
In the event, these novels, for all their talk about inevitable futures, are
much less secure in their representation of the past as the prehistory of the
present and the future than they might otherwise have been. From this perspective, nineteenth-century literature amounts to much more than a history of the progress of progress—the history that we can find described in
the pages of Bancroft's writing. It is not "made in the image of the present."[16] It is an archive and an agent of an unlikely modernity that is and
was no less real for having been so. To the extent that this literature can
imagine impossible experiences of time while also participating in the self-
reflexivity of modernity—to this extent the modernity that this literature
describes has in fact already happened.

In addition to drawing from Lukács and Dekker, my interest in locating the historical romance in relationship to modernity rather than the premodern past that it ostensibly represents recalls Gould's introduction to
Covenant and Republic, McGill's view of Hawthorne's realism, and Jeffrey
Insko's arguments about Catharine Sedgwick's "anachronistic imaginings."
Gould proposes that, "[b]y locating the [historical romance's] 'historicity'
in the seventeenth century, critics of this historical literature of New England consistently have assumed a stable relationship between text and context, a fact that ultimately obscures the many ways in which these novels do
not merely make analogies between past and present but actually inscribe
contemporary history."[17] Similarly, McGill rejects the view that *The House
of the Seven Gables* is overly concerned with departing from the real of its
moment. She writes that "Hawthorne is a good deal more interested in the
representation of ordinary life than his defensive identification of his text
as a Romance in his 'Preface' would suggest," and she points out that Hawthorne considered this particular novel to be a modern one.[18] Just as sugges-
tively, Insko emphasizes how the historicist methods of many contemporary literary historians force a linear model of historical time onto texts that

actually set out to criticize precisely that notion. He shows how literature such as Sedgwick's *Hope Leslie* engages in a "non-colonizing form of presentism" concerned with envisioning a "nonteleological" model of "multicultural democracy."[19] In this respect, he reads this and other writing in relation to the present tense of its composition.

In proposing that the historical romance tells us much more about modernity's new order of time than it does about the premodern, however, I am equally interested in discerning how this literature contributes to the character of modernity by drawing forward certain anachronistic epic, messianic, and other literary temporalities. Those legions of American readers who engaged (and continue to read) historical romances were (and are) the products of a curious experience: this literature allows its readers to imagine and inhabit impossible relationships that cross naturalized chronological boundaries separating past, present, and future. Indeed, it invites readers to take up identificatory positions that are more in conflict with each other than they are complementary, and it facilitates the emergence of curious creatures: the imperial democrat, the colonizing postcolonial, the revolutionary conservative. If the intended pedagogical function of American historical fiction was to train its readers into a close identification with the nation, then in this respect its actual impact was something rather different.

This chapter explores these features of the national historical romance in relationship to Hawthorne's *The House of the Seven Gables* and *The Scarlet Letter*, Catharine Sedgwick's *Hope Leslie*, and Joseph C. Hart's *Miriam Coffin*. Before turning to my readings of these texts, a few thoughts on the issue of the novel versus romance and romance versus historical romance distinctions. My arguments here follow the simple if unconventional rule that the American historical romance is distinguished neither by its topical focus nor even exactly by its form. *The House of the Seven Gables* treats the Puritan and early national past, for instance, but its primary interest is the quite recent 1840s. I have nevertheless chosen to include it in this discussion of the historical romance, where others class it either as a novel or a romance. I have permitted myself to take this minor liberty, because a telling feature links *The House of the Seven Gables* to the other romances, novels, and historical romances germane to this discussion: an attraction to performing a social diagnostics of the experience of modernity and in particular the experience of modern time. The texts traditionally classed in each of these categories are acutely time conscious and deeply committed to parsing how the new features of time relate to the past and future fortunes of the nation. To put this in a slightly different way: if the historicity of the historical romance resides anywhere in particular, it is in its diagnostic disposition vis-à-vis the temporalities of modernity—in the time consciousness of modernity it displays. The recurrent formal features that shadow particular iterations of these genres—resistance to process as progress, for example—follow in some measure from this impulse to diagnose and do justice to the modernity that is their broadest subject matter. I would then hazard to suggest that the effort to distinguish novel from romance from historical romance is symptomatic of a scholarly reluctance to concede the reality of the conjuncture that these texts inscribe.[20] That is to say, the ongoing effort to sort novels, romances, and historical romances into different buckets is an effort to preserve a separate domain of the real—the province of the realist novel—in which time can take only one form and to separate it from the impossibly fanciful world of the romance, where the single increment of time can both flit and assume a stable form—a world in which the past and the future stand at equal removes from the present and are equally accessible to us.

It is to this world that we now turn.

Parables of the Market

The House of the Seven Gables is a parable of the market revolution. With its main tale set in the 1840s and introduced from the perspective of the 1850s, this intricate novel recounts the downfall of the patrician New England Pyncheon family and their (re)integration with their long-oppressed plebeian antitypes, the Maules. The action of the tale opens with one of the former family's late representatives, the aging Hepzibah Pyncheon, reluctantly entering the surging market economy. Or rather, we witness the market economy and the appurtenances of modernity penetrating the Pyncheon family home. Pressed to desperate measures by the promised return of her unjustly incarcerated and failing brother Clifford, whom she alone must support, Hepzibah opens a cent shop in one corner of the storied family home. Although her first encounter with market culture does not come to pass until some pages into the novel, once it does, we quickly discover that this meeting will not be a happy one. Hawthorne's Pyncheon family epitomizes a dislocated social class. As Henry James suggests, they depict the "end of an old race."[21] Accordingly, Hepzibah's feeble attempt to secure a minor income capable of supporting her brother and herself yields her little more than tears and inconsolable distress. She cannot master the sunny disposition required of a cent-shop huckstress. When she tries to stock the shop window, she badly fumbles the task. When her first customers arrive, she takes their money with a grasp rather than a welcoming open palm. In one of this novel's many scenes of Hepzibah's humiliation by modern life, her clutching fist is made to resemble the clenched palm of an organ-grinder's monkey.

Nor is she our only indication that this novel will be dedicated to diagnosing a "transition from one structure of society, and one system of belief and knowledge, to another."[22] As Henry James remarks of Hawthorne's compositional tendencies, here Hepzibah and her companions are "figures rather than characters—they are all pictures rather than persons."[23] These several pictures resolve into a composite portrait of the consequences of modernity—its beneficiaries and its victims. Although the story opens with Hepzibah's inadvertent scowl scaring away her customers, she is soon rescued from the trials of the market by the arrival of her country cousin: the doe-eyed, young Phoebe Pyncheon. As Gillian Brown and Meredith McGill explain, Hawthorne's Phoebe is ripped from the pages of domestic fiction. She is all rosy cheeks and beaming countenance; the sunny disposition captured in her name literally lights the dark rooms of the Pyncheon home. More important, Phoebe's domestic skills have been honed in the countryside to a state of level perfection. Like other young women displaced by the economic desiccation of the rural countryside, she might just as well have found herself the inmate of Melville's "Tartarus of Maids" or incarcerated in a Lowell mill. She recalls the character of Robin from Hawthorne's "My Kinsman, Major Molineux," and she points to an experience of societal displacement depressingly common in 1840s New England.[24] As Brown eloquently argues, however, Phoebe's masterly domestic skills make her an essential addition to both the logic of Hawthorne's novel and the diegetic world of the Pyncheon household. She manages magically to translate her domestic economy to the market economy, quickly conquering the shopkeeper's role that her dear old cousin Hepzibah can only struggle to comprehend. As Brown suggests, "The trials of the market are so thoroughly overcome [with Phoebe's help] that the reality of free enterprise democracy seems to disappear in the [novel's] closing scene."[25] Her translation of domesticity into market success, Brown continues, epitomizes a "domestic ideology" that "[f]orwards and foster[s] the succession of one economic mode by another."[26] Moreover, Phoebe is not the only newcomer set loose by the market economy who washes up on the shores of the Pyncheon family home. In addition to her cent shop, Hepzibah's only other apparent source of income is her boarder, Holgrave, who turns out to be a Maule and who winds up marrying Phoebe. As Walter Benn Michaels has argued, Holgrave recalls the many "propertyless young men whose geographic mobility was produced by hopes of a corresponding economic mobility."[27] His mobility and initial anonymity mark Holgrave as a product of the market sensibility, and his chosen trades certify him as a thoroughly modern man. He sets up shop as an itinerant daguerreotypist, while at the same time acquiring the habit of writing for the burgeoning periodical trade. All of this supplements what we learn is Holgrave's attraction to the changeable and radical ideas of modern political philosophy.

The tenor of the novel as a whole has led critics old and new to observe that it inclines toward social diagnostics, while at the same time encouraging readers to seek remedy from the dislocations of market culture and modernity in literature's comforting embrace—especially the "picturesque effect" of the romance genre.[28] Although these are not Henry James's explicit concerns, for example, he does remark that Hawthorne's characters "are all types, to the author's mind, of something general, of something that is bound up with history."[29] Where James suggests that the novel indicts the course of history, A. N. Kaul proposes that "[t]his story is . . . Hawthorne's parable of [the] leveling democracy in America" that follows the economic restructuring of the Jacksonian period.[30] But it is Michael Gilmore's "The Artist and the Marketplace" that definitively sets the terms for how we now understand this novel. Gilmore suggests that the novel's preoccupation with the market, its costs, and its consequences speak to Hawthorne's own frustration with the restructuring of the literary realm toward market-driven creativity. For Gilmore, the emergence of a national literary marketplace drives Hawthorne to allegorize his experience of market dispossession, and Hawthorne "us[es] Hepzibah to explore his own ambivalence about courting the public in order to make money."[31] Walter Benn Michaels extends this argument to suggest that Hawthorne's disquisition on romance in the preface represents an attempt to theorize a form of literary production in which an author holds a fee-simple title to his literary property. As Michaels remarks, "The fate of property [literary and otherwise] in *House* suggests the appeal of a title based on neither labor nor wealth and hence free from the risk of appropriation."[32] Most recently, Meredith McGill has encouraged us to read the generic instability of this novel (more on which later) as the sign of Hawthorne's struggle to accommodate himself to the decline of the "culture of reprinting" that McGill recounts and the rise of a new national literary marketplace.

This novel's interest in the consequences of market culture extends to its pointed concern for the way the market economy changes the order of time in the New England community it describes. Like other historical romancers, Hawthorne sometimes seems to want to represent the past and present as irremediably distinct, and his self-conscious account of cotemporalities in the preface can start to recede from view. It might have been eclipsed by a personal interest in the progress of progress, but it seems much more likely that this wavering commitment represents a level of sensitivity to a literary marketplace that demanded such wares. For instance, Jonathan Arac points to Hawthorne's ties to John L. O'Sullivan's Democrats and his participation in O'Sullivan's *Democratic Review* coterie. He proposes that George Bancroft's "extensive [historiographic] narrative with its well-defined shape and its repeated narrative guidance to the reader was clearly coherent with his commitment to the [Democratic] party of the people," and especially to that party's vision of the linear march of progress carrying the nation well into the future.[33] Although Arac suggests that Hawthorne's scattered technique "conflic[ts] with his Democratic allegiance," Hawthorne's narrator often does provide similar "narrative guidance to the reader" that tries to seal over the novel's generally "scattered" form.[34] His frequent addresses to the reader emphasize the work's linear qualities and stress the currents of progress defining the nation at large, putting us on the terrain of the nationalistic novel. "[W]e shall commence the real action of our tale," Hawthorne writes in the second paragraph of chapter 1, "at an epoch not very remote from the present day."[35] These early lines encourage Hawthorne's reader to imagine that "we" share the same "present," and this "we" depends absolutely upon the imaginary shared present that the novel formally articulates. Passages of this kind intersperse Hawthorne's writing.

"We" arrive at the threshold of the story's first major event, the opening of Hepzibah's tiny dry-goods shop, for example, not long after the "commence[ment]" of Hawthorne's tale. As Hepzibah opens her shop on the ground floor of the family's home, we steal "upon [her] at the instant of time when the patrician lady is to be transformed into the plebeian woman":[36] "The inevitable moment was not much longer to be delayed. The sunshine might now be seen stealing down the front of the opposite house, from the windows of which came a reflected gleam, struggling through the boughs of the elm-tree, and enlightening the interior of the shop, more distinctly than heretofore. The town appeared to be waking-up. A baker's cart had already rattled through the street, chasing away the latest vestige of night's sanctity with the jingle-jangle of its dissonant bells. A milkman was distributing the contents of his cans from door to door; and the harsh peal of a fisherman's conch-shell was heard far off, around the corner."[37] Here Hawthorne enumerates a collection of events occurring simultaneously, across time, at the same moment; he also distributes our attention among these events. In so doing, he invites us to imagine Hepzibah's community as sharing equally the fraction of time just prior to her "moment" of disgrace. At this penultimate "instant," Hepzibah, the milkman, and the fisherman blowing the conch shell are physically dispersed; they can neither see nor touch one another. By contrast, Hawthorne's reader sees them simultaneously acting, and in this respect, his reader envisions and imaginatively inhabits a community whose articulating link is time. In an analogous scene much later in the novel, Hepzibah and her brother, Clifford, try to flee the suffocating effects of their home, as well as their potential implication in the sudden death of their cousin Jaffrey. During their attempted escape they board a train, and Clifford strikes up a conversation with a stranger. Clifford and his new friend discuss what Clifford takes to be modernity's most fascinating artifact, electricity, and its most recent embodiment, the telegraph. As he muses on this new form of communication, Clifford makes the following remarks: " 'Is it a fact—or have I dreamt it—that, by means of electricity, the world of matter has become a great nerve, vibrating thousands of miles in a breathless point of time! Rather, the globe is a vast head, a brain, instinct with intelligence! Or, shall we say, it is itself a thought, nothing but thought, and no longer the substance which we deemed it?' "[38] Clifford attributes to the telegraph much the same effect achieved in the previous quotation: he suggests that the telegraph produces an experience of simultaneity, "a breathless point of time," unavailable prior to its invention. Physical distance, traditionally the strongest barrier to community, immediately dissolves in the face of this new technology: the "globe" becomes a "vast" and single "head," the globe "is itself a thought, nothing but thought, and no longer" finite or restricted by its materiality. The experience of a "breathless point of time" links an atomized world into a community that transcends and outmodes local experience. On a first reading, Hawthorne's considered linkage of Hepzibah, the milkman, and the conch blower suggests that the moment has passed when the inhabitants of Salem live separate and uncoordinated lives, while also providing Hawthorne's reader with an opportunity to identify with this unitary community. Social barriers might separate Salemites, but a higher order of time—one associated with modernity, egalitarian democracy, and the market revolution—links them to one another and to Hawthorne's reader. In the second example, Clifford explicitly emphasizes how technological advance allows Americans to transcend division and localism. His example of the telegraph exemplifies the view that the nation has undergone a transformation of time that signals its shift from the premodern to the modern.

Yet there is also a more "subtile" map of time at play here, and it offers a competing image of modern time.[39] As I discussed briefly in Chapter 1, Benedict Anderson's "print capitalism" thesis imagines readers participating in "transverse, cross-time" relationships. This is another way of saying that print culture provides a virtual experience of synchronic coincidence that underwrites fantasies of social simultaneity with one's national community. Here Anderson follows the once-dominant anthropological practice of suggesting that modern time is about "coincidence, and measured by clock and calendar."[40] Anderson also contends that such "transverse, cross-time relationships" significantly predominate in the modern West, with other experiences of time figuring as the vestigial residue of past social worlds.[41] The premodern West and non-Western cultures do, however, experience a different kind of imagined simultaneity: the "simultaneity of past and future in an instantaneous present."[42] This copresence of past and future, or "simultaneity-along-time," which is contrasted with the "simultaneity-across-time" associated with modernity, resembles the Augustinian holy city where redeemed Christians drawn from all historical moments congregate in a place not subject to linear time. Premoderns were less interested in those standing next to them than they were in their contemporaneity with ancestors and descendants. The transition to modernity entails a move from "simultaneity-along-time" to "simultaneity-across-time"—the generalized replacement of one temporality with another.

Yet Hawthorne's novel indicates what happens when these two kinds of simultaneity become bedfellows. Although, like other writing of its kind, *The House of the Seven Gables* articulates the simultaneity-across-time associated with modernity (as it does in the examples just cited), it is also very much about simultaneity-along-time. It is, after all, the story of a curse and the haunting of the Pyncheon family. The book explains early on that town gossip attributes any and all of the Pyncheon family's misfortunes to the "sins of the fathers." We also learn that the Puritan patriarch of the family in the New World, Colonel Pyncheon, expropriated the land on which the house was built. By way of a scheme, the details of which are lost to history, Colonel Pyncheon managed to have the land's original owner, Old Matthew Maule, displaced and sent to the gallows during the Salem witch trials. From the gallows, old Matthew Maule cursed Colonel Pyncheon and his descendants, saying they would all drink blood. And they do. The colonel dies the first morning the house is to be opened to the public as he chokes in the froth of his own blood. Famously, old Colonel Pyncheon's likeness comes to stamp the family profile and personality for decades to come, with generation after generation following the colonel's path in life and in manner of death: "His character, indeed, might be traced all the way down, as distinctly as if the Colonel himself, a little diluted, had been gifted with a sort of intermittent immortality on earth."[43] Over the centuries-long life of the house, the Pyncheon family's fortunes wax and wane. Periodically a new Pyncheon just as greedy and persistent as the first Colonel Pyncheon arrives. At these moments the townspeople remark, " 'Here is the old Pyncheon come again! Now the Seven Gables will be new-shingled!' "[44] This seemingly off-hand proposition, in which the past inhabits the present, grows increasingly important, as we discover simultaneity-along-time working at cross-purposes with simultaneity-across-time. For example, the original owner of the house, Matthew Maule, also inhabits the novel's present tense: "[O]ld Matthew Maule, it is to be feared, trode downward from his own age to a far later one, planting a heavy footstep, all the way, on the conscience of a Pyncheon."[45]

The most remarkable case of the past living in the present is Judge Jaffrey Pyncheon—the modern-day Pyncheon cousin and nemesis of Clifford who embodies the worst acquisitive traits and duplicities encouraged by the market revolution. Just prior to the scene of her social disgrace at the penny shop, Hepzibah glances out at the street after having spent the afternoon gazing at the portrait of the Puritan Colonel Pyncheon that keeps watch over the parlor. As she does so, she sees Judge Jaffrey passing. The proximity of these two events—her gazing at the painting and her glancing out at the street to see her cousin Jaffrey—precipitates Hepzibah's acute awareness of an uncanny resemblance between ancestor and descendent. She realizes that "the face of [her ancestor's portrait] enable[d] her to read more accurately, and to a greater depth" her cousin Jaffrey's face.[46] This is in fact the intrigue of this romance. In a gesture that recalls Irving's George/ George portrait and Dr. Paris's Thaumatrope, *The House of the Seven Gables* emphasizes Jaffrey's resemblance to the colonel and offers it as a significant commentary on the nature of time. In "The Pyncheon of Today," this intrigue persists when we see Phoebe, the country cousin, taking a turn at the shop counter. Her unpleasant cousin, Jaffrey, arrives hoping to see the newly free Clifford. Upon Jaffrey's arrival, the narrator relates the following:

The fantasy would not quit [Phoebe], that the original Puritan, of whom she had heard so many somber traditions—the progenitor of the whole race of New England Pyncheons, the founder of the House of the Seven Gables, and who had died so strangely in it—had now stept into the shop. In these days of off-hand equipment, the matter was easily enough arranged. On his arrival from the other world, he had merely found it necessary to spend a quarter-of-an-hour at a barber's, who had trimmed down the Puritan's full beard into a pair of grizzled whiskers; then, patronizing a ready-made clothing establishment, he had exchanged his velvet doublet and sable cloak, with the richly worked band under his chin, for a white collar and cravat, coat, vest, and pantaloons; and, lastly, putting aside his steel-hilted broadsword to take up a gold-headed cane, the Colonel Pyncheon, of two centuries ago, steps forward as the Judge, of the passing moment![47]

In a passage that distinctly recalls Irving's account of the historical afterimage, this lengthy break in the flow of the narrative ends up summoning into the present tense a visitor from the past, a visitor who is a peculiar kind of visitation. Hawthorne takes care to render Colonel Pyncheon the equal of his descendant Phoebe. This is not a Dickensian Christmas past figure who wears antiquated clothing that marks his distinction from the present moment. This is instead an example of the kind of simultaneity-along-time that Anderson associates with the premodern. With the aid of the contrivance of manufactured "off-hand" clothing, the past, in the body of Colonel Pyncheon, and its future, in the person of Judge Jaffrey Pyncheon, are made one in an instantaneous present. Although the chapter's title, "The Pyncheon of Today," would seem to refer to Phoebe, it also applies to the colonel. The same character both is and is not the colonel; the same character both is and is not Judge Jaffrey. The novelistic emphasis on Judge Jaffrey's contemporaneity with his three cousins strains against an equal sense of his simultaneity with the colonel, producing a distinctly inaccessible present.

The narrator describes a similar encounter between Hepzibah and Jaffrey. Near the story's climax, and immediately prior to the moment of Jaffrey's death, he arrives at the Seven Gables and demands that Hepzibah allow him to see Clifford. He is convinced that Clifford holds the secret to a long-standing mystery about lands for which the family has inadequate proof of their ownership. Hepzibah at first refuses Jaffrey's request, fearing that his overbearing greed will crush Clifford's sensitive spirit. Hepzibah eventually relents and agrees to the meeting, but not before venting decades of frustration and anger at Jaffrey. The narrator describes Hepzibah's thoughts as she recovers from this outburst: "Hepzibah almost adopted the insane belief, that it was her old Puritan ancestor, and not the modern Judge, on whom she had just been wreaking the bitterness of her heart. Never did a man show stronger proof of the lineage attributed to him, than Judge Pyncheon, at this crisis, by his unmistakable resemblance to the picture in the inner room."[48] As Jaffrey waits to confer with Clifford, Hepzibah feels the weight of the moment: "Her colloquy with [Jaffrey] who so perfectly represented the person and attributes of the founder of the family, had called back the dreary past. It weighed upon her heart. . . . The whole [family history] seemed little else but a series of calamity, reproducing itself in successive generations, with one general hue, and varying in little save the outline."[49] Hepzibah feels her heart burdened by a past that is all too present. She also finds herself distraught to see that her family's future cannot help but to embody the past. Hepzibah cannot foresee her family being rewarded with the historical forgetfulness that comes with linear time. All that she can envision is a similarity—a simultaneity—of past and future in an eternal present.

In a final wry example, Hawthorne introduces the sad assembly of chickens roosting in the gardens at the Pyncheon home, who, in their depravity, encapsulate this novel's major issues, as Hawthorne himself concedes. They are a tense and skinny crew, these chickens, comprising "Chanticleer himself," his "two wives," and one small offspring. This young chicken, the narrator remarks, "looked small enough to be still in the egg, and, at the same time, sufficiently old, withered, wizened, and experienced to have been the founder of the antiquated race."[50] The narrator continues, "Instead of being the youngest of the family, [this chicken] rather seemed to have aggregated into itself the ages, not only of those living specimens of the breed, but of all its forefathers and fore-mothers, whose united excellencies and oddities were squeezed into its little body."[51] This account of the chicken coop imagines a little body, a single present tense into which all of the ages are gathered. It imagines the past and the future inhabiting the same physical space, the very same present.

As the combination of these examples would suggest, *The House of the Seven Gables* is about simultaneity-along-time: the simultaneity of past and future in an instantaneous and eternal present. It is also about simultaneity-across-time: the experience of moments of time that are shared by the three cousins, as well as by Hepzibah and her townspeople. Most significantly, it persistently traces and reproduces the simultaneity of both experiences of simultaneity, favoring neither diachronic nor synchronic simultaneity. In other words, it articulates what Partha Chatterjee has called the "heterogeneous time of modernity."[52] We might wish to understand the Pyncheons as cousins of those moderns Fredric Jameson has described, who have a comparatist perspective on time born of their experience of a changing world on the brink of an inevitable, new homogeneous order of time.[53] Yet Chatterjee proposes that nationalism and capitalism have long asked us to believe that only one experience of time is ultimately available in modernity; their self-fulfilling prophecies deceptively proclaim that progressive time will replace all other temporalities as capitalism makes its way across the globe. For writers on the postcolonial condition, however, this notion of a homogeneous time is pure and simple fantasy. Chatterjee remarks, for example, that "[p]eople can only imagine themselves in . . . homogeneous time; they do not live in it."[54] For Chatterjee, heterogeneous time defines modernity, and homogeneous time is a pernicious utopian construct at odds with lived experience. Adapting Chatterjee, we can say that *The House of the Seven Gables* gives the lie to the utopian time of nationalism, and it demonstrates how the "comparatist" perspective on time that Jameson describes might be thought of as something other than the prehistory of a present tense in which that perspective has been replaced—that is, as a specific experience of modernity that is still with us today in the form and experience of this literature.

In this context, consider once again the passage that immediately anticipates Hepzibah's entry into her ill-fated cent shop and the market culture of modernity. In this scene, Hawthorne offers us a vision of synchronic simultaneity in the image he provides of a waking commercial culture. We see the milk vendor circuiting the town and leaving bottles neatly on doorsteps. The baker "jingles" past each household, forcing its tenants into the dawning day. Finally, we have the image of the fisherman blowing his conch shell. This last is a curious literary figure. Hawthorne's recourse to this space-transcending sound provides a final, capping image that on first sight simply secures the connection linking the residents of Salem in a way that the more space-bound milkman or baker could not: the two tradesmen on land must ply their wares one house at a time, and their relationships to their customers are consequently more serial than they are simultaneous. The fisherman blowing his conch shell achieves the image of a group of community members knit into a single fabric that these two others simply cannot. Yet why a fisherman blowing a conch shell and not a church bell ringing? What is the significance of this particular kind of sonority? Here Hawthorne's conch shell effectively delivers his reader into the precinct of the epic. The ancient epic the *Mahabharata* famously features Arjuna's blowing of a conch shell as the heroic call to battle. A considered analysis of this ancient text is beyond the scope of this chapter.[55] However, it is worth noting that Hawthorne's redeployment of the conch shell in the context of his novel has the effect of drawing his reader in two directions at once. That is to say, at one and the same time, Hawthorne's reader inhabits a present-tense characterized by two types of simultaneity—much like the one enjoyed by his characters. We are implicated in the experience of synchronic simultaneity associated with the novel genre, while at the same time we are drawn into a relationship with the ancient past associated with the epic. That relationship comes about by virtue of a literary device that draws into the present a genre—the epic—and a temporality—diachronic simultaneity—often considered extinguished by modernity.[56] This single figure of the sonorous conch shell confirms, in other words, Gregg Crane's sense that the historical romance has something of the epic about it.[57] It also forces us to question precisely where Hawthorne is asking his readers to live and who it is asking them—or allowing them—to be. In this context, "American" seems far too restrictive an answer. *The House of the Seven Gables* draws us across the conventional chronological and cartographical distinctions associated with the modern nation-state while at the same time working to facilitate those distinctions.

The presence of the epic in Hawthorne's novel—this generic indeterminacy—points us toward Meredith McGill's recent discussion of this novel in terms of its genre trouble. According to McGill, we can read much of the difficulty of this novel, including its resistance to process as progress, as a symptom of a major shift in the American literary marketplace. McGill compellingly argues that, prior to the 1850s, the U.S. literary marketplace—if it can be called a national one—operated according to the demands of a reprint culture organized around the almost infinite reproducibility of uncopyrighted and uncopyrightable literary property. By this account, *The House of the Seven Gables* represents Hawthorne's attempt to recast himself as a properly national literary commodity and a full-fledged novelist so as to accommodate himself to the emerging national literary marketplace. In order to do so, Hawthorne must dissociate himself from the outmoded market for reprint culture, which was where, in fact, his literary reputation was first made. As McGill demonstrates, the long-standing myth of Hawthorne's anonymous struggle for artistic success was largely a story of the author's own invention. McGill also suggests "some of the reasons why Hawthorne himself might have eagerly, if ironically, claimed the distinction of early obscurity," one of the primary reasons being "the desire to distance himself from his participation in mass-cultural and feminized forms such as the eclectic magazine, the gift book, the children's book, and the women's periodical."[58] Or as she puts it elsewhere, "Attempting to move beyond short fiction into the territory of the modern novel, Hawthorne is troubled by his dependence on literary forms that suddenly appear to him to be minor and insignificant."[59] Despite this overweening desire to separate himself from feminized and outmoded forms associated with an earlier mode of literary production, *The House of the Seven Gables* "depends," McGill proposes, "on the literary forms it tries to disavow."[60] In a moment of keen sensitivity to the way genres are transported from one moment to another—the way that the formal traits of a given genre are always borrowed, and often borrowed from a different present tense—McGill suggests that the culture of reprinting and its distinctive literary forms are "carried forward into the national culture that replaces it by the force of its repudiation."[61] Here a particular instance of market pressure produces the opposite of homogenization. The market produces the "confliction of fictions" that Richard Brodhead associates with this period's writing.[62]

I want to extend McGill's argument to its point of maximum applicability. McGill details the significant effects of Hawthorne's multiplication of generic precedents. She focuses in particular on the sketch, which, as she argues, "make[s] nothing happen" and which underwrites a Hawthornean "poetics of repose"—an aesthetic comfortable for the rising bourgeoisie.[63] The poetics of repose that Hawthorne enacts in his sketches and then transports into his *House* is "an anti-dramatic balance of narrative energies that brokers a powerful compromise with his middle-class readers, offering them fanciful speculation that is tempered but not overwhelmed by didacticism."[64] As McGill argues, however, Hawthorne also has recourse to other forms such as the gothic tale. In her attention to the concatenated generic form of this novel, McGill recalls earlier readings by sometimes less sympathetic critics. Trollope, for example, objected to the novel's ending with the marriage of Phoebe and Holgrave. He writes, "The love-scene, and the hurrying up of the marriage, and all the dollars which they inherit from the wicked Judge, and the 'handsome dark-green barouche,' prepared for their departure, which is altogether unfitted to the idea which the reader has formed respecting them, are quite unlike Hawthorne, and would seem almost to have been added by some every-day, beef-and-ale, realistic novelist, into whose hands the unfinished story had unfortunately fallen."[65] From

McGill's perspective, the point might be that Trollope misses the extent to which Hawthorne was in certain respects very much an "every-day, beef-and-ale, realistic novelist"—just as he was a writer of children's books, a sketch writer, a romancer, a biographer, and more. In 1851, Edwin Percy Whipple similarly identifies an unfolding recognition of Hawthorne's multigeneric talents: "[W]e have seen Hawthorne likened for this quality to Goldsmith, and for that to [Washington] Irving, and for still another to Dickens; and some critics have given him the preference over all whom he seems to resemble."[66] Whipple is speaking here perhaps of George Bailey Loring's elaborate review of *The Scarlet Letter* for the *Massachusetts Quarterly* in 1850, which includes this long sentence: "It seems useless now to speak of his humour, subtile and delicate as Charles Lamb's; of his pathos, deep as Richter's; of his penetration into the human heart, clearer than that of Goldsmith or Crabbe; of his apt and telling words, which Pope might have envied; of his description, graphic as Scott's or Dickens's; of the delicious lanes he opens, on either hand, and leaves you alone to explore, masking his work with the fine '*faciebat*' which removes all limit from all high art, and gives every man scope to advance and develop."[67] Between Whipple and Loring, we have a Hawthorne who is humorist, romancer, realist novelist, poet, and master of the sketch combined. These qualities lead Richard H. Millington to propose that in this novel Hawthorne "operate[s] within an established range of genres ('Novel,' 'Romance,' 'Tale,' 'Legend') and effects (the 'picturesque')."[68] Given this lasting sense that there is more here than either novel or romance can alone name, the addition of the epic to the mix seems entirely plausible. Whether we credit Hawthorne with a special talent for capacious description or (as Lukács would) a proximity to daily life that underwrites a sensitivity to the machinations of the social, we can be sure that with his turn to each of these genres Hawthorne draws a range of temporalities into his diegetic present tense. It is precisely this generic instability of his novel that makes it a rich artifact for something we might call literary social history.

If there is a clear precedent for thinking about *The House of the Seven Gables* in terms of generic and temporal instability, we should not limit our sense of the viability of such a critical model for thinking about Hawthorne's more conventional historical romances. Hawthorne's famous preface to *The Scarlet Letter*, "The Custom-House," for example, offers a similar account of the conflict of times articulated in *The House of the Seven Gables*. As is widely known, this preface offers a genealogy of the story, tracing it to the author's discovery of a sheaf of manuscript pages and a glowing scarlet letter secreted therein. In what is perhaps the most striking instance of the simultaneity-along-time, or diachronic simultaneity, just described, and certainly one of the best known, Hawthorne's author-narrator describes the moment when he physically recoils from the touch of the scarlet letter: "While . . . perplexed,—and cogitating, among other hypotheses, whether the letter might not have been one of those decorations which the white men used to contrive, in order to take the eyes of Indians,—I happened to place it on my breast. It seemed to me,—the reader may smile, but must not doubt my word,—it seemed to me, then, that I experienced a sensation not altogether physical, yet almost so, as of burning heat; and as if the letter were not of red cloth, but red-hot iron. I shuddered, and involuntarily let it fall upon the floor."[69] In this archetypal scene, Hawthorne envisions a "sensation not altogether physical, yet almost so" that connects the writer, as he was during his time at the Custom-House, with Hester Prynne, as we come to know her later in the novel, and also to the reader of *The Scarlet Letter*. An interval of at least one hundred years collapses here, and Hawthorne's author-narrator, as well as his reader, stand in the presence of Hester's shame. It is not merely memory that he describes, but a scenario of simultaneity supposed to be cognitively unavailable after the advent of modernity.

This familiar scene is not the only one that resembles the double-timed modernity already demonstrated to be at issue in *The House of the Seven Gables*. Nor is it the only experience of time that Hawthorne's Custom-House preface describes. As is the case with *The House of the Seven Gables*, "The Custom-House" threads together two and more accounts of time in its short pages. Very early in the preface, Hawthorne's author-narrator characterizes his relationship to the town of Salem, which is his family home and the place he lived as he wrote the book:

The figure of [my] first [Salem] ancestor, invested by family tradition with a dim and dusky grandeur, was present to my boyish imagination, as far back as I can remember. It still haunts me, and induces a sort of home-feeling with the past, which I scarcely claim in reference to the present phase of the town. I seem to have a stronger claim in residence here on account of this grave, bearded, sable-cloaked, and steeple-crowned progenitor,—who came so early, with his Bible and his sword, and trode the unworn street with such a stately port, and made so large a figure, as a man of war and peace,—a stronger claim than for myself, whose name is seldom heard and my face hardly known.[70]

Hawthorne's author-narrator describes a "home-feeling with the past," an intimacy with moments already gone, that secures his relationship to the town. His claim to be *of* Salem derives not from his residence *in* Salem, especially not "the present phase of the town." He considers himself a Salemite by virtue of his intimacy with his ancestral past. Hawthorne's author-narrator continues on to imagine a conversation taking place among his ancestors, described here as literally inhabiting the same interval of time as himself:

No aim, that I have ever cherished, would [my ancestors] recognize as laudable; no success of mine . . . would they deem otherwise than worthless, if not positively disgraceful. "What is he?" murmurs one gray shadow of my forefathers to the other. "A writer of storybooks! What kind of a business in life,—what mode of glorifying God, or being serviceable to mankind in his day and generation,—may that be? Why, the degenerate fellow might as well have been a fiddler!" Such are the compliments bandied between my great-grandsires and myself, across the gulf of time! And yet, let them scorn me as they will, strong traits of their nature have intertwined themselves with mine.[71]

Although the penultimate sentence invokes a supposed "gulf of time" separating himself from his ancestors, Hawthorne's author-narrator nevertheless just as forcibly envisions a closing of that gulf with his comments about the way "strong traits of their nature" intertwine in his own personality. There is, moreover, good evidence to suggest that the narrator we encounter is in fact burdened with a sense that he must find some new way to be "serviceable to mankind in his day and generation." We have more than this narrator's word that he and his ancestors are intertwined.

Neither is the narrator himself the only instance of a persistent intimacy with the past that appears in this preface. Turning to his companions in the Custom-House, the narrator depicts a group of men who live in past and present at one and the same time. These elderly men, once soldiers and men of influence but now confined to the feminized space of the Custom-House, are themselves vehicles for past experience to live in the present: "[T]he frozen witticisms of past generations were thawed out, and came bubbling with laughter from their lips. Externally, the jollity of aged men has much in common with the mirth of children; the intellect, any more than a deep sense of humor, has little to do with the matter; it is, with both, a gleam that plays upon the surface, and imparts a sunny and cheery aspect alike to the green branch, and gray, mouldering trunk. In one case, however it is real sunshine; in the other, it more resembles the phosphorescent glow of decaying wood."[72] Hawthorne describes his narrator's companions in terms hostile to simplistic accounts of linear time, which would suggest that the old self-evidently consign themselves to the past by virtue of their appearance. It is, he suggests, mainly impossible to determine whether they stand at the beginning or the end of their lives merely by reading their surface. The "arrow" of time is here Janus-faced, and Hawthorne's inhabitants of the Custom-House inhabit a unique temporality untouched by progress.

This sense of a past having access to the present continues with the author-narrator's description of the conversations at the Custom-House. In particular, he describes the accounts of long-ago feasts in terms that suggest they are much more than casual reminiscences and that even suggest how the author-narrator conceives the function of storytelling: "[These] reminiscences of good cheer, however ancient the date of the actual banquet, seemed to bring the savor of pig or turkey under one's very nostrils. There were flavors on his palate, that had lingered there not less than sixty or seventy years, and were still apparently as fresh as that of the mutton-chop which he had just devoured for his breakfast. I have heard him smack his lips over dinners, every guest at which, except himself, had long been food for worms."[73] The office of the storyteller is to effect a diachronic collapse and therefore to undo what we often take to be the work of narrative—that is, the projection of a linear time line along which each event may be plotted. In one final image, we see echoes of the scene when Colonel Pyncheon, in the person of Jaffrey Pyncheon, visits Phoebe. Reflecting on the work of his Salem predecessor, "Mr. Surveyor Pue," and the story of the scarlet letter, Hawthorne's narrator comments, "There seemed to be here the groundwork of a tale. It impressed me as if the ancient Surveyor, in his garb of a hundred years gone by, and wearing his immortal wig,—which was buried with him, but did not perish in the grave,—had met me in the deserted chamber of the Custom-House."[74] This is a relationship to the past more familiar than alienated. Hawthorne even goes so far as to conjure the gruesome image of the surveyor's wig persisting across the many years separating mid-nineteenth-century Salem from colonial Salem. This physical detail is the final piece of evidence for a sense that the past and present live as one.

These several instances of diachronic synchrony, as it were, cohabit uneasily with an equally powerful articulation of the time of linear progress. The challenge of Hawthorne's Custom-House preface resides, as it did in *The House of the Seven Gables*, in the fact that the two temporalities overlap without synchronizing. Although the work of analysis demands that we separate out two strands of temporal articulation, the fact remains that the novel itself emerges from the overlap of the two rather than from their detachment. Put another way, Jeffrey Insko has recently argued that in Catharine Sedgwick's romances "the linearity of historical time becomes entangled, like a triple helix, a strand of DNA, as three different moments are woven together."[75] It is an elegant metaphor that comes extremely close to naming the complex temporality of the romance. Still, the difficulty of the romance, as well as the fragility of its cultural nationalism, extends from an incommensurable quality elided in the image of a "weaving together" of different moments into a single strand. We see the oddity of this particular conflict of time even in the previous quotation that describes the author-narrator's "home-feeling with the past." This passage emphasizes, as I have suggested, the persistence of the past in the present and their seemingly impossible intimacy. Yet we must also acknowledge that portion of the quotation which invokes the notion of a linear unfolding of time, when Hawthorne writes of his "boyish imagination": "[The figure of my first ancestor] still haunts me, and induces a sort of home-feeling with the past, which I scarcely claim in reference to the present phase of the town."[76] The narrator's "home-feeling with the past" is stronger than his home feeling with the present, but he also claims this to be the case because Salem has changed so radically since his childhood. In other words, the narrator's intimacy with the past contrasts with his alienation from a present characterized by the temporality of progress. Yet, if his alienation from the present derives from the press of change underway since his childhood, how can he simultaneously imagine a home feeling with the past that depends upon the notion of temporal stasis? Here, as in *The House of the Seven Gables*, Hawthorne wants to have it both ways, and in fact he achieves that with a remarkable level of success. Rather than merely an instance of narrative confusion, we might regard this moment in Hawthorne's romance as a key to the nature of American modernity.

These images should also press us to think through exactly what Hawthorne's *House* did for its readers, for he wrote *The House of the Seven Gables* from and about a moment when the industrial book, periodical culture, and literature's other printed avatars had become articles of everyday life—the moment of "print capitalism." Indeed, it would not have been entirely surprising had Hawthorne added a slim volume or two, or a "penny paper," to the roster of goods for sale at Hepzibah's "little shopwindow." As Hawthorne describes it, though, hers is a curious shop. It includes certain "articles . . . of a description and outward form, which could hardly have been known" in earlier days: "bits of delectable candy, neatly done up in white paper," a "party of leaden dragoons," "a package of lucifer-matches," and, of course, "Jim Crow[,] seen executing his world-renowned dance, in gingerbread."⁷⁷ But this merchant's space—the zenith of market culture—also has the air of an anachronism. Indeed, as Hawthorne explains, the shop was first opened by one of Hepzibah's dissolute ancestors who spent his fortunes on trivialities. Thus it is that the most self-evident figure of market culture in this novel—Hepzibah's little shop window—articulates the peculiar simultaneous simultaneities seen elsewhere: "[I]t was incontrovertibly evident that somebody had taken the shop and fixtures of the long retired and forgotten Mr. Pyncheon, and was about to renew the enterprise of the departed worthy, with a different set of customers."⁷⁸ Ultimately, we do get a sense that the emergence of a thing called print culture might have something important to do with this modernity. Hawthorne finally provides us with a figure of print when Hepzibah and Clifford take their train ride. At this moment, Clifford reflects on the scene around him: "It seemed marvellous how all these people could remain so quietly in their seats, while so much noisy strength was at work in their behalf. Some, with tickets in their hats, (long travelers these, before whom lay a hundred miles of railroad,) had plunged into the English scenery and adventures of pamphlet-novels, and were keeping company with dukes and earls. Others, whose briefer span forbade their devoting themselves to studies so abstruse, beguiled the tedium of the way with penny-papers."⁷⁹ Print capitalism—the novel and the newspaper—is writ rather small and sordid in this passage. Here novels are about "keeping company" not with those around you but with those at distant removes who occupy different national traditions and different geographies. This experience of modernity is about keeping company in new ways with untoward and unexpected fellow travelers—"dukes and earls" rather than one's fellow Americans. Writing in his journal on May 5, 1850, Hawthorne had this to say, however, about the arrival of his train from Portsmouth to Concord at a station in Newcastle—a sleepy and degraded village not much larger than a pinpoint on a map. The quotation is a long one, but it bears full repeating:

How much life has come at once into this lonely place! Four or five long cars, each, perhaps, with fifty people in it; reading newspapers, reading pamphlet novels, chatting, sleeping; all this vision of passing life! A moment passes, while the baggage men are putting on the trunks and packages; then the bell strikes a few times, and away goes the train again; quickly out of sight of those who remain behind, while a solitude of hours again broods over the Station House, which, for an instant, has thus been put in communication with far-off cities, and then has only itself, with the old black, ruinous church, and the black old farm-house, both built years and years ago, before railroads were ever dreamed of. Meantime, the passenger, stepping from the solitary station-house into the train, finds himself in the midst of a new world, all in a moment; he rushes out of the solitude into a village; thence through woods and hills; into a large inland town; along beside the Merrimack, which has overflowed its banks, and eddies along, turbid as a vast mud-puddle, sometimes almost laving the door-step of a house, and with trees standing in the flood, half-way up their trunks. Boys, with newspapers to sell, or apples, lozenges &c; many passengers departing and entering, at each new-station; the more permanent passenger, with his check or ticket stuck in his hatband, where the conductor may see it. A party of girls, playing at ball with a young man; altogether, it is a scene of stirring life, with which a person, who had been waiting long for the train to come by, might find it difficult at once to amalgamate himself.

It is a somber, brooding day, and begins to rain as the cars pass onward. In a little more than two hours, we find ourselves in Boston, surrounded by eager hackmen.[80]

Read alongside the train-ride scene in *The House of the Seven Gables* and the idea of modern print capitalism, this passage may surprise us with its emphasis on the way the technologies of modernity produce a heightened sense of *dis*connection. We see people "reading newspapers, reading pamphlet novels, chatting, sleeping." We see the railroad bell striking in a manner that for any historian of modern clock time anticipates the coordination of national time forced by the needs of national rail schedules later in the century.[81] And we see how "for an instant" the Station House has been "put in communication with far-off cities." Yet there is at least as much poignant solitude here as there is a knitting together of faraway people and places; there is as much immanence as there is transcendence of space through time. This town has seen better days, and the rush of the market appears not to have been a friend of "this lonely place." The citizens of market culture arrive with their newspapers and their novels, but when all is said and done they leave behind a "solitude of hours" that "broods over the Station House." A "person" finds it "difficult to amalgamate himself" with this world. The last line of this passage captures the decisive forgetfulness that isolates this town: "In a little more than two hours, we find ourselves in Boston, surrounded by eager hackmen."[82] No memory persists of the people and places brought, for an instant, into "communication with far-off cities." In an important way, Hawthorne's journal entry points to the impossible modernity his novel enacts and the magnificent fragment it becomes. Both are epitomized in his image of the Merrimack. Instead of a rushing river of time, Hawthorne describes "the Merrimack, which has overflowed its banks, and eddies along, turbid as a vast mud-puddle."[83]

This vision captures and reduplicates modernity's new order of time: it is out of control, disturbingly full rather than empty, eddying like "a vast mud-puddle." As Rufus Griswold might suggest, it stands at the conjuncture of the rivers of time, and it might as easily turn back as move forward. Less conveyance than convergence, it provides little indication of what the future holds for the people of America. It is not a reliable predictor of their glorious destiny.

How to Split a Live Chicken in Two

When our attention shifts from this novel's genre trouble to its literary figures, we are reminded of just how difficult it is to cleave the various temporalities of modernity from each other. Hawthorne's dialect writing in particular involves the discrepant experience of time that he theorizes in the novel's preface, and it shows the inconceivably tight fit between the two temporalities entailed in that experience. And although dialect writing might not be the first trait we associate with the historical romance, it does appear throughout this literature. My interest in this figure stems mainly from the strong degree to which, when read against the grain, it counters the very project of people sorting that it would seem to exemplify. As I read it, the figure of dialect writing ends up troubling the project of social consolidation envisaged in those "narrative guidance[s] to the reader," and it even makes it difficult to comfortably inhabit one or another of the racial categories it would seem to invoke and re-create.[84]

As readers familiar with this novel will remember, the "Alice Pyncheon" chapter recounts the "legend" of an eighteenth-century Pyncheon and her doom at the hands of a conjuring member of the Maule family. They might not remember from this chapter one of the novel's oddest images: a black Pyncheon servant named Scipio. Scipio appears briefly at the start of the chapter, where he refers to the current Pyncheon as "massa," describes himself as "a nigga," and characterizes the Seven Gables as a "berry good house."[85] Early reviews of Hawthorne's romance overlook this moment of dialect writing, and while Hepzibah's Jim Crow gingerbread man has received his fair share of attention in later criticism, less has been said about Scipio. In ways that suggest the prevalence of the trope of dialect writing in the 1840s and 1850s, as well as the selective vision of Hawthorne's reviewers, the *Democratic Review*, for example, applauds Hawthorne's resistance to the popular taste for "idioms and barbarisms," writing, "[Hawthorne's] delineation of New-England manners, conversations and language, are governed by good taste in avoiding to adulterate the conversation of ordinary people with idioms and barbarisms, which rarely have existence in New-England. That the works of Mr. Hawthorne will go down to other generations, conveying a truthful picture of the manners of our times, there can be no doubt."[86] This reviewer's inability to acknowledge Hawthorne's dialect writing as such recalls a broader predisposition to overlook nineteenth-century dialect writing unless it appears in a very limited range of sources. Although dialect writing can be found in historical romances, African American life writing, political journalism, and elsewhere, we tend to think of it as the exclusive property of literary regionalists and late nineteenth-century African American writers. This oversight has the effect of limiting our understanding of this trope and these genres, for dialect writing tells a very specific story about modernity.

Dialect writing's critics have proposed many ways to think about its aesthetic, political, and historical significance. Its earliest critics, such as the *Democratic Review* writer, objected to dialect writing because it reproduced a subliterate voice. This view was as common among intellectually conservative European American critics as it was with the mid to late nineteenth-century African American bourgeoisie. This latter group was troubled by dialect writing's breach of middle-class decorum. Others have reclaimed dialect writing as a realistic and faithful reproduction of what Richard Brodhead has called "[e]thnically deformed speech."[87] They associate the best dialect writing with a respect for local life and a kind of ethnographic veracity. More recently, dialect writing has been shown to produce—rather than realistically reproduce—the ethnic and racial difference it claims to document.[88] Rather than think of dialect writing in strictly mimetic terms, this last view demands that we acknowledge the capacity of literary form to impact our experience of the social world. Here I take a slightly broader view that shifts us away from thinking about dialect writing in relationship to either its fidelity to or divergence from the protocols of spoken language. I propose to read dialect writing as a kind of instantaneous chronicle of American modernity. Dialect writing's unacknowledged central mechanism is, I propose, the comparison of one form of writing to a standard form of writing always implicitly cited by this trope. As I will illustrate, moreover, dialect writing also articulates the linear time conventionally associated with modernity to the diachronic simultaneity of the premodern.

This coarticulation of two kinds of time occurs, for example, in the dialect writing that opens the Alice Pyncheon chapter—a story that digresses from the main narrative about the Pyncheons of the 1840s and considers instead the fate of the seemingly eighteenth-century Alice. The anticipation of Alice's story begins in the chapter titled "The Daguerreotypist," which immediately precedes the Alice Pyncheon chapter. In the former, we encounter Holgrave conversing in the garden with the young Phoebe Pyncheon. Their talk turns to the "curse" haunting Phoebe's kinfolk, and it accentuates the resemblance between the antagonist of Hawthorne's main tale, Jaffrey, and his colonial predecessor, the Puritan colonel. Their conversation also underscores how colonial and premodern America struggled with an uneasy experience of time as repetition that was later supplanted by linear progress. After much discussion of the family's misfortunes, the daguerreotypist's chapter closes with Holgrave's telling Phoebe that he has "'marvellous gifts of writing . . . stories'" and has "'put an incident of the Pyncheon family-history, with which [he happens] to be acquainted, into the form of a legend, and mean[s] to publish it in a magazine.'"[89] We may read this device in terms of McGill's account of how the very forms that Hawthorne had sought to leave behind find their way into *The House of the Seven Gables*. It is as though Hawthorne has determined to recycle one of his own unpublished manuscripts, something left over from the culture of reprinting. Given the periodical context, it should not surprise us to find that Holgrave's "legend" includes the novel's only significant instance of dialect writing: although literary history associates the figure of dialect writing primarily with the periodical press of the late nineteenth century, it defines this medium as early as the 1820s.[90] In the event, Holgrave concludes his buildup to Alice's story by framing it as a "legend," which further suggests how the events of Alice's chapter are meant to antedate the advent of modern time. Holgrave then reveals a "roll of manuscript" and "beg[ins] to read," whereupon the Alice Pyncheon chapter opens with this peculiar episode from the apocrypha of the Pyncheon curse:[91]

There was a message brought, one day, from the worshipful Gervayse Pyncheon to young Matthew Maule, the carpenter, desiring his immediate presence at the House of the Seven Gables.

"And what does your master want with me?" said the carpenter to Mr. Pyncheon's black servant. "Does the house need any repair? Well it may, by this time; and no blame to my father who built it, neither! I was reading the old Colonel's tombstone, no longer ago than last Sabbath; and reckoning from that date, the house has stood seven-and-thirty years. No wonder if there should be a job to do on the roof."

"Don't know what Massa wants," answered Scipio. "The house is a berry good house, and old Colonel Pyncheon think so, too, I reckon;—else why the old man haunt it so, and frighten a poor nigga, as he does?"

"Well, well, friend Scipio; let your master know that I'm coming," said the carpenter with a laugh. "For a fair, workmanlike job, he'll find me his man. And so the house is haunted, is it? It will take a tighter workman than I am, to keep the spirits out of the seven gables. Even if the Colonel would be quit," he added, muttering to himself, "my old grandfather, the wizard, will be pretty sure to stick to the Pyncheons, as long as their walls hold together!"

"What's that you mutter to yourself, Matthew Maule?" asked Scipio. "And what for do you look so black at me?"

"No matter, darkey!" said the carpenter. "Do you think nobody is to look black but yourself? Go tell your master I'm coming; and if you happen to see Mistress Alice, his daughter, give Matthew Maule's humble respects to her. She has brought a fair face from Italy—fair, and gentle, and proud,—has that same Alice Pyncheon!"

"He talk of Mistress Alice!" cried Scipio, as he returned from his errand. "The low carpenter-man! He no business so much as to look at her a great way off!"[92]

These opening lines of the Alice Pyncheon chapter build upon the daguerreotypist's chapter's hint regarding the "legendary" qualities of Alice's story. Matthew Maule and Scipio emphasize the constancy of the house, and its haunting is a similar collapse of past and present. The three generations of Pyncheons look more and more like a single cast of characters. The difference of past from present is radically absent here as the premodern temporality of diachronic simultaneity appears to eclipse the time of linear progress.

In the face of this incipient homogenization of time, however, Hawthorne's dialect writing manages to preserve a split register of time to the extent that it actives in its reader a contradictory experience. In the moment that one reads dialect writing, that is to say, one understands the dialect written on the page as a compromised declension of standard written language. In other words, Scipio's "dialect" implies a language that had to have come before it. This prior language is not vernacular "speech," as one might logically suppose; it is instead the standard of written language that this dialect writing presupposes as its point of departure. In reading Scipio's response to the carpenter's initial questions about the house, we see the marks on the page: "massa," "berry," and "nigga." Equally present is the point of comparison from which those marks imply they developed: "master," "very," and "nigger." Although those prior marks are not graphically apparent, they are no less present in the moment of reading than the ones we do see. In this sense, Scipio's "dialect" entails a past and present that are different and so formally articulates the linear temporality being concealed at the level of statement. At the level of a formal figure, in other words, this dialect writing desublimates the temporality of linear progress being subsumed at the level of narrative exposition. Scipio's "dialect" in this way marks the insistent coarticulation of a linear temporality obscured at the level of statement in Hawthorne's opening lines of his chapter about Alice Pyncheon: Scipio comments that the "house is a berry good house, and old Colonel Pyncheon think so, too, I reckon;—else why the old man haunt it so and frighten a poor nigga, as he does?" Both halves of this rhetorical question indicate the absence of linear time. Scipio suggests that even thirty-seven years after Matthew Maule's grandfather laid the last shingle, the House of the Seven Gables shows virtually no signs of wear; its first owner and its builder, Colonel Pyncheon and Matthew Maule's grand-father, continue to reside there in spirit. Yet the very manner of communi-cating these notions requires the reader to experience past and present as fundamentally different, and in doing it reactivates the linear temporality that is otherwise prohibited from rising to legibility. Secreted in the single event of Scipio's "dialect" are two noncoincident temporalities.

Outside of the romance genre, dialect writing repeatedly stages, and in even more obvious ways, this phenomenon of temporal copresence, as it does in August Baldwin Longstreet's *Georgia Scenes*, an 1835 classic of Southwestern humor. Typically lauded as realist or condemned for its stere-otyping depictions of poor whites and African Americans, Longstreet's col-lection of sketches and tales has been said either to record or to have se-cured emergent racial hierarchies. Yet Longstreet's dialect writing signifies just how precarious is national (or racial) identity if we trace it to an experi-ence of literature. In this collection of previously published sketches, Long-street's past experience with critics who disliked his dialect writing plainly informs his manner of self-presentation. Longstreet anticipates a new round of criticism in the following caveat, which appears in the author's preface to *Georgia Scenes*: "I cannot conclude these introductory remarks without reminding [my contemporaries] who have taken exceptions to the coarse, inelegant, and sometimes ungrammatical language which the writer represents himself as occasionally using, *that it is the language accommo-dated to the capacity of the person to whom he represents himself as speak-ing*."[93] James E. Kibler Jr., the editor of a 1992 reprint of *Georgia Scenes*, resurrects this last phrase in his editor's introduction, where he praises Longstreet's writing because his "ear was particularly keen" and "his realis-tic dialogue rich with carefully rendered Georgia dialect."[94] He also dubs

Longstreet "the founder and first practitioner of the school of Realism in America."[95] Kibler describes dialect writing as an auditory realism, an attempt to capture on the page the experience of the ear. Summoning Longstreet himself to defend this position, Kibler quotes the author's original preface at length, presenting it as the key to Longstreet's dialect writing. The most telling of Kibler's authorizing quotations is an excerpt from the 1835 caveat from Longstreet quoted earlier. It comes nested in the following statement, written by Kibler: "About the language, [Longstreet's] preface states: *'it is language accommodated to the capacity of the person . . . speaking.'* In other words, [Longstreet] tells us clearly that this will be a book of *real* life, taken from the real life—written from close observation of character— and that 'mere fancy' will enter into it only in the process of *combining the realities.*"[96] Dialect writing signals to Kibler the "close observation of character" and fidelity to "real life" required of a skillful artist. Dialect writing succeeds where more fanciful efforts fail because it hews to the truth, mimicking it rather than obscuring it. And in Kibler's view, Longstreet himself understood precisely this special quality of dialect writing. Like any number of commentators on the significance of dialect writing, Kibler reads it as the work of a self-nominated realist.

The most compelling insight given in Longstreet's preface disappears when Kibler renovates Longstreet's caveat with an ellipsis that implies that dialect writing has to do with the "real" sounds of local life. When we reinsert the excised "to whom he represents himself as speaking" into this passage and read it to the letter, Longstreet's proposal parses very differently. In his original, Longstreet tells us that the language he uses is "accommodated to the capacity of the person to whom he [as author] represents himself [as narrator] as speaking"[97] That is, Longstreet suggests that his dialect writing is accommodated to a speaker who appears only in writing, that speaker "to whom he [the author] represents himself [the narrator] as speaking." If we take Longstreet at his word, his dialect writing is not accommodated to a real encounter, or even to an embodied person who secures the claim to realism. Rather Longstreet tells us that his dialect as narrator is the dialect that he, the writer, has contrived as an imagined response to an equally contrived character existing only in and as writing. We might wish to compare Longstreet's dialect writing to a standard of spoken language, but the narrator's occasional dialect is really related only to the dialect given his fictional interlocutors. Moreover, in a text-based environment, one free of any spoken signs, the only point of comparison we have for making sense of this dialect is the standard orthography that surrounds it.

We might take as a Southwestern humorist's passing joke this, Longstreet's enigmatic statement regarding his own realism, but a more serious engagement with this passage illuminates dialect writing's signifying mechanism. Taken quite literally, Longstreet's statement indicates that dialect writing is neither vernacular speech nor a post hoc record of vernacular speech. In fact, the comparative axis in Longstreet's dialect writing—in any dialect writing—is not voice to writing but writing to other writing. Longstreet's dialect writing only ever responds to, and becomes significant in relationship to, the standard written language of other fictional interlocutors. In this sense, dialect writing is a figure possible only in writing, as the name might suggest. Saying that dialect writing is not speech is not to say that it has no signified or outside event to which it gives us access but rather to require that we rethink its evidentiary significance. In truth, dialect writing articulates the heterogeneity of "local" time dominating the moment of its writing, and it reactivates the reader's experience of locality. This is because dialect writing requires its reader to engage two temporalities at once, as it subtly figures the coeval nature of these seemingly incompatible rhythms. In one of Longstreet's best-known stories, "The Character of a Native Georgian," for instance, a prolonged tour through a Georgia town finds Longstreet's narrator accompanying a white, gentlemanly "native Georgian" to an open-air market. Once there, the white "native Georgian" "beset[s] an old negro woman to sell him the half of a living chicken":

> "Do, my good mauma, sell it to me," said he; "my wife is very sick, and is longing for chicken pie, and this is all the money I have . . . and it's just what a half chicken comes to at your own price."
> "Ki, massa! how gwine cut live chicken in two?"
> "I don't want you to cut it in two alive; kill it, clean it, and then divide it."
> "Name o' God! what sort o' chance got to clean chicken in de market-house! Whay de water for scall um and wash um?"
> "Don't scald it at all; just pick it, so."
> "Ech-ech! Fedder fly all ober de buckera-man meat, he come bang me fo' true. No, massa, I mighty sorry for your wife, but I no cutty chicken open."[98]

The tradition that would have us understand dialect writing as a mimetic realism would ask us to read this passage as figuring a variant of standard speech. Either the apostrophes closing the two *o*'s would be interpreted as signifying a vernacular speech habit of dropping *f*'s from the end of a word, or the entire passage would be read as a racist misrepresentation of vernacular speech. More broadly, critical accounts of the cultural work of dialect writing would have us emphasize the social hierarchy figured in the linguistic differentiation of dialect from "standard" English. Yet the so-called dialect here also implies something it is not, but without which it could not be itself. What makes this passage dialect writing is that in the moment we read it, we understand it as departing from a standard written language that we assume precedes it. This passage of dialect writing implies a "pure[ly] anterio[r]" language that had to come before it: not vernacular speech but the standard of written language supposed by this dialect writing and from which it departs. In this sense, dialect writing can be diagrammed as

> "Ki, massa! how gwine cut live chicken in two?"
> "How am I going to cut a live chicken in two?"
> the difference between these two.[99]

We know Longstreet's f's are "missing" only because we also know they are/were there. No object can disappear in the way that these f's appear to have done unless they are understood as having been there in the first place. What this suggests is that dialect writing figures not only itself but also that "first place"; those f's are absent, but then again they are not. In this sense dialect writing is both the marks that we see on the page and those that we don't see; those we don't see are just as present in the figure of dialect writing as those we do see. Dialect writing figures both past and present at once and also figures them as different.

This figuration would suggest that the apparently unitary "moment" of dialect writing is itself divided into a past and a present that differ. In the flicker of an instant, dialect writing requires us to perceive both a standard language and a dialect; dialect writing requires its reader to perceive both its past and its present in the single moment of reading. This flickering quality is dialect writing at work. Dialect writing attests, moreover, to the abiding presence of a temporality wherein past and present are endlessly differentiated. The insistent return of this temporality would matter little were it not for the fact that in the scene from *The House of the Seven Gables* quoted earlier, as in Southwestern humor, dialect writing is supposed to help chronicle the presence of a premodern temporality disarticulated from change and progress. At the level of a trope, in other words, this dialect writing is figuring the presence of a temporality incommensurable with the temporality being described at the level of statement. The point here is not, however, that dialect writing gives us access to the univocal truth about time in the moment it describes. The point is that when it is read carefully and against the grain, this period's literature, especially in moments of figurative excess such as this one, can be seen to articulate temporalities that we might otherwise think of as impossible adjuncts. Southwestern humor, for instance, repeatedly insists that it chronicles the singular rhythm, the unique tempo of a region where little changes; it simultaneously describes these local times as always already lost, because progress and the stasis of the old Southwest cannot cohabit. Yet the dialect writing that dominates this and other regional literatures reveals that there is no single rhythm, no single local time encompassing the experience of the Southwest, the Southwestern humorists, or, indeed, America. Instead, this literature confirms that linear progress and other forms of time can be coeval; one does not necessarily cede to the other. It materializes at precisely those moments when the homogeneous time traditionally identified with modernity looms on the horizon. Dialect writing debuts just as what has been posed as a conflict between premodern and modern, black and white, Indian and settler—in a word, *irreconcilable* temporalities appear on the brink of resolution, just as one temporality is about to overwrite all others. At these moments, dialect writing announces a failure to transition to homogeneous time, because dialect writing articulates at the level of form a temporality (or temporalities) being obscured at the level of statement. In doing so, dialect writing expresses the heterogeneous time of modernity.

"Temporal Affairs Were Suspended"

In *Hope Leslie*, Catharine Maria Sedgwick anticipates Hawthorne when she invokes and repudiates—often in the same stretch of writing—a form of American cultural nationalism based on a commitment to the idea of "progress."[100] Sedgwick's novel points to a shift in New England from a premodern to a modern experience of time, and she marks this regional transition as coincident with the Atlantic seaboard's larger transformation from a collection of localized colonies into a tightly bound nation. This consolidation of a specifically Anglo-American colonial culture and its transformation into a nation by the work of colonialism and capitalism was for Sedgwick documented in the seventeenth-century histories authored by John Winthrop, William Bradford, and William Hubbard that Sedgwick consulted in her researches for this novel.[101] Sedgwick describes the arrival of this new national coherence as the welcome moment when egalitarian Enlightenment reason reached North America and as therefore the era when it became newly possible to see the error of the superstitions and in- humane colonialism of the Puritans. Indeed, on the evidence of her novel alone, Sedgwick would seem to confirm George Dekker's claim that "the faith at least of the early romancers was that [contemporary history] already had the shape and meaning of an inevitable progress from savagery to civili- zation."[102] She also appears to validate Emily Budick's view that "[t]hrough their historical fictions," early romancers "hoped to restore their readers to the historical consciousness they lacked and to shared responsibility in the national venture."[103] Yet Sedgwick's attention to the excesses of colonial racism aimed at indigenous North Americans, as well as her mourning of the lost potential for a multiracial nation, undercut any easy sense that she was certain about the inevitability of "progress" in America. In this respect, her commitment to American cultural nationalism appears to be at best an ambivalent loyalty. Yet the criticism on Sedgwick has tended to cut in the direction of cultural nationalism—if in a feminist key.

In early reviews of Sedgwick's romance, for instance, *The American Ladies Magazine* claimed to be "particularly pleased that a *lady* had entered the ranks of those contributing to a fledgling American literature," while the *North American Review* closed its account of Sedgwick's novel with a "concluding appeal that Sedgwick continue her efforts 'for the public's sake, and for the honor of our youthful literature.'"[104] In 1842, upon the republication of *Hope Leslie*, Godey's *Lady's Book* made the following state- ment: "It is gratifying to see the unrivalled talents of such a writer [as Sedg- wick] devoted to so patriotic an object as that of increasing the interest of the American people in the history of their own country. The best pens among our female writers, we are happy to notice, are chiefly devoted to national subjects. While the lady writers are thus patriotic, we need not de- spair of ultimately building up a sound and elegant national literature."[105] For these contemporaries, Sedgwick's novel represents precisely the kind of "indigenous" literature a new nation requires. As Philip Gould argues, Sedgwick's late twentieth-century champions—feminist literary critics and historians—adopt similar terms of approbation. In her introduction to *Hope Leslie*, for example, Mary Kelley writes, "Spurred by the enormous popularity of Sir Walter Scott's historical novels, Sedgwick sought to re- cover her nation's past, to kindle interest in its early inhabitants, and to foster a cultural identity other than that derived from the former mother country."[106] Judith Fetterley understands the novel in similar terms: "Responding, like Cooper, to the call for a distinctively American literature, [Sedgwick] rivaled him in her own day as the writer who could answer Sydney Smith's sneering question, '[W]ho in the four quarters of the globe reads an American book?' by putting America on the literary map. Moreover, like her contemporary, Lydia Huntley Sigourney, she created a space for the woman writer to participate in creating an American literature and hence in constructing the new Republic."[107] Here Sedgwick participates in the creation of a "new Republic" where there was not one before, and Fetterley concludes that in *Hope Leslie* "the construction of America falls to the decidedly unromantic [character] Hope Leslie and to her 'brother' Everell."[108] As Ezra Tawil has argued regarding scholarship on the frontier romance, Sedgwick's novel is made to seem to be "a progressive revision of the racist male prototype."[109]

This sense that *Hope Leslie* provided the basis of "a cultural identity other than that derived from the former mother country," as Kelley describes it, is notable in the context of *Hope Leslie*, because like Hawthorne's novels, its cultural nationalism is betrayed by its form. In addition to the complications already discussed, *Hope Leslie* points us in the direction of a revolutionary messianic form of time that the novel associates with the violence of interracial war. The modernity of this novel begins to come into view, for example, as early as Sedgwick's preface. It functions as a conventional apologia and seeks to forestall critics who would deride Sedgwick for her inattention to the finer grain of historical fact. Although this preface lacks a detailed statement of her aesthetic program, it does offer a short account of her method. She writes, "The following volumes are not offered to the reading public as being in any degree an historical narrative, or a relation of real events. Real characters and real events are, however, alluded to; and this course, if not strictly necessary, was found very convenient in the execution of the author's design, which was to illustrate not the history, but the character of the times."[110] Sedgwick actually resembles Hawthorne here, in that she describes her own work as more or less founded in fact but willing to take the liberty of invention that Hawthorne describes as the license available to the writer of the romance as opposed to that of the realist novel. Anticipating those critics who would second-guess her depiction of Magawisca, the heroic Indian "maiden," as a woman of high virtue, Sedgwick defends her tale as follows: "[I]t may be sufficient to remark, that in such delineations, we are confined not to the actual, but the possible."[111] This category of the "possible" is Sedgwick's way of suggesting that her work is historically plausible, even if it is not always factually precise. It also anticipates Hawthorne's commitment to the "probable," as opposed to the actual, in his *Seven Gables* preface. Sedgwick's preface concludes, moreover, with remarks that suggest she intends her work as suited to the needs of the coalescing nation: "These volumes are so far from being intended as a substitute for genuine history, that the ambition of the writer would be fully gratified if, by this work, any of our young countrymen should be stimulated to investigate the early history of their native land."[112] With a strategy of narratorial interpellation that defines this work as a whole, in which Sedgwick's author-narrator often directly addresses her reader and emphasizes the reader's proper role as a national-racial subject, Sedgwick here represents her novel as what Lauren Berlant might call an article of national fantasy.

In crucial respects, however, *Hope Leslie* also traces the conflict of times seen throughout the writing already considered. As is the case with Irving and Hawthorne, for example, Sedgwick's novel often adopts a diagnostic rhetoric of American modernity organized around depicting the before and after of modernization. *Hope Leslie* effects this contrast through its repeated thematization of the idea of worldwide historical progress and the benefits of Enlightenment reason and through the novel's attention to "premodern" timekeeping measures. The thematization of progress and Enlightenment begins early on in *Hope Leslie,* when we are introduced to the adoptive father of the novel's eponymous heroine in the person of William Fletcher. Fletcher, one of the early Puritan settlers, was, as Sedgwick's author-narrator explains, of an "ardent temperament" and found himself "disappointed at the slow operation [in the colony] of principles" that were transparently for the good of all.[113] In this respect, Fletcher was ill-suited to his errand in the wilderness, for the character of his age did not speak well of the "character of man." In one of her many messages from the future, as Jeffrey Insko describes them, Sedgwick's author-narrator compares her own time to that of the Puritans: "The character of man, and the institutions of society, are yet very far from their possible and desired perfection. Still, how far is the present age in advance of that which drove reformers to a dreary wilderness!—of that which hanged quakers?—of that which condemned to death, as witches, innocent, unoffending old women! But it is unnecessary to heighten the glory of our risen day by comparing it with the preceding twilight. To return to Mr. Fletcher."[114] Unnecessary they may have been, but apparently such comparisons distinctly appealed to Sedgwick's inclinations as a writer and her sense of the course of history. They occur throughout the novel, and they describe contemporary New England as being decidedly different from the colonial environment of its ancestors and also as a decided improvement upon the Puritan experience. Like Hawthorne, Sedgwick often casts the witch-hunting Puritans in contrast to the reason of the modern nation, and her author-narrator describes even the geography itself in distinct contrast to its former state: "The wigwams which constituted the [Indian] village," she writes, "gave place to the clumsy, but more convenient dwelling of the pilgrims," thanks to the economic and social industry of the more recently arrived white settlers.[115] Anticipating the rise of market culture and its appurtenances, Sedgwick writes, "Where there are now contiguous rows of shops, filled with the merchandise of the east, the manufactures of Europe, the rival fabrics of our own country, and the fruits of the tropics; where now stands the stately hall of justice—the academy—the bank—churches, orthodox and heretic, and all the symbols of a rich and populous community—were, at the early period of our history, a few log-houses, planted around a fort, defended by a slight embankment and palisade."[116] Like Rip Van Winkle's post-Revolutionary Hudson Valley village, Sedgwick's nineteenth-century New England has lost its sleepily local character and is instead one node on a national-global commercial network: instead of "a few log-houses, planted around a fort," New England boasts not only significant commerce and civilization but also connections to "our own country," the "tropics," the "east," and Europe.

Although Sedgwick distinguishes the colonial past from the American national present in these ways, she also sees the rising glory of America, as the eighteenth-century poets called it, anticipated in the founding of the Puritan colony itself. Indeed, Sedgwick traces the emergence of the temporality of progress, and its characteristic force of "change," to the moment of colonial founding. In her account of Hope Leslie's visit to the home of the noble workman, Digby, Sedgwick uses the opportunity of Digby's serflike presence to mark the significant political changes under way in the early seventeenth century. After Hope worries aloud whether her disobedience in the face of patriarchal colonial authority represents a sinful failing, Digby reassures her that she is simply one instance of a spirit already set free elsewhere in the mother land. "'No, no, Miss Hope,'" Digby remarks, "'I watch the motion of the straws—I know which way the wind blows'": "'Thought and will are set free. It was but the other day, so to speak, in the days of good queen Bess, as they called her, when, if her majesty did but raise her hand, the parliament folks were all down on their knees to her; and now, thank God, the poorest and the lowest of us only kneel to Him who made us. Times are changed—there is a new spirit in the world—

chains are broken—fetters are knocked off—and the liberty set forth in the blessed world, is now felt to be every man's birth-right.' "[117] Digby's comments suggest that, even in the pre-Revolutionary colonial environment of the socially repressive and patriarchal New England British colonies, the "spirit" of "change" can be felt as a blowing wind.

This attention to the press of progress is reinforced by Sedgwick's focused attention on the implicitly premodern timekeeping measures of colonial New England. Sedgwick describes a relationship to the sun, the moon, candles, and hourglasses that, while not completely unfamiliar to Sedgwick's readers, would have registered with her more affluent audience in particular as a sign of the antiquity of Sedgwick's characters. Michael O'Malley suggests that, "[b]y the 1830s, a sense of time rooted in nature confronted a seemingly arbitrary time based on commerce, revealing itself in machine movements and the linear progress of invention."[118] Although private "[c]locks were still relatively rare in 1826," they would have been less so for the incipiently middle-class urban women (and men) who sought out Sedgwick's writing, for the standing clock was fast becoming a central feature of the affluent domestic interior.[119] It seems significant, then, that Sedgwick so closely marks the passage of time in her novel according to the heavenly and nonmechanical timekeeping measures that remained a staple part of rural life into the 1860s.

One of the first instances of this attention to premodern measures of time comes in a letter from Mrs. Fletcher to Mr. Fletcher while he is away from home on the business of retrieving their newly adopted daughter, Hope. (Hope's sister, Faith, has already arrived at the Fletcher homestead.) The letter, headed "Springfield, 1636," recounts news from the home front, as it were, including the behavior of their children and servants.[120] Of the servant Darby she remarks, "'Darby, who is ever a dawdler, having gone, last Saturday, with the cart to the village, dilly-dallied about there, and did not set out on his return till the sun was quite down, both to the eye and by the kalender. Accordingly, early on the following Monday, he was summoned before Mr. Pynchon.'"[121] Mrs. Fletcher's attention to the measures of the sun and the calendar is part of the more generally antiquarian feel of this letter, with its anachronistic, or perhaps merely irregular, spelling and its reference to the judicial predispositions of the Puritan clergy. Shortly thereafter in the narrative, as Mr. Fletcher and the family's new charge, Hope Leslie, approach the frontier home of the Fletchers, Fletcher's wife and children await their arrival. On this, "one of the most beautiful afternoons of the month of May," "[a]ll was joy in Mrs. Fletcher's dwelling."[122]

Fletcher's son, Everell, can barely manage his excitement: "'My dear mother,' said Everell, 'it is now quite time to look out for father and Hope Leslie. I have turned the hour-glass three times since dinner, and counted all the sands I think.'"[123] During this interval of waiting, the decidedly un-mechanical hourglass, which turns only with the aid of the human hand, provides Everell's primary sense of duration. Much later in the novel, a teenage Hope Leslie sits with her companion, Esther, who is a much more docile, pliant, and patient Christian than Hope could ever expect to be: "'Do, Esther, look at the candles,' [Hope] whispered; 'don't you think it must be nine o'clock?'" "'Oh, hush!'" Esther responds, "'no, not yet eight.'"[124] Schooled in reading the duration of light as a marker of time, Hope turns to the candles rather than to a watch. Significantly, each of the measures of time described is connected to some form of cycle, whether the Puritan "kalender," or almanac, which was concerned more with the sea-sonal and diurnal cycles of planting, as the reference to the eye and the sun suggests; the hourglass, which must always begin where it ends and which had long-standing associations with the cycle of life, as its appearance on early American tombstones indicates; or the candle, which measures finite rather than infinite duration and which bears a strong association with the cycle of labor by hand required to produce it.

Yet Sedgwick also mobilizes the formal devices of the realist novel, marrying her claims about American modernity to her version of novelistic writing. In this respect, Mary Kelley is right to suggest that Sedgwick "blends the conventions of romance with historical realism."[125] Through-out this novel, Sedgwick's narrative interpolations, which come at the start and the close of almost every chapter, attempt to set right order—which is to say linear order—to the course of diegetic time. In the following passage, from the opening of the first volume's chapter 3, we see, for example, Sedg-wick linking her rhetoric of progress and American modernity to a careful management of diegetic time. After having closed the previous chapter in the late evening, Sedgwick's author-narrator opens with, "On the following morning Mr. Fletcher set out for Boston, and escaping all perils by flood and field, he arrived there at the expiration of nine days, having accom-plished the journey, now the affair of a single day, with unusual expedi-tion."[126] Unwilling to let a single hour go unaccounted, Sedgwick resets her narrative clock after nearly every chapter break. She also employs that most important device of spatiotemporal mapping: the "meanwhile." In the pre-viously quoted chapter, Sedgwick links Mr. Fletcher to his people back home by virtue of this formulation: "Mr. Fletcher was detained, at first by business, and afterwards by ill-health, much longer than he had expected, and the fall, winter, and earliest months of spring wore away before he was able to set his face homeward. In the mean time, his little community at Bethel proceeded more harmoniously than could have been hoped from the discordant materials of which it was composed."[127] Here the collectivizing effect of the "In the mean time" not only connects Mr. Fletcher to his "little community" in a moment of protonational simultaneity; this phrase appears to lend its binding influence to the "little community" itself, producing a people surprisingly "harmonious[s]" even in the face of their "discordant" composition.

Such moments are not difficult to come by in *Hope Leslie*. Chapter 4 of volume 1 concludes with the following: "The alarm was spread through the village, and in a brief space Mr. Pynchon with six armed men were pressing towards the fatal scene. In the meantime, the tragedy was proceeding at Bethel."[128] A later chapter that treats Magawisca's fate ends with, "There we must leave [Magawisca], and join that fearful company who were gathered together to witness what they believed to be the execution of exact and necessary justice."[129] Still later, Sedgwick's author-narrator, seeking to reinforce the linear shape of a narrative that spans more than a decade, once again intervenes: "As our fair readers are not apt to be observant of dates, it may be useful to remind them that Miss Leslie's letter was written in October. In the following May, two ships, from the mother country, anchored at the same time in Boston-Bay."[130] In a scene that recalls the premium placed on the space of the domestic interior in the realist novel, we are told the following: "[W]hile the governor was looking over a letter of introduction, presented to him by Everell's chance acquaintance, who had announced himself with the name Sir Philip Gardiner, the young ladies withdrew to their own apartment."[131] Finally, near the story's end, we are told that, "[w]hile all this business was transpiring, Hope Leslie, wearied by the fatigues, agitations, and protracted vigil of the preceding night, was sleeping most profoundly."[132] In each of these instances, some version of the "meanwhile" provides a sense of a shared temporality divisible into passing instants, each of which is shared by the novel's characters, and the novel's readers as well.

In several memorable instances, Sedgwick manages an exceedingly deft maneuver that marries her rhetoric of progress to these formal effects, producing what would seem to be analogously linear (and progressive) historical and diegetic timescapes. An especially crucial chapter near the novel's end, for example, finds Hope Leslie, her cousin, and Governor Winthrop's family, who are Hope's and her cousin's benefactors, at home in the Winthrop mansion. She characteristically sets the scene with an account of the difference separating the practices of the Puritan settlers from those of Sedgwick's readers. "At the period of history," Sedgwick writes, "twelve o'clock was the hour appointed for dinner; we believe in the mother country—certainly in the colony then, as now, every where in the interior of our states, this natural division of time was maintained. Our magistrates did not then claim any exemption from the strict rules of simplicity and frugality that were imposed on the humble citizens, and Governor Winthrop's meridian meal, though it might have been somewhat superior in other luxuries, had no more of the luxury of time bestowed on it, than that of the honest artisans and tradesmen about him."[133] Here Sedgwick orients us by having us clock in, as it were, at the point of noon. In this way she reasserts the singularity of a narrative line that is decidedly digressive, as her narrative interpolations repeatedly admit. It is not only we, her readers, who are ordered by this particular clock. Sedgwick's narrator asserts the regularity of time in the colonial moment, an episode when even the highest governing official obeys the custom of the country. In doing so, she depicts a dinner hour that resembles the event of newspaper reading in Hegel's account of modernity.[134] This same chapter continues, moreover, and draws the graph of linear time and space even more tightly and restrictively around Sedgwick's narrative and her reader: "It now drew near the hour of two, the time appointed for the interview of the Governor with Sir Philip; the dinner was over, the table removed, and all orderly and quiet in the parlor, when Jennet, in her retreat, heard Miss [Hope] Leslie and Mr. Everell Fletcher enter, and though the weather was warm, close the door after them. A slight hint is sufficient for the wary and wise, and Jennet, on hearing the door shut, forebore to make any noise, which should apprise the parties of her proximity."[135] Still projected into an alien past, by virtue of Sedgwick's earlier marker of this moment as happening during an earlier "period of history," we find ourselves in a carefully mapped diegetic world whose constituent members inhabit a single point of time in common. Jennet's physical proximity to Hope and Everell is in many respects less important than her temporal coincidence with them.

Sedgwick's seemingly rigorous attention to the Aristotelian unities has been lost on a number of her critics. Writing in the *American Monthly Magazine* of January 1836, one of Sedgwick's early reviewers complained that her stories bordered on chaos. "It is not Miss Sedgwick's great gift," this reviewer writes, "to contrive the incidents of a story." The reviewer continues, "It is, however, true that she does not give us the old hackneyed routine. But in avoiding this, her drama wants a regular beginning, middle, and end; it is often improbable, and sometimes inconsistent; and we never read one of her stories without smiling at a certain spirit of adventure, which always comes out somewhere in the conduct of her young girls."[136] For this reviewer, Sedgwick's writing is a compromised pleasure; the energetic appeal of her young female heroines does not completely outweigh her inability to articulate a single narrative line that hews to the orderly and predictable unfolding the reviewer desires. Much later, Michael Davitt Bell would write the following comments about *Hope Leslie*, a work he finds valuable primarily as an illustration of the conventional historical romance at its most hackneyed. "*Hope Leslie* is doubly conventional," Bell writes, "For one thing it embodies a conventional 19th century attitude toward history, a belief in 'progress'—a belief that history, in the words of [David] Levin [in *History as Romantic Art*], 'had been a movement from the "artificial" toward the "natural."' *Hope Leslie* is also conventional in that it expresses this attitude toward history by means of a conventional marriage plot, found again and again in the historical romance, in which historical progress becomes identified with the romantic attachment of hero and heroine."[137] Bell's claim that *Hope Leslie* is "doubly conventional" would lead us to expect him to have little trouble parsing the novel's plot; if romance conventions were in fact so clearly at play, this novel should be a straightforward read. Yet *Hope Leslie*'s significant "shortcoming" is, Bell argues, its decidedly "confusing" plot.[138] He complains that the novel's "abundance of material leads to a good deal of confusion," even if "all the confusion of plot" cannot obscure "her book's central, essentially simple, symbolic concern" with American progress.[139] Even more recently, Sedgwick's romance prompts Jeffrey Insko to ask whether *Hope Leslie* might not question "the very notion of time" as "chronological succession."[140] Even Sedgwick herself repeatedly apologizes, in the midst of her intensely focused effort to bring the predictable order of linear progress to the page, for her repeated digressions: "We return from our long digression to the party we left in Governor Winthrop's parlour."[141] Then fifteen pages later: "After having favoured our readers with this long skipping-place, we resume the thread of our narrative."[142] And near the start of the second volume: "But to return to our individual concerns."[143] Finally, blaming the character Hope for the nature of her narrative, Sedgwick's author-narrator remarks, "There we must leave [Robin] to achieve, in due time, an object involving most momentous consequences, while we follow on the trail of our heroine, whose excursive habits have so often compelled us to deviate from the straight line of narration."[144] These comments encourage us to cast our thoughts back to Hawthorne's resistance to process as progress. Indeed, these comments suggest that, like Hawthorne's critics, Sedgwick's reviewers and even the author herself identify without quite naming the heterogeneous time articulated in and through this romance.

If we have seen *Hope Leslie* at its most conventionally novelistic, it should not surprise us to learn that it also involves the simultaneity-along-time associated with the premodern. This diachronic simultaneity encroaches especially on those moments when Sedgwick most deliberately deploys her rhetoric of historical progress and American modernity. For example, shortly after the previously quoted passage that marks the difference of contemporary New England from colonial Massachusetts by referencing its global commerce, the following passage offers a competing sense of the relationship between premodern and modern New England: "The mansions of the [early colony's] proprietors were rather more spacious and artificial than those of their more humble associates, and were built on the well-known model of the modest dwelling illustrated by the birth of Milton—a form still abounding in the eastern parts of Massachusetts, and presenting to the eye of a New-Englander the familiar aspect of an awkward friendly country cousin."[145] Despite having just asserted that the order of progress has rendered the colonial past alien to her readers, Sedgwick's author-narrator concedes here a certain past living in the present in the forms of the houses themselves. As elsewhere, Sedgwick's narrator seeks to deny the coeval nature of linear progress and diachronic simultaneity—the copresence of which allows the past and present to be different and the same—by associating the persistence of the past in the present with a rural order of time signified by the mention of the "friendly country cousin." Sedgwick's romance would assign diachronic simultaneity, or the persistence of the past in the present, to a geographic locale and locally defined lifestyle expected to disappear very soon. The fact remains, however, that these two orders of time are articulated within the pages of the same book and thus live in the same diegetic present tense; their competition in fact defines the very nature of reading during this period.

In a passage that even more forcefully recalls Hawthorne's "hauntings," William Fletcher, upon meeting his new adoptee, Hope Leslie, writes to his wife of the uncanny resemblance between past and future generations, on the order of Hawthorne's Pyncheons. "So much was [Fletcher] impressed with the resemblance" between Hope and her mother "that he said, in a letter to his wife, that it reminded him of the heathen doctrine of metemsychosis—and he could almost believe the spirit of the mother was transferred to the bosom of the child."[146] Like Hawthorne's Colonel Pyncheon, who reemerges in the body of his descendant Jaffrey, Hope's mother persists into the present by virtue of Hope's physical presence. Finally, as the customs of New England's Puritan ancestors endure in the rural housing styles of the 1820s, so, too, does Sedgwick's community share with its founders a single funereal practice: "We shall now leave the little community, assembled at Bethel, to perform the last offices for one who had been among them an example of all the most attractive virtues of woman. The funeral ceremony was then, as it still is, among the descendants of pilgrims, a simple affectionate service; a gathering of the people—men, women, and children, as one family, to the house of mourning."[147] The very syntax of Sedgwick's sentence here points out the indistinctness of past and present rather than their difference: it describes a single funeral service at which past and present, ancestors and descendants gather together in a moment of mournful intimacy. These two temporalities—one involving linear progress and the other a persistence of the past in the present—often occur simultaneously in the space of a single narrative interval. Here the conjunctural effect of these distinct temporalities, which we saw at play in Hawthorne, and which is implicitly at work throughout the romance genre, is impossible to ignore. For instance, the chapter that Sedgwick's author-narrator characterizes as a "long skipping-place" opens with a description of the customary activities of a Sunday in colonial New England: "The observance of the Sabbath began with the puritans, as it still does with a great portion of their descendants, on Saturday night. At the going down of the sun on Saturday, all temporal affairs were suspended; and so zealously did our fathers maintain the letter, as well as the spirit of the law, that, according to a vulgar tradition in Connecticut, no beer was brewed in the latter part of the week, lest it should presume to *work* on Sunday."[148] Sedgwick's suggestion here that "all temporal affairs are suspended" functions in two complementary ways. It describes a supposed suspension of linear time that allows the past to persist into the present. It also indicates that under normal conditions the "new" is always coming into being. This passage implies, in other words, that past and present always differ if time, or the "temporal," is in play; it suggests that in this incipiently Enlightenment colony, the time of linear progress is the order of the day. In this way, Sedgwick's narrator seeks to restrict our notion of what counts as time by substituting one temporality—the time of linear progress—for time as a whole.

Put another way, Sedgwick's reference to this passage as a "skipping-place" implies that it describes a temporal hiatus, when in fact it portrays merely a declension of time that allows for diachronic simultaneity. This passage acts as a simultaneous disavowal and discovery of adjunct temporalities.

As Sedgwick's characterization of the Puritan sabbath continues, her narrator increasingly emphasizes the persistence of the past in the present, while simultaneously invoking a rhetoric of progress and predicting that the time of progress will ultimately supplant the premodern temporality that allows the past to endure into the present. Addressing Sedgwick's contemporaries, her narrator states, "It must be confessed that the tendency of the current age is to laxity; and so rapidly is the wholesome strictness of primitive times abating, that, should some antiquary, fifty years hence, in exploring his garret rubbish, chance to cast his eye on our humble pages, he may be surprised to learn, that even now the Sabbath is observed, in the interior of New-England, with an almost judaical severity."[149] This passage forecasts an ultimately triumphant spirit of restlessness and change, while at the same time suggesting that at least some quarters of New England have remained immune to the unfolding of the new and the different. These areas experience time as their forefathers did, which, in Sedgwick's terms, is to say not at all. In the New England interior, little has changed from the era of the Puritans to Sedgwick's own age; these lands would appear to be deprived of linear time. At the same time, Sedgwick predicts the ultimate disappearance of such experiences under the growing weight of linear progress. As with Sedgwick's other narrated references to the ways of rural people, which are quoted earlier, Sedgwick seeks here to assign the premodern temporality she describes to the contemporary hinterlands. She attempts, in other words, to deny the coeval nature of supposedly premodern and modern orders of time by assigning them different addresses. Eventually Sedgwick describes Saturday afternoon's "uncommon bustle," the "bidding of the church-bell" on Sunday, and the village bell's "twilight walk" at the close of the sabbath. Like Hawthorne's recourse to epic convention, this description does little to indicate whether the scene described is Sedgwick's own era or that of colonial New England, and it finally closes with the following: "After having favoured our readers with this long skipping-place, we resume the thread of our narrative. We have passed over eight days, which glided away without supplying any events to the historian of our heroine's life; though even then the thread was spinning that was to form the woof of her destiny."[150] Suggesting that her description of "customary" activities threatens her larger project, Sedgwick reassures her readers that "the thread was spinning" and that the new continued to unfold. She thus associates the project of historical narrative itself with representing time as the continuous elaboration of new and different moments. We are encouraged to overlook any evidence that time might have more than one expression and to view with suspicion any articulation of time that suggests it does.

As with Hawthorne's introduction to the story of Alice Pyncheon, this supposed skipping place, where the notion that past and present are the same threatens to overwhelm the notion that they are different, includes one of *Hope Leslie*'s only significant examples of dialect writing: "On Saturday afternoon an uncommon bustle is apparent. The great class of procrastinators are hurrying to and fro to complete the lagging business of the week. The good mothers, like Burns' matron, are plying their needles, making 'auld claes look amaist as weel's the new;' while the domestics, or help, (we prefer the national descriptive term) are wielding with might and main, their brooms, and *mops*, to make all *tidy* for the Sabbath."[151] In the midst of her meditation on the constancy of New England culture, Sedgwick turns to an eighteenth-century Scottish dialect poet and applies his dialect writing to the "good mothers" of seventeenth-century New England. The quotation from Burns and the sentence it occupies are deceptively similar to the rest of this chapter's initial paragraphs; it also recalls Scipio's comments on the constancy of the House of the Seven Gables. At the level of statement, it undermines the notion that past and present differ, claiming that the old will look as good as the new. Again, however, as in Hawthorne, the dialect writing in which this claim is realized articulates a very distinct experience of time. Here, as elsewhere, dialect writing figures even the single moment as divided, and while the old might look almost as good as new, the old is also never actually the same as that new. In Sedgwick's romance, as in Hawthorne's, dialect writing persistently reminds us that time has more than one manifestation and that these are realized at the level of literary form. In order to speak of time in the romance, we must therefore always modify that term. *The House of the Seven Gables*, *The Scarlet Letter*, and *Hope Leslie* include temporalities but no single time.

I have so far described the temporal heterogeneity of this literature as articulating a kind of double-timed modernity in which synchronic simultaneity subsists alongside simultaneity-along-time. In many respects, these are conventional enough ways of conceiving of time: lines and circles, progress and stasis, modern and premodern. Now, however, I turn to what I will be calling revolutionary messianic time, which repeatedly flares in

Sedgwick's novel and elsewhere in this period's literature. At key moments that address the history and the impact of violent political struggle in British North America and the United States, American writing has a habit of articulating an experience of time in which the past and the future are drawn into the same single "present." Here the biblical metaphor of Judgment Day is illuminating. On Judgment Day, as it is traditionally conceived, the three temporal aspects—past, present, and future—that define earthly, or secular, time cease to apply. On this day, the entire past history of the world joins all of its potential futures, and they are gathered together in the sight of God. This ingathering of infinity, as it were, provides an opportunity for the distribution of pure and equal justice. Rather than be judged against the standards, morals, and actions of those who share(d) one's chronological interval of earthly time, this judgment is an absolute one: one's actions are reckoned alongside all that has been and all that ever will be. In this view, real justice is possible only in the messianic moment, because only in that moment can the scales of measure be calibrated to an absolute standard. In the Judeo-Christian tradition, this moment awaits the arrival of the Messiah. In the American historical romance, however, it emerges from the concentrated political struggle attendant upon the colonization of North America. These romances suggest that the irruption of bloody political struggle escapes containment by any single chronological interval: these struggles affect not only the future, as one might expect, but also the past. Indeed, these moments of revolutionary messianism draw the future and the past into the present, and they initiate an earthly process of distributive justice. These romances suggest, in other words, that violent political struggle changes the very structure of time. The compelling implication here is that time is a sociopolitical effect whose nature changes according to human activity.

In *Hope Leslie*, this revolutionary messianic time extends outward from two of the most significant moments in the plot. It first radiates out and then back in again from the moment in volume 1 when the Mohawks raid the Fletcher homestead during Mr. Fletcher's absence in order to recapture Magawisca and Oneco, the daughter and son of the Pequod chief, Mononotto. It also bleeds out from the moment when Sir Philip Gardiner's kidnapping plot ends with his ship, its crew, and his spurned lover Rosa blown to the heavens. In the first instance, the Mohawk and Pequod Indians ally to take their revenge on the Puritans for the earlier massacre of the Pequods, at which time Magawisca and Oneco were taken prisoner. During the raid, the Indians brutally kill Mrs. Fletcher, her three daughters, and her baby boy; they kidnap Faith Leslie, Hope's younger sister, who preceded Hope to the Fletcher household; and they also kidnap, with the intent to kill, the young Everell Fletcher, whom Magawisca later saves from execution at the hands of her father. Although the events of the attack occupy fewer than three pages, it is present in the narrative anticipation and the recollected memory of the novel and its characters for several additional chapters. Well before the Pequod-Mohawk alliance takes its revenge, for example, Mrs. Fletcher writes to her husband, in a letter already quoted, telling of her recent "forebodings." She remarks:

"There hath been some alarm here within the last few days, on account of certain Indians who have been seen lurking in the woods around us. They are reported not to have a friendly appearance. We have been advised to remove, for the present, to the Fort; but as I feel no apprehension, I shall not disarrange my family by taking a step that would savour more of fear than prudence. I say I feel no apprehension— yet I must confess it—I have a cowardly womanish spirit, and fear is set in motion by the very mention of danger. There are vague forebodings hanging about me, and I cannot drive them away even by the thought that your presence, my honoured husband, will soon relieve me from all agitating apprehensions, and repair all the faults of my poor judgment."[152]

Here Mrs. Fletcher discounts her "apprehensions," attributing them to her "cowardly womanish spirit," but as we learn several pages later when the Indians attack, she has in fact discerned agents from the future in the outline of her present. Mrs. Fletcher's experience of the future in the present finds a corollary among Sedgwick's Pequods in the person of Magawisca's mother, Monoco, as we learn when Magawisca recounts the story of the destruction of her people at the hands of the English. During a conversation with Everell Fletcher before the attack on the Fletcher household, Magawisca recalls the fatal day of the earlier English raid on her people. Magawisca explains that a "warning spirit" that day visited Monoco: "'My mother was in her hut with her children, not sleeping, for my brother Samoset had lingered behind his companions, and had not yet returned from the watersport. The warning spirit, that ever keeps its station at a mother's pillow, whispered that some evil was near; and my mother, bidding me lie still with the little ones, went forth in quest of my brother. All the servants of the Great Spirit spoke to my mother's ear and eye of danger and death. The moon, as she sunk behind the hills, appeared a ball of fire; strange lights darted through the air; to my mother's eye they seemed fiery arrows; to her ear the air was filled with death-sighs.'"[153] In language that recalls Puritan accounts of celestial and providential signs, Magawisca's mother experiences the massacre of the Pequods in advance of its "actual" unfolding. Monoco also shares this relationship to the future with a fellow Pequod, Cushmakin, who himself has lately suffered a "darkness" spreading over his "soul."[154] Here the parallel between Mrs. Fletcher and Monoco is clear. The massacre of the Pequods precedes the attack on the Fletcher household by a period of several months: the latter is the retribution for the former. Yet Mrs. Fletcher and Monoco encounter similar warnings from the future. This representation of an experience common to an Indian mother and a white one underscores Sedgwick's (wavering) commitment to a multiracial feminist humanism. More to the point, it indicates how the violent conflict that was colonization (re)structured the three aspects of time.

Indeed, when Sedgwick's narrator describes the immediate consequence of the Pequod attack on the Fletchers, we are offered a view of just how much political violence affects our experience of quotidian, historical, and narrative time. Arriving at the Fletcher homestead, after having heard a horn signaling an attack, the servants Digby and Hutton search in vain for any survivors. Overcome by the scene, Digby laments, " 'Not one—not one spared!' "[155] Stepping from a secret hiding place, the dissolute female servant Jennet replies, " 'Yes, one.' "[156] Encouraged by his discovery of Jennet, Digby demands that she supply him with details. " 'How long,' Digby inquired, 'have [the attackers and the kidnapped] been gone? how long since you heard the last sound?' "[157] Jennet replies, " 'That's more than mortal man, or woman either, in my case, could tell, Mr. Digby. Do you think, when a body seems to feel a scalping knife in their heads, they can reckon time? No; hours are minutes, and minutes hours, in such a case.' "[158] Digby turns in disgust from Jennet, and Sedgwick's author-narrator appears just as contemptuous of her. Yet the ensuing dialogue actually confirms Jennet's sense that, at the point of a knife, or, as in Sedgwick's case, faced with the enormity of politically motivated massacre, the ability to "reckon time" either escapes us or is transformed in striking ways, as the following passage demonstrates. Preparing to pursue the attackers, Digby turns to his companion, Hutton: " 'Are you ready, Hutton?' asked Digby, impatiently": " 'Ready!—yes, I am ready, but what is the use, Digby? what are we two against a host? and, besides, you know not how long they have been gone.' 'Not very long,' said Digby, shuddering and pointing to blood that was trickling, drop by drop, from the edge of the flooring to the step."[159] The grains of the hourglass that we earlier saw Everell count in anticipation of his father's arrival are here transformed into the spill of human blood. We might on the one hand regard Digby's bloody "timepiece" as an indication of his hunter's instincts and a sign of the frontier spirit associated with the Puritan settlement. In this reading, the freshly shed blood would signify to Digby in much the same way the blood of a wounded stag might allow him to track his prey. On the other hand, in the context of this particular blood-bath, the pungent naturalism of using the flow of human blood as a time-keeping measure would seem more to alienate us from that naturalism than to confirm it. Here the intervention of warlike violence produces a super-natural order of time, but one that is no less real for being so.

According to *Hope Leslie*, the anticipatory relationship to the fu-ture—or rather the future's intrusion upon the present—and this supernat-ural alienation of time from its familiar measures are not the only ways in which violence transforms the shape of temporal experience. In the events that directly follow the Indian attack on the Fletcher household, in fact, we see how this revolutionary messianic time forces the future and the past to inhabit the same present. Seeking to shelter Everell Fletcher, who was cap-tured in the Indian raid, from murder at the hands of her father, Mono-notto, Magawisca attempts to intervene on his behalf with Mononotto. After pleading her case, she discovers to her dismay that "her father's pur-pose was not to be shaken."[160] Upon this discovery, Magawisca's relation-ship to the future is transfigured: "She looked at Everell, and already felt the horrors of the captive's fate—the scorching fires, and the torturing knives; and when her father commanded the party to move onward, she uttered a piercing shriek."[161] Mononotto proceeds to chide Magawisca for her response, suggesting that "'cries and screams are for children and cow-ards.'"[162] Yet Magawisca shrieks here not so much from fear as from her felt experience of the future. This future is much more than a fearsome possibility; this future is already Magawisca's present. Only two paragraphs later, we see the order of appearance reversed, such that Everell's past comes to inhabit his present: "Everell had observed, and understood [Magawis-ca's] intercession, for, though her words were uttered in her own tongue, there was no mistaking her significant manner; but he was indifferent to the success of her appeal. He still felt the dying grasp of his mother—still heard his slaughtered sisters cry to him for help—and, in the agony of his mind, he was incapable of an emotion of hope, or fear."[163] Where the im-pending brutality of Everell's execution precipitates in Magawisca a visita-tion from the future, the recent events of the Fletcher massacre encourages the past to occupy Everell's present tense. Here the "present" is the inter-section of past and future. All of history meets in these episodes of revolutionary messianic time. A similar passage occurs much later in the narrative, upon Everell Fletcher's return to New England after a long sojourn in England intended to help him recover from the tragic loss of his mother and siblings. Invited to a dinner at Governor Winthrop's mansion, he arrives only to discover that there are also Indians invited to the table that day. He is overcome with emotion, and Hope notes his dismay. In reply to her request to know what "ails" him, he responds, " 'Nothing, nothing,' said Everell, wishing to avoid observation, and turning towards the window: he then added in explanation to Hope, who followed him, 'these are the first Indians I have seen since my return, and they brought, too vividly to mind, my dear mother's death.' "[164] Despite the fact that these Indians had no hand in his mother's and his siblings' deaths, Everell feels his present penetrated by his past. Lest this point escape us, Sedgwick also addresses it earlier, in those moments just described when Everell's execution (and his escape) await him: "Everell had escaped death from his savage captors, but while it was comparatively distant, he thought he was indifferent to it, or rather, he believed he should welcome it as a release from the horrible recollection of the massacre at Bethel, which haunted him day and night. But now that his fate seemed inevitable, nature was appalled, and shrunk from it; and the impassive spirit, for a moment, endured a pang that there cannot be in any 'corp'ral sufferance.' The avenues of sense were closed, and past and future were present to the mind, as if it were already invested with the attributes of its eternity."[165] As Sedgwick indicates, Everell's impending death and his recent exposure to the clash between the Puritans and the Indian alliance produce in him an experience comparable to the moment predicted for the arrival of the Messiah. Notwithstanding the fact that Everell remains tied to this mortal life, he encounters a "messianic moment," one when "past and future were present to the mind," a corporeal moment invested with the temporal collapse supposedly reserved for that which is beyond any " 'corp'ral sufferance.' "

Sedgwick later confirms the political significance, and derivation, of this unique temporality in a comment that comes in one of Hope Leslie's letters to Everell Fletcher. Hope recounts a recent trip up the mountain with Everell's father and "Mr. Holioke." In a scene that eventually attributes the naming of Mt. Holyoke to Hope Leslie, and its namesake's frolics to her sense of "levity," Mr. Holioke and Hope Leslie banter about the romantic associations of the landscape. Hope comments, " 'He must have a torpid imagination, and a cold heart, I think, who does not fancy these vast forests filled with invisible intelligences.' " She then recalls Mr. Holioke's response: " 'While I was pondering on this thought, Mr. Holioke, who seldom indulges in a fanciful suggestion, said to your father, "The Romans, you know, brother Fletcher, had their Cenotapha, empty sepulchers, in honour of those who died in their country's cause, and mouldered on distant soil. Why may we not have ours? and surmise that the spirits of those who have died for liberty and religion, have come before us in this wilderness, and taken possession in the name of the Lord?" ' "[166] Mr. Holioke suggests that the distinctly political struggle for "liberty and religion" has reordered the course of historical time, so much so that their chronological predecessors are actually undertaking the seventeenth-century Puritan errand. The struggle for liberty, which was, by the time of Sedgwick's writing, presumed to be the link connecting generations of colonial, Revolutionary, and post-Revolutionary Americans, serves to effect a contemporary past, present, and future.

The Opening of Genre

Joseph C. Hart's internationally successful historical romance, *Miriam Coffin, or the Whale-Fishermen*, provides a useful counterpoint to *Hope Leslie*, *The House of the Seven Gables*, and *The Scarlet Letter*, highlighting by comparison important features of the romances already discussed. Where Sedgwick's and Hawthorne's arguments about American modernity sometimes emerge at the level of implication, Hart quite explicitly frames his tale as the story of a modernity secured by print capitalism and market culture. The ostensible subject of this romance is, as its title would suggest, the community of whale fishermen, sheep farmers, and merchants of Nantucket as they struggle through the early days of the American Revolution. *Miriam Coffin*'s equal concerns are to tell the story of a striking change in time, to identify this new order of time with the simultaneous ascent of a modern order of print, and to trace its impact on the social configuration of American life. The eponymous antiheroine of this novel finds herself compelled to engage in her own version of market capitalism. With her seagoing husband trapped overseas in England by the war, Miriam must manage his affairs. Less troubled by the rigors of the market than Hepzibah, Coffin goes so far as to trade with the British. And as Phoebe Pyncheon turned her domestic skills to the demands of the market, so Miriam takes the famed mercantile skills of an eighteenth-century whaling wife and turns it to her new circumstance. She is both a financial success and a political embarrassment to her neighbors and her husband.

The real interest of the tale in this context is its mobilization of several figures of print to underwrite its story of Nantucket's transformation. Hart's introduction to *Miriam Coffin* is a fictional account of the author's meeting with an old Nantucket sailor who, we are told, actually wrote the tale. This "singular being," Hart explains, "had been represented by the people of the town as possessing a remarkably retentive memory,— particularly in what related to the early history of the island."[167] Like Hawthorne in "The Custom-House," Hart describes himself as the handmaiden editor of *Miriam Coffin* and recalls that he had the good fortune of meeting this wizened old sailor at his hut on Nantucket. In Hart's account of their meeting, the sailor rapidly summarizes eighty-odd years of Nantucket history, viewed from the vantage point of the 1830s, and then opens a secret cabinet to reveal the handiwork of his later years: the manuscript for *Miriam Coffin*. During the chowder and polite conversation that precede this unveiling, the sailor explains that for many years the isolation of the island and the peculiarity of its white settlers ensured the persistence of premodern experiences of time. "'To the introduction of Quakerism'" at the beginning of the eighteenth century, the sailor says:

> "and its unvarying customs, together with the unyielding manners of the Puritans to which the islanders had been accustomed, and which still lingered about them even after their change of faith, added to their isolated situation, is perhaps to be attributed the unchangeableness of the ways and habits of the Nantucket people. It is the last hold of the simple manners of our English ancestors in America. In this respect Nantucket is to the rest of America, what Iceland is to the Northern nations of Europe. For while all has undergone a change, I will not say for the better, in the continental countries, these two islands continue to exhibit the manners, customs, dress and language of their ancestors, in much of their pristine purity."[168]

Before the Revolution and up until recent times, Nantucket escaped the currents of modernity gripping Britain, Europe, and their North American colonies. Thanks to Nantucket's odd location and cultural history, early white islanders long existed as their ancestors did before them, sharing across generations a common set of "manners, customs, dress and language." Unlike the rest of the Anglo and European world, Nantucketers remained largely untouched by the technological change, immigration, and economic shifts transforming daily life elsewhere.

The sailor then relays that, more recently, Nantucket has been the site of unwonted developments. The island may have long been the last outpost of "the simple manners of our English ancestors in America," but "'[t]he spirit of resistless change is . . . abroad in Nantucket . . . and I grieve to say the few years last past have worked a wonderful change in the people. . . . [N]ot a single custom of our ancestors is adhered to in its ancient purity,— all—all is giving way before the spirit of innovation that now stalks abroad in the island,—prostrating all that is venerable for its antiquity, and good as being the delight of our fathers!' "[169] Although Nantucket's isolation and cultural homogeneity long set it apart from the mainland, this once remote and internally consistent island has finally fallen prey to linear time. Every moment is entirely, unrecognizably new and distinct. Hart's informant objects to the island's being always different, never the same, constantly in motion; "the spirit of resistless change" is his idiomatic expression for the advent of progressive time.

Hart's introduction closes without explaining just what occasioned this transformation. However, as the narrative proper unfolds, Hart draws the line separating old from new Nantucket with several signal accounts of print culture. Chapter 1 closes, for example, with the Quaker sea captain Jethro Coffin and his wife, the book's namesake, Miriam, debating an island trauma. During a brutal storm, a crucial Nantucket lighthouse has collapsed. Jethro favors lightning as the cause of the collapse, Miriam wind. An argument ensues, and after as much strife as the author can feasibly grant a Revolutionary-era Quaker couple, we learn in a narrative aside that "[t]he authority of Jethro, touching the agency of the lightning, did not prevail, although he attempted to sustain his position in an argument of great ingenuity, which the lack of printing-presses at Nantucket has prevented us from handing down to posterity."[170] Later in the narrative we meet the island's "last surviving" Nantucket Indian chief, Tashima. After a racist description of the "self-willed" downfall of the Nantucket Indians, we learn that even though Tashima knew his people were nearing extinction, this late eighteenth-century chief remained a dedicated teacher of the island's Native children. Focusing in particular on Tashima's linguistic endeavors, the narrator explains that Tashima was eager to see the language of the Nantucket Indians endure. In his pursuit of Nantucket linguistic survival, Tashima exploits all of the resources at his disposal, including ideograms, pictures, and letters. "The characters adopted by Tashima for the instruction of his pupils, were," we learn, "in addition to his pictures, the Roman letters; and the alphabet, so far as it was necessary for conveying Indian sounds, was substantially the same as our own."[171] Hart next reports that detailed accounts of Tashima's work and the language of the Nantucket Indians are unavailable; unfortunately, "Tashima's numerous books and lessons were all in manuscript; and it is to be regretted that the printer was never called in to aid in their preservation. They would have furnished delicious *morceaux* for the literary wranglers and philologists of the present day; but, at the time we write of, a printing-press was unknown at Nantucket. Even in Boston, which some of its people still insist upon calling the 'Literary Emporium,' that persevering printer, Benjamin Franklin, could scarcely find support for his little 'Weekly News-Letter.'"[172] In both of these passages, Hart portrays print capitalism as a crucial marker of the difference of Revolutionary-era Nantucket from its early national descendant. Hart's interleaved comments as narrator, which more than once remind us that Nantucket formerly had no indigenous press, mark the transformation to homogeneous time and national outpost as contemporaneous with the transition to print capitalism. It requires very little effort to read print capitalism as an agent of nationalism here; the challenge is to find something other than homogeneous time in this literature—to read against rather than with the rhetoric of American modernity that it deploys.

Despite the American historical romance's lasting (self-)association with the advent of a national literature and its confirmed "nationalistic tenor," this genre remains an elusive one.[173] Its best-known male practitioners have occupied the "hermeneutic center" of the American literary canon for some time, and women romancers have more recently claimed a place at the core of American literary history.[174] Yet the question of which specific qualities define the historical romance has remained curiously open. The history of this openness usefully tracks the shifting fortunes of writing from the first half of the nineteenth century. As I mentioned at the start of this chapter, Richard Chase and Lionel Trilling describe the American romance as constitutionally averse to representing the facts of the real world. They emphasized a distinctly American "sacrifice" of writing's "relation" to the actual events of history. For these men, the historical romance's turn to the past was of less interest than its curiosity about the eternal complications of human cognition.[175] Later critics press us to acknowledge the romance's engagement with contemporary politics and U.S. political history. Here the historical romance engages American history in order to retrospectively rewrite colonial history as the triumph of American national identity. It revises after the fact the political meaning of the American Revolution and early American Republicanism. Jonathan Arac combines these two positions, arguing that a "story of the nation's colonial beginnings" emerged during the time of Andrew Jackson's two-term presidency and "looked forward to [the nation's] future as a model for the world." In Jacksonian America "there was no fully operative national culture"; the emergence of historical narratives was, he explains, "part of the process by which the nation was forming itself and not merely a reflection of an accomplished fact."[176] Yet he also sorts Hawthorne's historical romances into a separate category termed "literary narrative." In *Nineteenth-Century American Romance*, Emily Budick remarks that, "[u]nlike the nations of Europe[,] the United States did not arrive in the 19th century after a centuries-long evolution toward modernity. Rather, its origins constituted a historically locatable moment of rupture with another cultural and political entity."[177] Americans turned this seeming handicap to their favor by positing a new, specifically American cultural practice whose defining quality would be its break with a tradition that it would nonetheless be required to retell as historical narrative: "The consequence of America's literary independence [would] be nothing less than the birth of the nation and of a new human being to go with it," and one of the most important places in which this "new human being" would be conceived was in the pages of the American historical romance.[178] The romance has also been identified with the construction of "primordial racial differences," which it then maps to broader claims about U.S. national identity.[179] In her discussion of frontier historical romances, for example, Dana Nelson describes the retrofitting of North American colonial history as the precipitating agent of a national community conceived as racially white. Nelson suggests that the authors of frontier narratives "deployed an American past to prove that there was *indeed* such a thing as an American book. . . . [These authors] strove to create a sense of historical depth and of national tradition for a young and self-conscious America."[180] Here novels mediate contemporary situations by "coalescing a national identity [and] establishing an ideal through which very diverse Anglo American readers could recognize themselves together."[181]

Although these views of the American historical romance conflict, they also collectively bring us a long way toward understanding the major significance of this literature. The historical romance is a "heterogeneous," "divide[d], subversiv[e]," and even "baffling" genre of writing;[182] it is a "fragile and unreliable mode" ill-suited to supplying the nation with a "coherent narrative shape"—ill-suited, in other words, to undertaking the "basic act of 'ideo-logy.'"[183] The historical romance is also a decided attempt to "enginee[r]" a national-racial community for "bourgeois and aristocratic readers,"[184] and a considered effort to "provid[e] the conditions of possibility of an Anglo-Saxonist nationalism and the fateful articulation of race and nation."[185] These two tendencies cannot be easily separated from each other, nor should they be. Chatterjee's remarks concerning utopian time indicate how we might conjoin these conflicting accounts of the romance, and they also help to refigure a classic distinction between the British novel and the American romance. Chase provides the standard twentieth-century formulation of this distinction in *The American Novel and Its Tradition*, in which he uses language derived from Hawthorne to argue that the American romance allows a "freedom from the conditions of actuality" unavailable in the British novel.[186] Romances "express dark and complex truths unavailable to [British] realism."[187] Unlike the novels of Austen or Dickens, the American romance, "tends to rest in contradictions and among extreme ranges of experience."[188] The American romance, Chase argues, is characterized by "disorder," and it is "fragmentary"; "radical disunities" and "polarities" dog Chase's American romance.[189] In coded language, Chase here traces the way the historical romance comprises more than one temporality, and he anticipates the lack of "synchrony" that David van Leer, Lauren Berlant, and others have identified with Hawthorne's writing. Although the language of transition and transformation runs throughout this genre, we might borrow from the collective wisdom of this critical tradition the sense that this literature does not evidence a historical moment standing on the cusp of homogeneous time. It offers us something else entirely.

Lauren Berlant has written that national identity, which emerges through a reader's engagement with cultural objects such as Hawthorne's writing, "provides . . . a translation of the historical subject into an 'Imaginary' realm of ideality and wholeness, where the subject becomes whole by being reconstituted as a *collective* subject, or citizen. . . . Such a promise of totality that overwrites the object status of individuals and property through a transformation of micro-spaces into larger, neutral, impermeable sites defines the utopian promise of the nation as such—all modern nations, not just America."[190] According to Berlant, a reader becomes American when his experience of the imagination allows him to feel that he has shed both his finite knowledge and his finite body. For Berlant, historical romances such as Hawthorne's do more than simply remind Americans of their nation's failures and triumphs; through the work of the imagination, they seek to relieve Americans of their determination by time. In this account, historical writing transports its readers to an "intermediate space" that resembles the zone of safety Hawthorne describes in his short tale, "The Haunted Mind": "Yesterday has already vanished among the shadows of the past; to-morrow has not yet emerged from the future. You have found an intermediate space, where the business of life does not intrude; where the passing moment lingers, and becomes truly the present; a spot where Father Time, when he thinks nobody is watching him, sits down by the wayside to take breath. Oh, that he would fall asleep, and let mortals live on without growing older!"[191] As is the case with Father Time's imagined sleep, the synchronic simultaneity afforded by literature is supposed to situate American readers outside of history and make them immune to all versions of time. The historical romance emerges, in this account, as what Hawthorne describes in "The Custom-House" as a neutral ground where time stops and where the imagination can transcend history's disaggregating and centrifugal pull. Although they might wish to do so, America's historical romancers did not provide this transporting experience by offering their readers access to the warm embrace of the scattered nation. They reassure us that "we" share the same "moment," and they seek to compensate us with the shelter of that imagined community. But the conflict of time traced in this literature forbids a consoling escape into the imagination. No matter what this literature might promise, it never takes us to that "spot where Father Time . . . sits down by the wayside to take breath."

A final melancholy passage from *The House of the Seven Gables* illustrates the dilemma faced by anyone reading this literature. On the morning that her shop is to open, Hepzibah stands before her bedroom mirror trying desperately to bring some sort of order to her personal appearance. Her efforts are thwarted by the fact that she is intensely nearsighted and owns no eyeglasses. In order to see her own face in the mirror, she must contract her brow, squint, and wear an unattractive scowl. Hepzibah is always scowling because of her nearsightedness, and so she becomes known to the town as a cross and angry person: "Her scowl—as the world, or such part of it as sometimes caught a transitory glimpse of her at the window, wickedly persisted in calling it—her scowl had done Miss Hepzibah a very ill-office, in establishing her character as an ill-tempered old maid; nor does it appear improbable, that, by often gazing at herself in a dim looking-glass, and perpetually encountering her own frown within its ghostly sphere, she had been led to interpret the expression almost as unjustly as the world did.— 'How miserably cross I look!'—she must often have whispered to herself; and ultimately have fancied herself so, by a sense of inevitable doom."[192] Nationalism has presented itself as the "inevitable doom" of American readers for some time now. This self-presentation dominates our image of the past. According to the logic of nationalism's utopian time, moreover, there is only one future to be had; we already know in advance what that future will be; and it will involve an attenuated process of self-abstraction away from the rewards and challenges of locality. Throughout this period's literature, however, we continue to encounter images such as this one of Hepzibah. Here Hepzibah figures for us a moment when one could not turn to the mirror of culture to discover who one was. The order(s) of time prohibited access to a clarified image of oneself. Indeed, Hepzibah recalls Irving's and Browere's George: her encounter with her mirror image yields only a murky reflection. At her mirror, Hepzibah encounters the same image of herself that we find even now: she figures the "perplexity of the living" in an era rendered inaccessible to itself.[193]

Chapter 3
Local Time: Southwestern Humor and Nineteenth-Century Literary Regionalism

One of the first outbreaks of nostalgia in America has gone largely unreported. From the seventeenth-century onward, European physicians documented viral plagues of this incapacitating disease. According to these doctors, this malady of the soul especially afflicted soldiers, poets, and philosophers. Its European observers thought nostalgia was a social ill worth fighting; they proposed radical treatments that included the burying of soldiers alive. Yet American doctors "proudly declared that the young nation remained healthy and didn't succumb to the nostalgic vice until the American Civil War."[1] In the historiography of nineteenth-century America, which mirrors the reports of these doctors, the conventional sign of the postbellum descent into nostalgia is the turn to literary regionalism associated with the likes of Sarah Orne Jewett and Charles Chesnutt. This writing trained the nation's attention on the (ostensible) decline of the people and the places that had formerly epitomized the American character and the American experience. In this perennially influential account of Reconstruction and Gilded Age America, literary regionalism tracks market culture's dissolution of the hardscrabble premarket peoples and the frozen-in-time geographic domains that had made America what it was. Literary regionalism's nostalgic antimodernism also functions in this narrative as the reverse signature of transatlantic modernity: "Toward the end of the nineteenth century," T. Jackson Lears writes, "many beneficiaries of modern culture began to feel as if they were its secret victims. Among the educated and affluent on both sides of the Atlantic, antimodern sentiments spread."[2] In postbellum literary regionalism, Lears argues, is to be found nostalgic antimodernism's motive force: "In republican mythology, the virtuous husbandman had long been counterposed to the corrupt cosmopolitan, but as rural populations declined, urban writers increasingly idealized farm life. A host of 'local color' writers imagined republican virtue in a wide variety of preindustrial communities."[3] This diagnosis of literary regional-ism identifies its provenance as the economic knitting together of the frac-tured postbellum nation.

Although its general outlines are correct, this is an overly restrictive measure of American modernity's compass. Especially if we plan to follow Lears in taking nostalgic literary regionalism as modernity's negative index, then it will be important to confess that the first signs of antimodern senti-ment appeared much earlier on the American literary scene. One might fea-sibly argue that nostalgia's first American outbreak dates to Irving's *Sketch-Book*. However, I want instead to offer a more modest relocation to the 1830s and to a literature that is organized around producing precisely the sense of "inhabitable backwardness"—the feeling of an "intact" local com-munity made "visitable in print"—more typically associated with the post-bellum emergence of the educated and affluent readership that Lears, Rich-ard Brodhead, Sandra Zagarell, and others have described.[4] Although feminist and African Americanist criticism has encouraged us to revalue postbellum regionalism's critique of market culture, the other nineteenth-century literary regionalists at issue here can make no such claim to political or moral acuity. This other literary regionalism is one of the most unseemly forms of writing to emerge from a century with no shortage of unseemli-ness on offer. I am speaking, of course, of the "humor" of the Old South-west.

Southwestern humor's tales and sketches depict a young America whose backwoods and frontier are peopled with rowdy crowds of dialect-speaking poor whites. Popular with middle-class white men, and written with them in mind, this writing represents America's first major outbreak of nostalgic antimodernism. From the 1830s through the early 1860s, the Southwestern humorists chronicled imaginary feats undertaken earlier, in the first three decades of the nineteenth century, by men like "Captain" Simon Suggs, the notoriously "shifty" would-be officer of an ad hoc infan-try company in Alabama; the "Big Bar of Arkansaw," a he-man of an Ar-kansas bear hunter; and "Old Stoke Stout," one of the few remaining genu-ine turkey hunters of Louisiana.[5] At the height of Southwestern humor's popularity, aspiring and middle-class white men found themselves standing on unstable social ground, and this literature promised the refuge of an en-hanced sense of white male fraternity.[6] The rise of the professions, the de-cline of the trades, the emergence of the "clerk" whose tale Thomas Augst has eloquently told—all of these contributed as much (or more) to the un-settling of these men's modes of self-understanding as it did to the lining of their pockets. In this context, Southwestern humor's depiction of rural white poverty figures as a kind of compensatory succor that anticipates the work of late-century literary regionalism. For Southwestern humor's readers and its authors, this was an episode of both real and perceived dislocation that had begun some time before and would continue into the future. This was the era of American modernity. More traditional forms of community were being replaced by the ambivalent rewards of the "national manhood" that Dana Nelson has described. At a time when these readers felt an acute need for the imagined fraternity of other white men, or the companionship of a leisured coterie of gentlemen sharing a single identity, Southwestern humor's writers and its publishers stepped in to fill the void. The first important venue for Southwestern humor, William T. Porter's periodical *The Spirit of the Times*, fancied itself, for example, the party organ of a transatlantic community of literate enfranchised men. According to Jonathan Arac, it "began from (and maintained) imaginative relations with British culture, and a metropolitan model stood behind its appeal to the far-flung corners of American leisure activity."[7] However, once the Panic of 1837 had "damaged the financial base for horse racing," Arac continues, "the journal shifted its emphasis away from news of the turf." It also redoubled its focus on a "distinctively American subject matter." With this shift, the *Spirit* embraced the predilections of the American Whigs, and it became "a focus of multiregional resistance to the presidency of Andrew Jackson."[8]

If Southwestern humor in this sense promised a big tent under which men of diverse regional backgrounds could gather, it also indicates the extent to which the ongoing effort to reembed them within new translocal networks often fell far short of its goal. If we follow Anthony Giddens's phenomenology, the "framework of experience" that defines the lives of men such as these during the *longue durée* of modernity is the loss of a deeply embedded sense of community. For Giddens, a dialectic between estrangement and new forms of intimacy defines the experience of modernity, and this dialectic follows from modernity's distanciation of time-space relationships:

All pre-modern cultures possessed modes of the calculation of time. The calendar, for example, was as distinctive a feature of agrarian states as the invention of writing. But the time reckoning which formed the basis of day-to-day life, certainly for the majority of the population, always linked time with place—and was usually imprecise and variable. No one could tell the time of day without reference to other socio-spatial markers: "when" was almost universally connected with "where" or identified by regular natural occurrences. The invention of the mechanical clock and its diffusion to virtually all members of the population (a phenomenon which dates at its earliest from the late eighteenth century) were of key significance in the separation of time from space.[9]

In this most standard of comparisons, premodern timekeeping is contingent upon naturally observable phenomena, and it is not subject to the rigors of scientifically verified measurement. The diurnal cycle organizes premodern life—as do animal migrations, the maturation of crops, and other biological markers. But these premodern measures are tied to specific local environments: although both indigenous North Americans and premodern Europeans measured time by the advance of the seasons, their measurements were not interchangeable. The swallows might come back to Capistrano every spring, but this particular measure of time's passage does not count for much in the landscape of the Celts. Modern modes of timekeeping are radical by comparison, because their universal metrics do not depend on local topography. They permit instead a measure of time disarticulated from the particularities of a specific locale. In conventional social theory, this process of distanciation pressures local communities into joining larger translocal aggregates such as the region or the nation: "The separating of time and space and their formation into standardised, 'empty' dimensions cut through the connections between social activity and its 'embedding' in the particularities of context and presence. Disembedded institutions greatly extend the scope of time-space distanciation and, to have this effect, depend upon coordination across time and space. This phenomenon serves to open up manifold possibilities of change by breaking free from the restraints of local habits and practices."[10] The new modes of time measurement (clock time and calendars) and spatial definition (geography and cartography) associated with modernity detach us from our specific locales, just as these measures themselves lose their contingency: Greenwich Mean Time is GMT in Greenwich or Guatemala. This time-space distanciation "frees" us—for better or for worse—from our social embeddedness. We no longer require the aid of local knowledge to make sense of the world around us. According to Giddens, however, the modern subject is not merely set free to wander in the disjointed space-time of modernity. That subject is "reembedded" in new distended networks. "It is simply not true," Giddens writes, "that in conditions of modernity we increasingly live in a 'world of strangers.' "[11] Instead, "intimate relationships can be sustained at a distance (regular and sustained contact can be made with other individuals at virtually any point on the earth's surface—as well as some below and above), and personal ties are continually forged with others with whom one was previously unacquainted."[12] Importantly, modernity's dialectic of disembedding and reembedding involves a continuously expanding scale of affiliation. Giddens identifies this process with technology's capacity to produce not only a new order of time but also the compression of space: "The very means of transportation which help to dissolve the connection between locality and kinship provide the possibility for reembedding, by making it easy to visit 'close' relatives who are far away."[13] Although Giddens would reject this assessment, his account of modernity obeys a certain narrative of progress. The local gives way to the regional, which in turn dissolves into the national. The expanded social scale that follows the compression of space transcends contingency.

In this chapter I offer a discussion of Southwestern humor that shifts the conversation about time-space distanciation and the categorical definition of the "local" away from this narrative of social becoming. I also indicate why it is crucial to undertake such a shift. By way of a discussion of literary regionalism, in other words, I propose a rethinking of the local as a category of analysis in this and other domains. My initial claim will be that we can read the two major episodes of nineteenth-century literary regionalism as related attempts to produce a progressive history of the time-space distanciation that Giddens describes. Both of these literatures aim at a historical sociology of modernity whose account of the distanciaton of time and space uncannily anticipates that of contemporary social theory. I also suggest that literary regionalism's diagnostics of modernity spatializes time in ways that Jürgen Habermas, Johannes Fabian, Walter Mignolo, and others have described in the context of European colonialism. Following Osborne, in particular, I will show how this spatialization of time works to differentiate both extranational and intranational space, and how in the process it (paradoxically) reinforces the image of an internally homogeneous national culture. Literary regionalism turns on this spatialization of time. In both of its major moments, nineteenth-century literary regionalism describes a nation characterized by an internal division of time. America always encompasses more than one point on the time line of civilization in this writing, and these different points embrace different orders of time. Importantly, however, this image of an internally divided national community only ever proposes to describe two temporalities—an emergent cosmopolitan one and a residual local one—and two geographic locales. What we might call national standard time is the effect of comparing these two: this binary comparison figures local time as the temporality to be transcended.

In figuring these two temporalities as competitors, in other words, this literature figures local time as the evolutionary loser. Literary regionalism's frame narrative, which typically identifies the subject of study as a lost locale, secures this characterization of local time as a ghostly revenant.

Clearly a different approach to the local is required. The narrative structure of Southwestern humor suggests a useful alternative that allows for the retention of the local as a category of analysis, but that does not counterpoise a resistant local community to a dominant national culture in a battle whose victor is determined in advance. My approach will be to concede the time-space distanciation that Giddens describes, while at the same time rejecting the idea that reembedding is its necessary dialectical other. Giddens has remarked that "[t]he locality in pre-modern contexts is the focus of, and contributes to, ontological security in ways that are substantially dissolved in circumstances of modernity."[14] While this might be the case, it does not follow that locality itself is dissolved. If modernity's distanciation of time and space cleared the way for a heterogeneous experience of time, it is also true that only a very specific understanding of the present endorses the idea that the process of reembedding actually came to pass. Indeed, this literature itself indicates how just those technologies typically identified with the reembedding process—that is, new modes of travel and the spread of "print culture"—engender an experience of deep locality that is reembedding's antipathetic opposite. Here, white male fraternity is a hopeless longing.

In this reading, literary regionalism mirrors other modern technologies in contributing to time's division into several coeval temporalities whose conflict structured the lives of its readers. When Southwestern humor reached into the far-flung corners of the nation, for example, it paradoxically introduced a force for deep locality into the lives of those white men who sought connections to a wider social network. Specifically, it compounded the experience of time as plural rather than singular that other modes of modern technology had already brought to bear in their daily lives. In this respect, Southwestern humor indicates that middle-class white men's desire for a consoling fraternity remained an unconsummated one and that if white male identity ultimately failed neatly to cohere, as Dana Nelson has argued, this failure had everything to do with the distanciation of time and space consequent upon modernity.[15] In this reading, too, literary regionalism's interest in modernity's technologies of travel is significant. On the one hand, Southwestern humor predictably describes the steamboat, the locomotive train, and other new travel technologies as agents of a new experience of time that was a force uniting groups that were (as one of these humorists put it) "as heterogeneous [as were] ever got together."[16] Yet this literature's keen interest in technological change and its commitment to ridiculing the hubris of invention—Twain's *A Connecticut Yankee in King Arthur's Court* is its descendant—guaranteed that these were no unambiguous portraits of technological triumph. Indeed, Southwestern humor ends up unselfconsciously conceding that the advance of capital's technologies fractures time into different temporalities. It also reduplicates for its reader a refracted narrative form consonant with these broad changes, and its interest in the figure of the storyteller highlights the important role that this narrative form plays in producing a season of unequal times. In short, although Southwestern humor's authors sought to consolidate a soothing fraternity of white men, they did more to help reorganize time in such a way that it retarded the reembedding process that any such fraternity would require. In this respect, it turns out that this particular mode of nostalgic antimodern literary regionalism did more to produce a desire for consolation than it did to console these men. Here middle-class white men fail to escape the contingency of the local, notwithstanding their access to Southwestern humor's fantasies of racial community.

In a broader sense, this analysis demands a rethinking of the term "local" itself. In conventional usage, the local features as a mere preamble to the national, but the way I conceive of the local forbids this logic of succession. If the national is thought to follow the local and replace it, then this is because history is thought to have only one track. It follows that in order for the national to realize itself, the local must ipso facto yield to the national. However, I want to imagine a local disarticulated from any historical relationship to other social forms such as the nation—ignoring for the moment even those recent injunctions that encourage us to view the local and the global as mutually constituting forms.[17] I want instead to conceptualize the local as a temporal conjuncture engendered by modernity's distanciation of time and space rather than as modernity's disfavored victim. In this context, Southwestern humor is especially useful. Its distasteful nostalgic antimodern sentiment gives the lie to most conventional conversations about literary regionalism: Does attending to the local validate and preserve a space of authentic resistance? Or does it produce a virtual figure that facilitates the destruction of the authentic? It is hard to muster the sympathetic identification with the authentic that such questions assume when the figure of authenticity is a would-be hustler who trades an underfed horse with camouflaged festering sores for what he later learns is a deaf, blind, and dying one. Yet Southwestern humor's very moral depravity might encourage us to ask other and better questions and lead us to conceive the local otherwise. It might allow us to see that the local is not just one—or even just two. As I intend to show, a reassessment of the finer details of literary regionalism can help us to understand the local as a contingent site of overdetermination inhospitable to the process of social reembedding.

A Place in Time

Southwestern humor is unconcerned with effacing its touristic relationship to the poor whites it describes, and in this respect alone it differs sharply from later nineteenth-century American regional literature. Despite its lasting association with backwoods and frontier life, and notwithstanding its ostensible interest in trenchantly local experiences, this genre works hard to represent its writers as, and to fashion its readers into, what in *Cultures of Letters* Richard Brodhead calls a supralocal class—or as Arjun Appadurai describes it, a group unencumbered by ties to "a situated community of kin, neighbors, friends, and enemies."[18] The postbellum New England regionalist Sarah Orne Jewett attempts, for example, to do justice to the premodern and premarket locals she describes by representing her cosmopolitan narrators as potentially the equals of the folk they visit on their travels to Maine. Compare this to Southwestern humor, which devotes itself to the unapologetic representation of its poor white subjects in caricature and which emerges from media explicitly concerned with fashioning their authors and readers into a single class of "gentlemen." Formally and anecdotally, Southwestern humor addresses its readers as men who have plenty in common with one another, but who share next to nothing with the poor whites this literature spends most of its time describing. At no point does Southwestern humor disguise its resolution to link its authors and its readers at the expense of the group that is its subject. Indeed, from the prefatory remarks opening the most popular collections of Southwestern humor, this literature sets out to separate describer from described, reader from read.[19]

Thomas Bangs Thorpe's highly successful *The Hive of "The Bee-Hunter,"* a collection of his previously published tales and sketches that appeared in 1854, opens, for instance, with a proud boast that both distinguishes Thorpe from the Southwest as a site of experience and argues for that site's availability as a subject of study. By way of introducing materials originally published in local and national periodicals, Thorpe brags that the sequestration of the Southwest in the "vast interior solitudes" of America has protected it from the homogenizing "trans-Atlantic influences" bearing down upon America's eastern seaboard. "The southwest," Thorpe explains, "with its primeval and evergreen forests, its unbounded prairies, and its many and continuous rivers, presents contributions of nature, which the pilgrims from every land, for the first time, behold with wonder and awe. Here, in their vast interior solitudes, far removed from trans-Atlantic influences, are alone to be found, in the more comparative infancy of our country, characters truly *sui generis*—truly American."[20] A New Yorker by birth, this transplanted editor of Louisiana's weekly *Concordia [Parish] Intelligencer* is specifically referring here to his adopted state, Arkansas, and Mississippi, but his opening gesture to the "southwest" also invokes the vast swath of land that writing such as Thorpe's was depicting as a region linked by common causes and shared experience: Georgia and Alabama, to be sure, and often Tennessee, Kentucky, and Missouri. From the 1830s through the early 1860s, Thorpe and his fellow Southwestern humorists renovated the public image of these areas, which had been previously known as the habitus of distinct local cultures. They worked hard at recasting these disparate places into a single "primeval" land where the American could be himself. Here alone, Thorpe suggests, can one find a "tru[e] American," because here alone is the nation in its authentic "infancy"; Southwestern humor captures the essence of America before the impositions of what its best-known legatee, Mark Twain, would famously call "sivilization." For thirty years, Thorpe, Augustus Baldwin Longstreet, Johnson Jones Hooper, George Washington Harris, and a host of other writers would hold up striking images of a region peopled with rough-and-ready poor whites, earthy Americans whose antics were as funny as their accents.

As a transplanted New Yorker emulating the life of a Mississippi Delta "gentleman," Thorpe's self-presentation in this context is telling. By his own standards of measure, and by those of his coterie, Thorpe falls far short of the "*sui generis*—truly American" characters he describes in such admiring terms; remarkably, Thorpe embraces this distinction. As Thorpe's preface suggests, his Southwestern humor is, on its face, preoccupied with the life of the uneducated poor white living robustly on the American frontier and along its inland rivers. Like his peer writers, Thorpe spends his time cataloguing the intrepid adventures of individuals such as the bee hunter of the book's title—men and women who, in their abler moments, wrestle "gators," tame "b[e]ars," outwit Yankees, and elude the national census taker. These are men and women who also just as often gouge each other's eyes out, run naked through public gatherings, go blind from a drinking binge, or otherwise abject themselves and their fellow poor whites in full view of their gentlemen neighbors. Yet here and throughout his writings, Thorpe himself emerges as a rather mannered cosmopolitan figure. Like most of his work, Thorpe's preface distances his authorial and editorial personae from his subjects, employing what critics of this genre typically call a narrative cordon sanitaire.[21] Thorpe's sketches and his editorial apparatus characteristically represent Thorpe as in but not of the brawling backwoods environment he describes, and in this Thorpe's writing is not alone. Like most Southwestern humor, Thorpe's writing carefully identifies Thorpe himself as one node on a web of imagined affiliation connecting genteel white men across the nation and, indeed, across the Anglo-European world. With rare exceptions, Southwestern humor shows its gentlemen authors and readers to be men who observe but do not succumb to the antics they describe, and in this respect they anticipate the class of tourists conventionally associated with the postbellum period and the nostalgic antimodernism of later literary regionalism.

The New York–based *Spirit of the Times*, the weekly "sporting journal" that first published many of the sketches collected in Thorpe's *Hive* and that enthusiastically solicited Southwestern humor, was also the venue originally, and perhaps most successfully, to carve out this position of protoethnographic observer for its authors and readers, not only in formal terms, but also in its mode and methods of publication. The *Spirit* spent its thirty-year run, from the mid-1830s to the early 1860s, publishing Southwestern humor, either original work submitted by author-correspondent subscribers from across the nation (but concentrated in the Southwest) or reprinted items culled out of newspapers from around the nation. Notwithstanding Thorpe's call to resist transatlanticism, the *Spirit* published its Southwestern humor alongside news from the "turf" and "chase" in England and continental Europe, as well as with miscellaneous items of interest to educated men traveling America's land and water highways in search of diversion. Although the paper shifted focus over the course of its run, it was always a self-proclaimed "gentleman's paper" geared toward men whose permanent homes might be far from the nation's coastal metropolises but who were hardly strangers to the entertainments and concerns of the circum-Atlantic city. The *Spirit*'s early readers, in particular, learned as much about the current theater offerings in London, New York, and New Orleans as they did about "Chunkey's Fight with the Panther." Porter's paper taught them how to gamble skillfully and in a gentlemanly fashion, and it told them where in the nation they might go to find the next round of betting. It told them, as well, how the horses were running in England. In short, the *Spirit of the Times* accustomed its authors and readers to navigating, and asked them to adopt, the social mores of a cosmopolitan lifestyle represented as common to their class of men internationally.

Yet like the passengers aboard the Mississippi steamboat in Thorpe's most widely republished story, "The Big Bear of Arkansas," the *Spirit*'s correspondent authors and readers were, in many respects, "as heterogeneous a crowd as was ever got together."[22] They submitted their reports from the far corners of the nation and even from its coastal cities, a geographic variety that ensured a wide range of cultural backgrounds and economic entanglements. At the same time, the men who wrote and read the *Spirit*'s Southwestern humor, as well as those who accessed it in its many collected and reprinted versions, were participants in a genre seemingly committed to fashioning them into a unitary cosmopolitan class.[23] In order not to highlight the differences between his northern and his southern readers and authors in an increasingly sectional America, Porter, the *Spirit*'s longtime editor, at one point went so far as to ban discussions of slavery from its pages, ensuring that racial difference rarely emerges as an explicit topic of debate and that African American characters have generally minor roles to play in these sketches, tales, and stories.

If the *Spirit* was Southwestern humor's most influential and enduring public distributor and advocate, this literature's formal strategies for attempting to fashion its authors, readers, and narrators into a delocalized class are predicted in the early writing of Augustus Baldwin Longstreet, the Georgia lawyer regarded as Southwestern humor's founding father. Longstreet's sketches of life in backwoods Georgia were originally published in the early 1830s, appearing as newspaper sketches in two conservative, states' rights local periodicals. These original publication venues lack the broad topical and geographical range seen in the *Spirit*, but Longstreet's sketches nevertheless introduce the two narrative protocols that would come to define Southwestern humor during this period, whether in the *Spirit* or elsewhere: the presence of a cosmopolitan narrator and an interest in what we might call "local time." In Southwestern humor's cosmopolitan narrator we meet a figure literally and metaphorically clothed in the garb of middle-class white masculinity who sets out to document—among other things—the peculiar temporality of the Old Southwest. In Longstreet's original sketches, and in the writing that followed his precedent, this narrator mediates between the reader and the scenes described, offering managed access to a panorama of rural life that is generally white and most often poor. Hennig Cohen and William Dillingham suggest that the authors of Southwestern humor, "more than they themselves perhaps realized, wanted to be recognized as gentlemen. Therefore from their detached position as narrators, they contrasted themselves with the common folk they observed and wrote about. They liked the folk but maintained their distance and their status."[24] Employing what Mary Louise Pratt terms manners and customs discourse, a feature of both the international travel writing Pratt describes and American literary regionalism, Longstreet's Southwestern humor inscribes the primary axis of difference organizing each tale as cosmopolitan narrator versus local subject, opening a space of identification for the reader of Southwestern humor, whom the narrator addresses as a man of the world—someone who, like Longstreet's two main narrators, Lyman Hall and Abram Baldwin, is amused but uncontaminated by the locals.[25] In the classic examples of Longstreet's writing, which were republished several times in a collected volume titled *Georgia Scenes*, we see Longstreet deploy Hall's and Baldwin's similarly urbane perspectives on rural Georgia and rural Georgians. Both narrators enter environments where their "dress, language, bearing, equipage, and manners are immediately recognized by the rural folks as distinctly different from their own. They are both almost always 'outsiders' in their stories. . . . And they are always 'travelling,' 'on the road,' 'on a visit,' 'in a remote part of one of the countries,' away at school, 'called by business to one of the frontier countries,' on a trip to Savannah, a guest at a party, invited on a foxhunt, etc."[26] Pascal Covici Jr. argues that this outsider's view mimics the history of the genre already alluded to here, pointing out that the authors of Southwestern humor were often "[l]awyers, judges, and doctors, educated on the Atlantic seaboard and suddenly thrust into the continent[;] they looked with wonder at the 'manners, customs, amusements, wit, dialect' so different from what they had left behind."[27] Like his narrators, Longstreet's reader watches the events of backwoods life—its "manners" and its "customs"—unfold at a distant remove. The structure of narration carves out a position the reader shares with other readers such as himself, those readers implied by the pages of a periodical such as the *Spirit of the Times*—a reader who travels, bets, and swaps stories along the way; a reader who knows his place as well as he knows the place of others.

We meet Longstreet's narrator Lyman Hall early in *Georgia Scenes* introducing a tale of "Georgia Theatrics." Hall's opening remarks frame this account of an intemperate, loud-mouthed, young shadowboxer as his first encounter with the "Dark Corner" of Lincoln, Georgia. "If my memory fail me not," Hall muses,

the 10th of June, 1809 found me, at about 11 o'clock in the forenoon, ascending a long and gentle slope in what was called "The Dark Corner" of Lincoln. I believe it took its name from the moral darkness which reigned over that portion of the country at the time of which I am speaking. If in this point of view it was but a shade darker than the rest of the county, it was inconceivably dark. If any man can name a trick or sin which had not been committed at the time of which I am speaking, in the very focus of the county's illumination (Lincolnton), he must himself be the most inventive of the tricky, and the very Judas of sinners. Since that time, however (all humour aside), Lincoln has become a living proof "that light shineth in darkness." Could I venture to mingle the solemn with the ludicrous, even for the purposes of honourable contrast, I could adduce from this county instances of the most numerous and wonderful transitions, from vice and folly to virtue and holiness, which have ever, perhaps, been witnessed since the days of the apostolic ministry.[28]

Hall's remarks, particularly his references to the "apostolic ministry," signal the character of his relationship to the locals of Lincoln. Hall is constitutionally different from, and more advanced than, these locals; like the biblical apostles, his role is that of missionary to the locals' natives. Indeed, his posture in relationship to the residents of the "Dark Corner" of Lincoln, and the region as a whole, allows him to discern shades of darkness.

Significantly, these remarks distance Longstreet's narrator and his reader from the events of the sketch itself by removing those events more in chronological terms than in geographic ones, thereby introducing the second narrative protocol defining Southwestern humor: a spatialization of time that keys a difference of social and economic standing separating cosmopolitan from local figures to a temporal difference that distinguishes the indeterminate geography of the cosmopolite spectator from the geography of the Southwest. Returning to Thorpe's prefatory remarks quoted earlier, we remember, for example, that Thorpe represents the Southwest as a place "primeval . . . which the pilgrims from every land, for the first time, behold with wonder and awe." Time is (or was?) peculiar in this Southwest. If every new "pilgrim" beholds the same vista, one gathers that the unfolding of linear progress characterizing Thorpe's moment and position does not apply to this region. Similarly, Hall represents Lincoln as a prehistory of his own, and his reader's, more temporally modern, temporally progressive moment, a present tense that not only chronologically but also qualitatively differs from the era of Hall's young shadowboxer.

In "The Dance," Abram Baldwin, Longstreet's other narrator, uses similar language to describe his visit to a celebration at a country squire's residence, employing the same strategy of temporal displacement seen in both Thorpe's preface and Hall's framing remarks. Explicitly contrasting his own background with the more humble circumstances of the squire and his neighbors, Baldwin explains that "[t]he squire's dwelling consisted of but one room, which answered the threefold purpose of dining-room, bed-room, and kitchen. The house was constructed of logs, and the floor was of *puncheons*; a term which, in Georgia, means split logs, with their faces a little smoothed with the axe or hatchet."[29] At these modest dwellings, where the split logs forming the floors are only "a little smoothed," the prepara-tions for the dance are already well underway by nine o'clock on the morn-ing Baldwin arrives. Anticipating the sentiments of his female friends at home, Baldwin sarcastically offers the following: "'What!' says some weakly, sickly, delicate, useless, affected, 'charming creature' of the city, 'dressed for a ball at 9 in the morning!' Even so, my delectable Miss Octavia Matilda Juliana Claudia Ipecacuanha: and what have you to say against it? If people must dance, is it not much more rational to employ the hour al-lotted to exercise in that amusement, than the hours sacred to repose and meditation?"[30] Where Hall glanced disapprovingly at the residents of the "Dark Corner" of Lincoln, Baldwin offers compliments, but compliments with similar implications for our understanding of the "frontier counties." In Baldwin's view, these hearty frontier girls compare favorably to the sim-pering "'charming creature' of the city." Breaking with the traditions of the Atlantic seaboard, "[t]he girls were met [at the dance] by Polly and Silvy Gibson at some distance from the house, who welcomed them—'with a kiss, of course'—oh, no; but with something much less equivocal: a hearty shake of the hand and smiling countenances, which had some meaning."[31] Baldwin admires these young women because they follow the unpretentious traditions of the old Republic. Yet, like Hall's treatment of Lincoln, Bald-win's description of "Polly" and "Silvy" as solid republicans places them chronologically anterior to those simpering "charming creature[s]" af-flicted with five names and eating disorders. In addition, Longstreet's narra-tor emphasizes that Polly and Silvy differ from his cosmopolitan readers not only in their manner of greeting but also in their relationship to time. Where a city girl reserves the evening hours for a dance, Polly and Sally alter the social structuring of time to accommodate the needs of life in the

Southwest, reserving nighttime for sleep. Their Southwest is not only a different geography; in manifold ways the experience of time in their Southwest differs from the cosmopolitan standards Longstreet assumes will be more familiar to his readers, even if his narrator disparages those standards himself.

Here Southwestern humor appears to acknowledge two orders of time, the cosmopolitan and the local, and in this sense it parts ways with the notion that modernity involves the triumph of linear progress. Southwestern humor would seem to acknowledge local communities and local peoples resistant to the binding force of American common time and to offer a responsive account of at least one American region and its exceptional staying power. Indeed, this is one of the standard readings of both ante- and post-bellum American literary regionalism—the idea that regionalism's representation of the locals as different from the cosmopolitan norm provides a pleasantly archival history of peoples and places who resisted the lures of nationalism and of capitalist culture writ large, exemplars who instruct those in the present seeking to hold on to established norms just how they might accomplish their goal. However, despite this literature's apparent interest in "local time," these passages actually demonstrate precisely the "denial of coevalness" and "allochronism" that Johannes Fabian documents in his study of anthropology's rendering of temporal difference, which takes its bearing from, among other things, nineteenth-century travel writing. In *Time and the Other*, Fabian explains that any logic of developmental difference—whether in the social scientific discourse he treats or in Southwestern humor's framing of the Southwest as both chronologically distant and a qualitatively different time zone—effectively represents linear progressive time as time in its natural state and as the always inevitable future-present.[32] That is, Hall's and Baldwin's comments, as well as Southwestern humor more generally, would appear to admit the difference between cosmopolitan and local temporalities, but they ultimately do so less to acknowledge a simultaneity, or coevalness, of competing experiences of time than they do to suggest that one party lags behind the other on a single chronology that is produced in the very act of comparison that marks these two moments as different. Southwestern humor's interest in local time does not, in other words, validate the persistence of that local time; rather it predicts the ineluctable—indeed, the often already accomplished—ascendance of cosmopolitan (linear progressive) time over local time, as we see taking place with Longstreet's narrators. If Southwestern humor allows for temporal difference, it is a strictly functional allowance: episodes of nonstandard, nonlinear time are assigned to a constantly disappearing past from which the pre-sumptively homogeneous and linear time of the present is represented as emerging or having already emerged. Southwestern humor always predicts the disappearance of local time, as Hall's comments do, by framing local time and temporal heterogeneity as vestigial anomalies that disappear in the face of an ineluctable "enlightenment" associated with modernity. Thus Southwestern humor routinely describes the events it recounts, and there-fore the alternate temporality of the Southwest, as consigned to the past and as the preamble to a present moment implicitly defined by the homogenous presence of linear progressive time; the experience of time characterizing that past may have been different from the experience of time in the pres-ent, but that experience is understood as always/already a lost one. As Cohen and Dillingham explain, "A sense of urgency characterizes a great deal of the writing of this time and place, urgency to get on paper some-thing of unique cultural significance that was rapidly disappearing. The stance of many writers is that of a cultural historian rather than a literary artist. . . . One of their strongest motivations was to preserve."[33] At these moments, Southwestern humor comes closest to underwriting an experi-ence of simultaneity: what identifies the present of these sketches and tales as such is the fact that the present's acknowledged members—Longstreet's narrators and his readers—share a single experience of time as linear prog-ress. As Peter Osborne has it, it is "in the repressed spatial premises of the concept of modernity that its political logic is to be found":[34] "[T]he idea of the *non-contemporaneousness* of geographically diverse, but *chronologically simultaneous* times, which . . . develops, in the context of colonial experi-ence, is the foundation for 'universal histories with a cosmopolitan intent.' Once the practice of such comparison was established in anthropology, co-lonial discourse *par excellence*, it was easily transferable to the relations be-tween particular social spheres and practices within different European countries themselves, and thereafter, once again, globally, in an expanding dialectic of differentiation and homogenization."[35] Like the European an-thropological writing that Osborne describes, Longstreet's figuring of a shared experience of time encourages his readers to imagine their shared tenancy of a single, instantaneous, and homogeneous moment: Southwest-ern humor constructs an image of a landscape in the present free of tempo-ral variety. Absent this shared experience of time, simultaneity is impossi-ble; in the present tense of Southwestern humor, it is taken for granted. In this context, the political significance of Hall's remarks in "Georgia Theat-rics" comes into focus. Hall begins with the comment, "If my memory fail me not, the 10th of June, 1809 found me, at about 11 o'clock in the forenoon [in] Lincoln." The obvious point here would not be that Longstreet's middle-class white male audience shares (or shared) June 10, 1809, with his narrator; the point would be to notice the rhetorically produced "present" of the story's telling, which seeks to offer its readers the sense of a common time. As the argument goes, this figuring of a homogeneous present moment of the story's telling shared by Hall and his readers allows—even effects—an experience of simultaneity. What this view does less to acknowledge is that this structure of narration often figures the present in common by figuring that present as unavailable in a temporally heterogeneous past. In this model the ultimate outcome is a coterie of readers lifted out of time, out of history, and into an imaginary space where they form a leisured fraternity of white gentlemen. Southwestern humor's narrative apparatus positions its audience as figures unconstrained by their contingency, sheltering them from the complexities of their own moment and relocating them to an imaginary "holistic" realm where they escape the impositions of time of any sort: this is the reward of imagined community, its consoling function in the face of contingency. It delivers an experience of eternity in life. The projection of heterogeneous time into the past figures a temporally homogeneous present; this figuration of a temporally homogeneous present allows readers to imagine themselves linked not only by shared interests but also by a shared experience of time. This experience of simultaneity replaces the capacity to feel one's own mortality with membership in a community that transcends time. Middle-class white men shed their burdensome embedding in history; faced with their changeable political fortunes, they take refuge in a life outside of time.

The Technology of Locality

This account of Southwestern humor as an experience of refuge and retreat is in many respects the story that this literature tells about itself. Read differently, it becomes clear that Southwestern humor lacks the capacity to unite its middle-class white male authors and readers in the homogeneous present tense that it claims to offer. This is especially true of Southwestern humor's interest in the relationship between travel technologies and the homogenization of time. Like the disembedded moderns whom social theories of modernity describe, and like the anthropological investigators whose work it would be to describe the still-embedded world, Southwestern humor's narrators are always on the move.[36] The resulting attention this genre pays to early America's mobility yields a picture of time as unpredictably multiform and conjunctural. Southwestern humor's genteel narrators, who manage its reader's access to the life of America's poor whites, are repeatedly associated with one or another form of travel: trains, carriages, boats, or other means of conveyance. While on their journeys, these narrators discover that technology produces a sense of radical disembedding in which the overlaying of different temporalities constitutes local time. These narrators and their readers discover that travel technologies distanciate time and space in such a way as to make time local and variable rather than predictably uniform. They also suggest the extent to which the local has no single time to call its own—that the local entails a surfeited sense of time. As Walter Blair explains, these tales and sketches are characteristically narrated by men who have "comic experiences while traveling, while attending to some sort of business in town, while enjoying a boisterous frolic or . . . while on a hunt."[37] As is the case with modernity, the condition of possibility for Southwestern humor is constant movement. Mirroring a broader period interest in the impact of travel technologies, such as Hawthorne's description of the elderly Pyncheons on a rushing train, Southwestern humor also represents these traveling narrators as symptomatic of the infrastructural changes accompanying the modernization of the United States immediately prior to the moment of Southwestern humor's publication and market culture's penetration of rural backwaters. This literature takes as one of its persistent themes the change wrought by early nineteenth-century innovations in travel, whether the "genius of Fulton," the opening of the Erie Canal, or the more prosaic improvement of roads and turnpikes that historians tell us characterized this period. Yet conventional accounts of literary regionalism encourage us to ignore the production of locality at issue in these discussions of travel.[38]

This production of locality happens nowhere more clearly, perhaps, than in Solomon Smith's "A Bully Boat and a Brag Captain: A Story of Steamboat Life on the Mississippi." In this story, the steamboat emerges as one of modernity's unpredictable technologies, and narrative is revealed to have no inherent relationship to linear time. Smith's story, which was first published in *The Spirit of the Times* and later collected in Porter's *Big Bear*, describes a night spent on a Mississippi River steamboat traveling upriver from New Orleans in 1827, nearly two decades before the narrator's self-acknowledged present tense. As Mark Twain would do later in the century, Smith depicts the riverboat and its culture as socially chaotic but maintains that this characteristic is proper to a frontier in the process of being settled by immigrants of all sorts. Smith's story also suggests that technological innovations such as the steamboat have effected, and continue to effect, wholesale changes in the way that all Americans live their lives. Echoing Longstreet's habit of framing the incidents he describes and the culture they characterize as consigned to the past, Smith opens his story with a quizzical address to the reader: "Does anyone remember the Caravan?"[39] With this initial gesture, Smith marks the present tense of his narrator and that narrator's addressees as qualitatively different from that of the *Caravan*, a distinction Smith then ties to inventions in the realm of travel that distinguish the narrator's moment from the world he describes. According to Smith's narrator, the *Caravan* was "what would now be considered a slow boat; —*then* [1827] she was regularly advertised as the 'fast running,' etc. Her regular trips from New Orleans to Natchez were usually made in from six to eight days; a trip made by her in five days was considered remarkable. A voyage from New Orleans to Vicksburg and back, including stoppages, generally entitled the officers and crew to a month's wages. Whether the Caravan ever achieved the feat of a voyage to the Falls, (Louisville,) I have never learned; if she did, she must have 'had a *time* of it!' "[40] Like Longstreet and like Porter's introduction to the *Big Bear* collection, Smith introduces his tale as a retelling of a moment from the prehistory of the present—a present defined by technological advance and social acceleration. In terms of speed, the *Caravan* pales in comparison to the riverboats that followed it, and even the entire era of the *Caravan* does not fare very well when measured against the present. In a footnote, the narrator remarks that the scene of riverboat card playing he is about to describe "took place seventeen years ago. Within the last ten years, although I have travelled on hundreds of boats, *I have not seen an officer of a boat play a card.*"[41] Again echoing Longstreet, Smith pairs social enlightenment—the taming of riverboat officers—with a transition into a new experience of time as linear progress.

The story opens as the captain and his crew prepare to play cards, with passengers looking on and a subordinate pilot taking the helm. The captain explains to this pilot that the ship is "about a half a mile from a woodyard." " 'But,' muttered the Captain, 'I don't much like to take wood of the yellow-faced old scoundrel who owns it—he always charges a quarter of a dollar more than any one else; however, there's no other chance.' " The ship proceeds to the designated point and ties up "alongside a good-sized woodpile."[42] After prolonged bargaining with the "yellow-faced old gentleman" over the price of a cord of wood, the captain finally agrees to buy the wood but complains about the price. The narrator continues, "In about half an hour we felt the Caravan commence paddling again. Supper was over, and I retired to my upper berth, situated alongside and overlooking the brag-table, where the Captain was deeply engaged, having now the *other* pilot as his principal opponent. We jogged on quietly—and seemed to be going at a good rate."[43] The card game goes on, and the captain occasionally asks about the stock of wood and how it burns. Eventually, another load of wood is required: "The game went on and the paddles kept moving. At 11 o'clock, it was reported to the Captain that we were nearing the wood-yard, the light being distinctly seen by the pilot on duty."[44] More dickering over price and changes of pilots ensue. Importantly, these passages from "A Bully Boat" ask readers to mark time using the same benchmarks as the riverboat passengers and crew, all of whom take for granted the nature and the character of time. In doing so, Smith's story sets the stage for its dis-mantling of the notion that technology produces homogeneously linear progressive time, as well as its rejection of the idea that narrative discourse bears witness to the presence of (or produces) such an experience of time.

As the story develops, Smith's characters—the captain, his pilots, the other gamblers on board, even the narrator—remain firm in their convic-tion that travel technologies such as the steamboat not only symbolize progress but also produce linear progressive time. They remain certain that they are moving upriver, even though they remain below deck for most of the story: time is assumed to yield change, because time here is understood to equal progress, the ostensible natural temporality of modernity. These characters metonymically link technology (the steamboat) to linear pro-gressive time, and linear progressive time to change (movement upriver). They are encouraged in this process by the introduction of clock time, which both Giddens and these men take to be a universal measure. This move on the part of Smith's characters—their naturalization of time as progress—mirrors and reinforces certain conventional readerly expecta-tions of narrative discourse triggered by the narrator's manner of storytell-ing. As the narrator spins his tale, he supplies a series of chronological markers: "[i]n about half an hour," "[a]t 11 o'clock," "[d]ay at length dawned." These markers encourage Smith's reader to imagine that chronol-ogy is more than simply a self-referential device: they invite the reader to adopt a perspective similar to that of Smith's characters, one that assumes chronology measures "change over time," as the historian's adage goes. These markers also elicit the expectation that narrative discourse—both the storytelling taking place on the boat and the storytelling that is Smith's story—signals the presence of linear progressive time. Said another way, Smith's chronological markers press us to adopt his characters' relationship to time, which in turn reinforces the view that narrative discourse traces the linear progress of time. Written narrative becomes linear progressive time's mode of concrete appearance in the world. Importantly, the timing mechanisms Smith describes also seem to indicate a condition of incomplete modernity. The time measures in this story oscillate between modernity's universal metrics and more contingent ones: for example, "[d]ay at length dawned." In a story that turns out to be very much about the distanciation of time and space, this is a significant overlay of different orders of time.

Smith's story eventually reveals the folly of an untested faith in travel technology, while also confounding any expectation that narrative discourse mirrors or produces an experience of time as linear progress. It also points to the fact that there is no such thing as a universal and contingency-transcending measure of time—not even (and perhaps especially not) when that measure takes its bearings from artificial technologies. "A Bully Boat" draws to a close in this way: "Day at length dawned. The brag-party broke up, and settlements were being made, during which operation the Captain's bragging propensities were exercised in cracking up the speed of his boat, which, by his reckoning, must have made at least sixty miles, and *would* have made many more, if he could have procured good wood."[45] The narrator joins the captain on deck for a final load of wood, and the central device of the tale is finally revealed: "After a quick glance at the landmarks around, the Captain bolted, and turned in to take some rest. The fact became apparent—the reader will probably have discovered it some time since—that *we had been all night at the same wood-yard!*"[46] The pilots' shift changes, the darkness of night, and the increasingly foggy river have prevented anyone from noticing that the *Caravan* has been running at a standstill throughout the night.

On the one hand, this story's opening lines rather predictably link technological improvement to the homogenization of time. On the other hand, it thwarts that very same expectation that time can be taken for granted as a predictable principle organizing the events of history. The story begins by implying that technology changes time in such a way that the *Caravan* captain's misapprehension of the relationship between time and travel would not happen in the narrator's present tense; with improvements to travel technologies, truly modern time, which is to say homogeneously linear progressive time, has emerged. The opening comparison between the *Caravan* and later steamboats distinguishes these later vehicles and their moment from the unpredictability of the past. At the story's end, Smith's narrator remarks that his modern reader would "probably [have] discovered" the confusion regarding the wood earlier than the captain did; the suggestion here is that technological advances make time transparently meaningful by rendering it homogeneous. Like everyone else on board the *Caravan*, however, the captain has faith in the technology of the steamboat as it existed in his day. Notwithstanding the story's effort to distinguish the moment of its telling from the events it describes, this parable haunts the narrator's, and the reader's, present tense. The hubris of the captain's technological faith corrodes the experience of simultaneity that Smith's narrator might potentially share with his reader, questioning the taken-for-granted accessibility of homogeneous time.

Joseph M. Field's "Stopping to Wood" describes a similar riverboat scenario, and it captures from its start the uneven distribution and effects of American capital's trade technologies. The story opens with a generically familiar chronological distancing of the narrator's present tense from that of the story being told, but his narrator also suggests that this distance may be deceptive: "In spite of the magic changes which have been wrought in the 'way of doing things' upon the western waters, the primitive mode of 'wooding' from the bank remains unaltered—as a sort of vagabond Indian in the midst of a settlement—as the gallows does in the light of civilization."[47] Field imagines a country transformed by the magical changes that technology has wrought, but he also suggests that the past continues to live on in the present even in the realm of technology. For Field, "the present mode is to be condemned as 'behind the time;' as tedious, slovenly, and unnecessary."[48] He also links this inaccessibility of the present to the process of temporal differentiation that Fabian describes: Field signals the present's temporally heterogeneous character by way of a racialist metaphor suited to the arguments of Indian removal, which would read the Indian himself as an instance of anachronism, one similar to the inhumane gallows in an otherwise civilized country.[49] Moreover, the metaphor ultimately suggests that while the "present mode" may simply be "behind the times," the larger present tense remains a divided one in the moment of the story's telling. This particular present tense contains more than one chronological instant. The story suggests that, on the one hand, modernity's travel technologies have radically changed the nature of America but that, on the other hand, they have not evened out all of the internal anachronisms of the current conjuncture: "Steamers have grown from pigmies to giants, speed has increased from a struggle to a 'rush,' yet the conception of a ready loaded truck, or a burden-swinging crane—despatching a 'cord' for every shoulder load, appears not to have entered the head of either wood dealer or captain."[50] For no good reason, because the technology of load transfer already exists, and in the context of an accelerated environment wherein "speed" has gone from being a "struggle" to a "rush," the untimely remnants of technologies past subsist side by side with the present culture of speed and progress. Field's story ties this technological anachronism to unequal and seemingly anachronistic labor models. As the riverboat pulls ashore to take its load of wood, "[t]he bank is reached—the boat made fast—gangways are formed—'Lively! men, lively!' cries the mate, and while the upper cabins pour out their crowds upon the boiler deck, the 'hands,' and the swarms of wild-looking passengers below (obliged by contract) dash among the brush. Now ensues a scene that tasks description!"[51] At a moment when market culture has overtaken the American interior, a form of labor unmediated by the market's money economy subsists alongside a new technology designedly linked to that economy. The "wild-looking passengers" pay not money but labor in exchange for their passage, and in this sense, that relationship produces a peculiar disjuncture between the progressing speed of modernity and the anachronistic remains of an older technology of travel. As a technology of trade and travel, the steamboat should march hand in hand with the money economy, but here it does not.

Like Solomon Smith's story, moreover, Field's "Stopping to Wood" rejects the simple equating of technology with travel upriver and the linear time of progress. After stopping to wood, this riverboat returns to its former task, which was a race with another "brag" captain. The two steamboats ply the river, and as one boat stops again to wood, the other approaches: "'Tis the rival steamer, sure enough; and once more she will pass during this detention. Now dash both mate and captain ashore to 'rush' the matter. The bell is struck for starting, as if to compel impossibility; the accumulated steam is let off in brief, impatient screams, and the passengers, sharing the wild excitement, add their cries."[52] This scene cites the gathering force, "compel[led] impossibility," and "wild excitement" of American modernity, and it describes a community brought together by just that gathering force. The two boats begin to race, and the story evolves into a tribute to linear progress. Yet even in the face of technology's growing force and its drive to elaborate history as an unfolding line, human frailty intervenes to yoke the travel of this boat back to contingent circumstance: "With a shout of rage the defeated pilot turns [the boat's] head—at the same moment snatching down his rifle and discharging it into the pilot-house of his opponent! Fury has now seized the thoughts of all, and the iron throats of the steamers are less hideous than the human ones beneath them. The wheel for a moment neglected, the thwarted monster has now 'taken a sheer in the wild current,' and, beyond the possibility of prevention, is driving on to the bank! A cry of terror rises aloft—the throng rush aft—the steam, every valve set free—makes the whole forest shiver, and, amid the fright, the tall chimneys, caught by the giant trees, are wrenched and torn out like tusks from a recoiling mastadon."[53] Travel technology here shears away from its promise to bring order to time. One human's rage interrupts the straight line of progress that is thematically and geographically linked to river travel, and his fury pitches the boat toward the shore. Time's straight arrow cannot save the boat and its passengers, for humans are capable of changing the nature and the course of time's flow. In so doing, they redouble (in a counterintuitive fashion) nature's "wild current," which runs not directly but obliquely against them. The result of this human collaboration with nature's oblique force anticipates Twain's explosive technologies of war: one of the prime artifacts of a progressive technology of travel, the steamboat, is transformed into an archaic "thwarted monster." The steamboat morphs into a "recoiling" prehistoric "mastadon" equipped with a gaping and belching "steam throat" of its own.

If "Stopping to Wood" recalls Solomon Smith's story in its reference to the fueling process, William Tappan Thompson's "The Coon-Hunt; or, A Fency Country" adopts its trope of failed movement. Thompson's story describes Tom Culpepper and Bill Sweeney's nighttime raccoon hunt—as well as the drinking that accompanies it. The story treats their inebriated attempt to traverse a certain stretch of Pineville, Georgia, recently fenced by one of their neighbors. As in Smith's story, they discover that their night of travel has availed them nothing. After many struggles, "they found out that *they had been climbin the same fence all night*, not more'n a hundred yards from whar they first cum to it."[54] The specifics of their adventure matter less than how they characterize the fences (or rather, the fence) that they encounter: "'Why,' ses Tom, 'it's old Sturlin's doins—you know he's always bildin fences and making infernal improvements, as he calls 'em.'"[55] In this context, E. P. Thompson's assessment of eighteenth-century "improvements" in the English countryside is telling. "[E]nclosure and agricultural improvement were both, in some sense," Thompson writes, "concerned with the efficient husbandry of the time of the labour-force."[56] The very "improvements" associated with progress end up thwarting the narrative line of the story, confusing any sense we might have of a unified chronotope of southern life. As with Smith's story, "The Coon-Hunt" uncouples narrative storytelling from linear progress.

In his introduction to the *Big Bear* collection, which includes Smith's story, William T. Porter accuses James Fenimore Cooper and the writers of his era of being irrelevant to the present, because their writing treats events "belon[ging] to an earlier period—before the genius of Fulton had covered the mighty rivers of the new world in the West with a substitute for the 'broad horns' and flat boats, which took the place of the frail canoes of the aboriginal inhabitants of those 'happy hunting grounds.'"[57] Like "A Bully Boat," the *Big Bear* stories taken together argue that "the genius of Fulton" has fundamentally altered the landscape of America, delivering a new experience of time to its inhabitants far and wide. Like Smith's tale, too, these stories also want to intimate that the relationship between time and travel will be (or is) increasingly transparent because of technological innovations such as Fulton's steam engine: in its more programmatic moments, Southwestern humor implies that transportation technology removes the local obstacles that previously refracted, or localized, time. Yet in Smith's story, in the *Big Bear* collection, and in Southwestern humor more generally, technology fails to clarify the relationship between time and travel. Southwestern humor's overweening interest in precisely those technologies of travel identified with modernity actually spotlights the declension of time— its localization—by technology. Like similar stories scattered throughout this genre, "A Bully Boat and a Brag Captain" addresses the declension of time into temporalities effected by technological apparatuses such as the steam engine. It acknowledges that time is always more oblique than not. These stories also imply that the cosmopolitan centers are just as subject to the localization of time as is the Southwest, because the metropole represents the acme of technological life. In this American modernity every area operates according to local time. And in this American modernity, the storytelling narrator has unpredictable effects.

The Ageable American

The "whole ethical system" of Johnson Jones Hooper's "Captain" Simon Suggs "lies snugly," Hooper explains, "in [Suggs's] favourite aphorism—'it is good to be shifty in a new country.'"[58] Suggs is a hardy provincial and a severe anti-Federalist. Like Suggs, many of Southwestern humor's most popular characters deliberately resist the encompassing embrace of the nation. In Hooper's stories, in particular, Suggs is notoriously hard to pin down and infamously uncommitted. Hooper collected these stories and republished them as a fictional campaign biography trumpeting "Captain" Simon Suggs for president—a project undertaken at the urging of William T. Porter. The irony surrounding Suggs's campaign biography was thick, because Suggs's primary commitment is to eluding the lures of national culture and the demands of market capitalism. In this he resembles many of the most popular characters in Southwestern humor who in their sober moments outwit the nation's accepted representatives: the census taker or the tax man or the surveyor.

This literature's interest in men and women who resist American nationalism and market culture's incursions has often led critics to read it as an artifact that conserves the temper and the tone of a locale facing up to modernity's leveling force. As Richard Brodhead explains, in this reading of nineteenth-century American literary regionalism: "The cultural work of nineteenth-century regionalism . . . has been assumed to be that of cultural elegy: the work of memorializing a cultural order passing from life at that moment and of fabricating, in the literary realm, a mentally possessable version of a loved thing lost in reality."[59] Although Brodhead's topic is postbellum regionalism, the description applies just as well to Southwestern humor. Regional writing always claims to preserve a threatened way of life with the permanence of writing. In this self-authorizing account of regional writing, the genre is an archive of the vanquished rather than the victors. This view has led critics to suggest that nineteenth-century literary regionalism is a form of subaltern history rendered in dialect. It is here that we find a sotto voce history of the nation—the stories of the rural poor, disenfranchised women, disenchanted immigrant whites. Yet this view has been recently condemned as naïve. In "The Reading of Regions," in particular, Brodhead focuses on postbellum regionalism's original publication venues: the quality newspapers and periodicals of Reconstruction and Gilded Age America. In this context, Brodhead suggests, Sarah Orne Jewett's writing ensured that coastal Maine would become a fully capitalized tourist destination. It did not protect Jewett's locals from the incursions of the metropole, notwithstanding its sympathetic portraiture. Like the vacationing tourist's sketch common to these periodicals, postbellum regionalism instead responded to "an elite need for the primitive made available as leisure outlet."[60] Brodhead suggests further that literary regionalism was instrumental to the consolidation of a translocal leisure class that depended for its sense of coherency upon the presence of primitive locals made "visitable in print."[61] Sandra Zagarell offers a similar account of Jewett's New England regionalism, with the proviso that a "shadow narrative" gives the lie to its portraits of quaint premodern locals.[62] Zagarell explains that even as Jewett's narrators "seek out 'simple country people,'" those people "both obstruct . . . efforts to learn about them and give evidence of lives embedded in the economic and social history of coastal Maine."[63] Although Jewett's readers, her narrators, and even Jewett herself might have wished to view places such as the fictional Deephaven, Maine, as "timeless and 'natural'" "pockets of the past," Jewett's writing acknowledges sub rosa "the inexorable disappearance of the region's traditions and people; it suggests that Deephaven may become a merely physical site whose contemplation gives cosmopolitan visitors a pleasurable sense of renewal inextricable from the full assimilation of Deephaven into postbellum America's economic and cultural infrastructure."[64] In Zagarell's view, Jewett's interest in coastal Maine signals that it has already been folded into the very market culture to which cosmopolites would have it stand opposed—a fact surmised by those locals Jewett seeks to ventriloquize.

In other words, the new consensus view is that nineteenth-century literary regionalism participates in the disappearance of the local in the face of modernity rather than working to preserve the local or to function as its advocate. Here literary regionalism is both an agent and evidence of the distanciation of time and space, and it reembeds Americans in broad new networks of affiliation. Nineteenth-century literary regionalism evidences a fait accompli history of nationalism and capitalism, in which local culture is the mere passageway to national culture.[65] Local time always gives way to an American common time. The choice (which is not a choice) is to resist or to be incorporated, with the former being no more than a prelude to the inevitable latter. This is the either-or logic of regionalism: either the local or the national must be homogeneous. There is, however, a third option. We might instead conceive of local time as more than one thing and, in doing so, dismantle the binary that allows for the rhetorical relocation of heterogeneous time and the local to an always already past moment which itself is produced in the act of comparing local and cosmopolitan orders of time. In this literature's most explicit logic, the local is always inching toward national inclusion. In this sense, there is no actual acknowledgment of alterity—either the past's alterity or that of the local. The local and the past are under permanent threat of erasure by the national and the present. The reverse effect of this relationship is that the present is itself assimilated to a triumphal history of supralocal culture. By acknowledging the multiplicity of time in the past, we go some way toward encountering the past as more than the prehistory of the present—a present whose own character is obscured in the process of comparing the national to the local. We encounter a radically different past absent the telos of the present, and the present itself looks different unburdened of the responsibility to figure the past as its prehistory.

In this context, we might turn to Johnson Jones Hooper's "Taking the Census" for an original view of the conditions that define the experience of deep locality. Appearing first in a periodical and then later as an addendum to Hooper's campaign biography of Suggs, "Taking the Census" caricatures "Hooper's 1840 job counting the reluctant residents of Tallapoosa County" in Alabama.[66] Hooper describes the experience of "assistant marshals" of the national government who undertook such work and comically relates the challenges they faced.[67] Hooper introduces the story with the following caveat:

> The collection of statistical information concerning the resource and industry of the country, by the assistant marshals who were employed to take the last census, was a very difficult work. The popular impression, that a tremendous tax would soon follow the minute investigation of the private affairs of the people, caused the census-taker to be viewed in no better light than that of a tax-gatherer; and the consequence was, that the information sought by him was either withheld entirely, or given with great reluctance. The returns, therefore, made by the marshals, exhibit a very imperfect view of the wealth and industrial progress of the country.[68]

Hooper captures the tension between the local and the national that has concerned us throughout this discussion of nineteenth-century regionalism. The locals of Tallapoosa County, as Hooper represents them, suspect national projects, such as the census, of bringing ill effects and so do everything in their power to thwart the census takers' efforts. Approaching the house of "a widow rather past the prime of life," for instance, the census takers find themselves under attack by a woman who refuses to understand herself—or to be understood—in terms dictated by "Washington City."[69] After dodging a hail of objects thrown from the window of the house, they modify their goals: "All this time we were perspiring through fear of the fierce guardians of the old widow's portal. At length, when the widow paused, we remarked that as she was determined not to answer questions about the produce of the farm, we would just set down the age, sex, and complexion of each member of her family."[70] This they attempt to do, but they meet resistance even when they manage to approach the widow and the children guarding the house. Unimpressed and offended by these representatives of the national government, the widow, Judy Tompkins, replies to their queries with outrage at the assumption that national governments deserve intimate knowledge of the local. Referring to U.S. president Martin van Buren, she threatens, " 'Kill him! kill him—oh—if I had him here by the years I reckon I would kill him. A pretty fellow to be eating his vittils out'n gold spoons that poor people's taxed for, and raisin' an army to get him made king of Ameriky—the oudacious, nasty stinking, old scamp!' She paused a moment, then resumed, 'And now, mister, jist put down what I tell you on that paper, and don't be telling no lies to send to Washington city. Jist put down "Judy Tompkins, ageable woman, and four children." ' "[71] Her suspicion of Van Buren and his representatives leads her to refuse all of the census takers' questions but two: her name and the number of others living in her house. In this sense, Judy Tompkins recalls those figures in Jewett's text who "obstruct . . . efforts to learn about them and give evidence of lives embedded in the economic and social history of coastal Maine."[72] The census takers want to know how Judy Tompkins and her children fit into the national frame, but she refuses to accommodate herself to that perspective. As the story continues, the census takers encounter similar characters everywhere they turn.

Yet the most significant of Judy Tompkins's statements is her brief self-designation as an "ageable woman." In this seemingly offhand comment we can read this character's most interesting affront to the protocols of nationalism. Here Tompkins attempts to detach herself from the nation by demurring from national time when she labels herself only "ageable." She does not assert the particularity of local time—that is, the difference of her locale from the cosmopolitan standard more familiar to the census takers. To do so would also be to position her local environment as the to-be-transcended, the difference in the past against which American common time always seeks to define itself. To do so would be to lay the rhetorical ground against which the figure of homogeneous time can come into view. It would be to accept a seductively phrased invitation to reembed herself in a broad translocal network. In a gesture both comical and perverse, Judy Tompkins instead identifies herself as an "ageable woman," which would seem to indicate that she has no time for the nation. Unlike Jewett's or Chesnutt's characters, she is neither likable nor noble, but in this context she is compellingly opaque.

There are other "ageable" characters in Southwestern humor. In Longstreet's "The Fight," we meet one Ransy Sniffle, who encourages the

dispute at the center of the story, which takes place, according to Longstreet, in the "younger days of the Republic."[73] Longstreet describes Sniffle
as follows:

Now there happened to reside in the county, just alluded to, a little fellow, by the
name of Ransy Sniffle: a sprout of Richmond, who, in his earlier days, had fed copi-
ously upon red clay and blackberries. This diet had given to Ransy a complexion
that a corpse would have disdained to own, and an abdominal rotundity that was
quite unprepossessing. Long spells of the fever and ague, too, in Ransy's youth, had
conspired with clay and blackberries, *to throw him quite out of the order of nature.*
His shoulders were fleshless and elevated; his head large and flat; his neck slim and
translucent; and *his arms, hands, fingers and feet, were lengthened out of all propor-
tion to the rest of his frame. His joints were large and his limbs small*; and as for flesh,
he could not with propriety be said to have any.[74]

Longstreet's Sniffle recalls Hawthorne's scrawny chicken. Divorced from
"the order of nature," his extremities grow at different rates: his "arms,
hands, fingers and feet" mismatch his body and one another. The joints
that connect his limbs are disproportionate to the limbs themselves. Ransy
Sniffle follows Judy Tompkins in his disconnection from the time of nature
and from that of the nation. Sniffle also indicates that the local is best understood as a site of temporal surfeit. He is "out of the order of nature,"
but he does obey other orders of time.

   According to "Interview with an Editor," Solomon Smith, the author
of "Bully Boat," was just as hard to place in chronological time as the
gangly Ransy Sniffle. In this story, Smith describes a visit to him from an
admirer portrayed as the editor William T. Porter. In this fictionalized visit,
the humor follows from a case of mistaken age. Having read writings attributed to "Old Sol," and having seen them associated with the traveling acting troupe managed by Solomon Smith, Porter arrives at Smith's hotel
room expecting an aged man to receive him. As it turns out, "Old Sol" is
merely one of Solomon Smith's stage personas, and so the man he meets is
"but thirty-four."[75] At the crux of the story, however, lies an exchange that
refuses the security of age dating in a manner that recalls Judy Tompkins
and Ransy Sniffle:

"Mr. Porter, I believe." "Yes, sir—your name is"—"Smith, sir—I am glad to see
you—heard of you frequently—always read your paper—by-the-by, got several
subscribers names to give you—much admired at the South—how d'ye do?" "Very
well—you are a younger brother, I presume?" "Yes, sir, there were eleven of us, and
I am the eighth." We here entered into a conversation for a few minutes concerning

the South—the theatres there—the bar—the race and race-courses, and the presidential question—on all of which subjects he appeared quite familiar. It being near time to go to press, we made a movement to go. "I will call again, when your brother is in." "My brother, sir?" "Yes, the *old* gentleman." "My dear sir, I have no brother in New York—none nearer than Cincinnati." "No! Did you not say you were the *younger* brother of *Old Sol?*" "Bless ye, no, sir—I am certainly a younger brother, but I am, nevertheless, the person you called in your last paper, the *old critter!*" "*You* Old Sol? Impossible! You have not a gray hair in your head—you cannot be more than thirty-five or forty, at most." "I am but thirty-four." "Well, old gentleman, any way you can fix it, you are welcome to New York."[76]

In this telling dialogue, something curious happens to the time of clocks and calendars associated with modernity. The story ends with Smith's forthright statement of his age: thirty-four. Yet the conversation that precedes it shadows that final statement. This conversation calls attention to the arbitrary nature of the time-date system that Smith and Porter bring to bear in this situation. In one sense, this scene merely identifies Smith's story as a case of Southwestern humor: "[T]he world of Southwestern humor is populated with those who do not know all they need to know, and the tension between knowledge and ignorance acts as the essential stimulant to laughter."[77] Yet we also learn that some forms of knowing are empty because the signifying mechanism upon which they rely has no "existential relationship" to time. Porter learns nothing when he learns that his interlocutor is the eighth child in a family of eleven. That knowledge alone, which is a knowledge about chronology and descent, tells nothing. As a result, Porter remains confused. In this context, Smith's remark—"I am but thirty-four"—lacks signifying force. If knowing a time count in a familial context says nothing, what could possibly be gleaned from the abstract designation "but thirty-four"? Although we know Solomon Smith's age, he is no more than "ageable."

These "ageable" characters return us finally to Captain Simon Suggs. Where Suggs suggests that it is good to be shifty in a new country, it is probably truer to the circumstance to say that it is required. Judy Tompkins, Ransy Sniffle, and Solomon Smith remain inaccessible because they are figures for the conjuncture. They are unresolved question marks that allegorize how modernity's coeval orders of time forbid the displaced easy access to social reembedding. Their interest for us therefore lies not in their escape from national time (they do not exactly escape) nor in their loyalty to a single local norm (these are not loyal people). Their interest lies in the fact that their unresolved qualities follow from a certain embeddedness in modernity's new order(s) of time. Modernity's distanciation of time and space produces these figures, but it does not reembed them in a single new order of time synchronized with broader translocal norms—quite the opposite. The distanciation of time and space leads them to inhabit several different orders of time. This is not an experience of freedom from contingency or transcendence of the local; neither is it a case of absolute determination. It is a scene of overdetermination: modernity's distanciation of time and space opens several avenues but guarantees passage on none. Tompkins, Sniffle, and Smith are not reduced to being only the addressees of national time, but neither are they defined by a singular local time either. These characters are the unequal sum of apples and oranges. It is not that Judy Tompkins has no time for the nation. The point is that she has too much. Here the local is not a site of resistance: it is a form of superaddition that no single clock can track.

Chapter 4
The Deprivation of Time in African American Life Writing

The fugitive slave narratives, spiritual autobiographies, and fictionalized biographies of African America faced a double demand. On the one hand, they were expected to detail the dehumanizing realities of slavery and racism. This first requirement explains the genre's recurring descriptions of blood-clotted whips, shredded flesh, and rape—not to mention segregation, prohibitions against literacy, and spiritual betrayal. On the other hand, these narratives were asked to certify the preternaturally durable humanity of enslaved and free African Americans. So to anticipate the charge that African Americans were unfit for immediate emancipation because they had been made inhuman, these narratives are leavened with tales of the resilient humanity of enslaved African Americans. In other words, the African American life narrative was expected to testify to the dehumanization and the humanity of African Americans at one and the same time.[1] We can trace that contradictory demand in this literature's effort to highlight the vague outlines of an experience of progress that might have been otherwise nearly indiscernible in the lives of this literature's subjects. Seeking to secure a place for African Americans in the family of man, the authors of these narratives most typically choose to depict the chronological evolution of individual African Americans away from the naïveté of childhood and into the maturity of adulthood. They also emphasize the maturation of the race as a whole, marrying a story of phylogeny to one of ontogeny. And they do so by attempting to structure the African American life narrative as linear and as characterized by progress. In other words, they attempt to write "autobiography as chronicle."[2] From Frederick Douglass to Harriet Jacobs and beyond, these authors sought to demonstrate the full evolution of individual African Americans and, more generally, African Americans as a people. As a result, these authors must, and do, carefully manage their public face when it comes to time. Given their particular political and aesthetic charge here, it should not surprise us as modern readers that these authors labor to adhere to the straight and narrow line. Nor should we be surprised when readers and later critics reaffirm this project: then as now the measure of the fully human amounts to an ideological measure figured in terms of linear progress. The narrative of the life as chronicle is, however, far from the full story of the life narrative. This literature explicitly concerns itself with linear time, and its authors gravitate toward this formal strategy out of a desire to certify the progress of African Americans. The life narrative nevertheless articulates a competition among linear time, what I will call laboring time and spirit time, and the revolutionary messianic time mentioned in our discussion of the historical romance. Indeed, these nonlinear modes of being in time characterize African American life writing as much as or more than linear progress did. The many direct addresses to the reader of the African American life narrative seek to make some of its times more legible than others, and it is in fact these many direct addresses that have structured our understanding of this genre.

If the African American life narrative articulates several different orders of time, some of them did aid nineteenth-century (and later) African American readers as they steeled themselves for an uninspiring experience of a civic-sphere present tense structured around the priorities of an unrepentant white racism. In articulating for its readers the parameters of revolutionary messianic time and of spirit time, in particular, these narratives provided a resource perhaps even more crucial than linear progress ever could have been. The logic of nineteenth-century race theory encouraged African Americans (and others) to envision one future: a manifest destiny in which hierarchies of race would guarantee the national homogeneity that John L. O'Sullivan envisioned by excluding African Americans from full and equal citizenship. Yet the spirit time and revolutionary messianic time that these narratives made conceptually available encouraged African Americans to regard the "future" as open to revision rather than as inevitably given. They even encouraged African Americans to imagine that a future messianic justice could intercede in the unbearable present tense. In other words, these narratives offer a resource of hope structured not around imperial occupation of the future, but rather addressed to the future's capacity to redress injustice in the present. These narratives did not, however, serve the role often attributed to them of helping to reconstruct a racial community capable of sheltering African Americans against the vicissitudes of history: the African American life narrative engenders an African American reading subject who is never securely raced—never quite complete. His encounter with the narrative of the life is not, I am suggesting, limited to an imagined experience of simultaneity with other African Americans. The African American subject who emerges from a reading of these pages does so "torn" by the conflict of time that is modernity. In addition to suggesting a different relationship on the part of African Americans to this literature, this view of the life narrative also complicates recent work that emphasizes the ways in which African American life narratives, which commonly include spectacles of African American bodies subjected to torture, serves to fashion white identity into a viable category of racial identification. In *Scenes of Subjection*, in particular, Saidiya Hartman has argued that the display of power rendered explicit in fugitive slave narratives served to solidify the boundaries of whiteness emerging in the nineteenth-century United States. Rejecting the sense that such displays were ambivalent and allowed the line between black and white to break down through a process of sympathetic identification, Hartman argues that, "[a]t the very least, the relations of chattel slavery served to enhance whiteness by racializing rights and entitlements, designating inferior and superior races, and gaining whites' dominion over blacks."[3] Notwithstanding the sophisticated terms of appraisal Hartman offers, the conflict of times articulated in and through the African American life narrative suggests that, while this genre's repeated narrative displays of tortured black bodies warrant our questioning attention, these narratives worked at least as hard to foreclose the consolidation of white racial identity as they did to confound the emergence of a coherent African American subjectivity. If the integrity of the African American reading subject is put into question by these narratives, then so is that of their white readers.

These narratives also shed significant light on the idea of modernity as radical rupture. If it is true for anyone that "the modes of life brought into being by modernity have swept us away from *all* traditional types of social order, in unprecedented fashion,"[4] and if the sense that modernity involves a "dramatic and unprecedented break between past and present" applies at all,[5] then surely it would seem that this conventional wisdom is true of the victims of the African slave trade. If for no one else, then at least for African Americans modernity involved a traumatic break with past ways of life and a distanciation of most conventional measures of time and space. In horrific ways, the great divide separating premodern from modern would seem to map most neatly to the experience of genealogical isolation and the middle passage that sets the terms for the African experience in the Americas. As

Christopher Miller has recently argued, the "middle passage" is a form of "rupture" that "begins with the African captives deprived of their last glimpse of their homeland, and this imposed blindness takes on tremendous symbolic weight" in African American literature.[6] "This crossing," Miller argues, "endured by so many million Africans, is (or should be) one of the prime figures in the collective memory of the modern world."[7] As Paul Gilroy would suggest, in fact, the middle passage is perhaps the most modern of all modernity's experiences.[8] Yet as long-standing conversations around the issue of African retentions in the Americas suggest, this idea of radical rupture has certain important limitations. Miller rightly points out the impossibility of a return to Africa in the context of the slave trade, and in particular France's policy of the *Exclusif*, and in this sense he describes an irreparable break. As others have demonstrated, moreover, much of the work of the Caribbean slave *barracoon* was to intermix indiscriminately people of different backgrounds so as to interrupt the retention of languages and cultural practices acquired on the African continent. Yet it is always worth asking to what extent the idea of persistence—if not return—might apply.

As it happens, persistence and retention are issues at play in the African American life narrative, but their conceptualization will need to take a different form than has sometimes defined criticism on this genre. Does the "literature of the slave" and of free people of color facilitate what Houston Baker famously calls a "journey back"? I suggest that the very modernity of this literature means that it does something rather different. I propose that if the African American life narrative does provide an avenue for a journey of sorts, then it is a circuitous one whose destination is not known. As an earlier generation of critics pointed out, this genre of writing draws from a variety of sources: if it is true that the double demand described earlier encouraged the writing of autobiography as chronicle, then the African American life narrative reproduces what I described in Chapter 1 as the peculiarly premodern/modern temporality of the European chronicle. Yet it is also true that, as Charles H. Nichols pointed out some time ago, the slave narrative borrows from a picaresque mode structured around fitful starts, periods of rumination, and, above all, no strong sense of a clear and present future. In the African American spiritual autobiography, moreover, one sees the adaptation of a form imported from a long tradition of Christian self-contemplation. In other words, the African American life narrative mirrors the other genres of writing considered here to the extent that it marries modern and premodern modes of being in time precisely in its effort to meet the demands of the present and to tell its impossible truth. The African American life narrative reaches back across modernity's great divide to access premodern European literary forms in an attempt to reckon with the ugliness of modernity. If the effect is to engender a journey, however, that journey takes the reader to a local present tense with an as yet unrealized future.

The Labor of Progress in the Fugitive Slave Narrative

The early African American life narrative inaugurates a literary tradition that has sought to document and overcome the natal alienation of people of African descent living in diaspora. African American literature has long taken as one of its primary concerns a condemnation of the efforts by slaveholders and other institutionally sanctioned racists to sever African American family ties, to obscure the birth dates of African Americans, and to reset the clock of daily African American life. The opening lines of Frederick Douglass's *Narrative of the Life of Frederick Douglass, An American Slave, Written by Himself* contain the canonical description of such processes of state-sanctioned social murder: "I was born in Tuckahoe, near Hillsborough, and about twelve miles from Easton, in Talbot county, Maryland. I have no accurate knowledge of my age, never having seen any authentic record containing it. By far the larger part of the slaves know as little of their ages as horses know of theirs, and it is the wish of most masters within my knowledge to keep their slaves thus ignorant."[9] According to Douglass here, to be a slave is to lack a birth date, a fully articulated family, and the genealogy the two together comprise.[10] To be a slave in this way is to live inhumanly; it is to descend to the level of a beast and to live a life untethered. In his classic comparatist account of slavery, *Slavery and Social Death*, Orlando Patterson suggests that this particular way of configuring—or deforming—an enslaved person's relationship to the past is one of the central features of the mechanics of both classical and modern slaveholding societies. According to Patterson, the enslaved are forced to endure a radical form of "secular excommunication."[11] The African American slave was, like those who preceded him in bonds, a "genealogical isolate": "Formally isolated in his social relations with those who lived, he also was culturally isolated from the social heritage of his ancestors. He has a past, to be sure. But a past is not a heritage. Everything has a history, including sticks and stones. Slaves differed from other human beings in that they were not allowed

freely to integrate the experience of their ancestors into their lives, to in-
form their understanding of social reality with the inherited meanings of
their . . . forbears, or to anchor the living present past in any conscious
community of memory."[12] Patterson argues that slaves have been repeatedly deprived of the knowledge of their social context and past that would
strengthen their social structures and kinship ties, as well as (re)establish
a nexus of African American sociopolitical power. Patterson describes this
deprivation as a process of "natal alienation": "[T]he term 'natal alienation'
. . . goes directly to the heart of what is critical in the slave's forced alienation, the loss of ties of birth in both ascending and descending generations.
It also has the important nuance of a loss of native status, of deracination.
It was this alienation of the slave from all formal, legally enforceable ties of
'blood,' and from any attachment to groups or localities other than those
chosen for him by the master, that gave the relation of slavery its peculiar
value to the master."[13] The slave, with no external attachments either to
limit him or to support him, functions as the ideal object of commodity
exchange: stripped of his past and the power it engenders, the slave emerges
as an empty vehicle prepared to effectuate the master's power.

Curiously, the study of African American literature has, for its part,
characterized this issue of natal alienation as an issue specifically of time.
Thus Henry Louis Gates Jr.'s seminal essay "The Literature of the Slave"
first addresses the slave narrative's widely acknowledged attention to literacy and then turns to the question of time under slavery. Gates argues:

Most fundamentally, we mark a human being's existence by his or her birth and
death dates, engraved in granite on every tombstone. Our idea of the self, it is fair
to argue, is as inextricably interwoven with our ideas of time as it is with uses of
language. In antebellum America, it was the deprivation of time in the life of the
slave that first signaled his or her status as a piece of property. . . . Within such a
time machine, as it were, not only had the slave no fixed reference points, but also
his or her own past could exist only as memory without support, as the text without
footnotes, as the clock without two hands. . . . A "slave" was he or she who, most
literally, stood outside of time.[14]

In this reading of the "literature of the slave," slavery compels African
Americans to enter a temporal desert that severs their ties to the family and
community members who might acknowledge their place "in time." As
Gates indicates here and elsewhere, his particular argument about the "deprivation of time in the life of the slave" follows from his perception that, in
the literature of the slave, "[s]laves . . . are those who cannot plot their

course by and who stand outside of the linear progression of the calendar."[15] For Gates, the literature of African American slaves chronicles a perversion of time's natural course, a process that robbed slaves of an unmediated relationship to time and its rewards, both of which are birthrights of the human. To be a slave is to lose access to the rewards of time itself, and to read the literature of the slave is to read evidence of that loss. We read the evidence of this loss, this deprivation, Gates would suggest, in these lines from Douglass's second narrative: "I never met with a slave who could tell me how old he was. Few slave-mothers know anything of the months of the year, nor of the days of the month. They keep no family records, with marriages, births, and deaths. They measure the ages of their children by spring time, winter time, harvest time, planting time, and the like; but these soon become undistinguishable and forgotten."[16] Expanding upon the theme he introduced in his first narrative, Douglass ponders a group of people who know little of "the months of the year" or "the days of the month." For Gates, these slave mothers who "keep no family records" symbolize an experience of lack, of temporal absence. The problem with this reading is that it figures linear progress as time in its state of nature. What this effectively does is to make absent what is transparently present in this moment: an experience of time that differs from the time of linear progress. In other words, when Gates summarizes this quotation as evidence of temporal lack, he actually projects absence into the scenario described here. In Gates's account, if there is no progress, there is no time: the two are one. Yet, in rereading Douglass's account, we discover "slave-mothers" were able to "measure the ages of their children by spring time, winter time, harvest time, planting time, and the like." For Gates, as for Douglass, these measures are inadequate because they "soon become undistinguishable and forgotten"; these measures do not track the linear progress of man, in which case they do not certify an engagement with time in its favored state. From a different perspective, however, the lines that reference these measures are hardly bereft of time. On the contrary, they detail two kinds of time, disavowing one and valorizing the other.

The disavowed time, which I call laboring time, recurs throughout Douglass's life writing, and it has two indivisible facets. In *My Bondage and My Freedom*, for example, Douglass recounts his life with the slave breaker, Mr. Covey. Discussing his removal to Covey's land, Douglass remarks, "I remained with Mr. Covey one year, (I cannot say I *lived* with him,) and during the first six months that I was there, I was whipped, either with sticks or cowskins, every week."[17] Douglass next reproduces a passage from his earlier life story, the *Narrative*, which he offers as representative of his experience with Mr. Covey: "If at any one time of my life, more than another, I was made to drink the bitterest dregs of slavery, that time was during the first six months of my stay with Mr. Covey. We were worked all weathers. It was never too hot or too cold; it could never rain, blow, snow, or hail too hard for us to work in the field. Work, work, work, was scarcely more the order of the day than of the night. The longest days were too short for him, and the shortest nights were too long for him."[18] By the conventional measures of premodern as opposed to modern orders of time, Douglass's description would appear inapt, to the extent that he describes slavery's labor in terms that fit better with the periodically very intense labor that E. P. Thompson contrasts with modern capitalism and that he defines as the "episodic" labor of those premodern agricultural labor systems based on seasonal cycles. The premodern "work pattern" with which slavery is conventionally associated, Thompson writes, "was one of alternate bouts of intense labour and of idleness,"[19] "and the irregularity of working day and week were framed, until the first decades of the nineteenth century, within the larger irregularity of the working year, punctuated by its traditional holidays, and fairs."[20] Yet Douglass's account also distinctly echoes the language of a former employee of one of what Thompson calls "the worst masters" of early industry. Thompson quotes the following passage as testimony to life in "those industries . . . where the new time-discipline was most rigorously imposed": "[W]e worked as long as we could see in summer time, and I could not say at what hour it was that we stopped. There was nobody but the master and master's son who had a watch, and we did not know the time."[21] We might do well to recall, then, Mark Smith's observations about clock time in the slaveholding South: "[T]he southern application of clock time and the practical effects it instigated were akin to the type of time employed under nineteenth-century industrial capitalism."[22] Douglass's life narratives work hard to frame his experience as a chronicle of progress, but at this particular juncture, Douglass's sensitivity to slavery's insidiousness leads him to acknowledge that, as in the mills that Thompson's subject describes, the repetitive, unbroken, and unremitting labor Douglass endures at Covey's produces a particular, and particularly brutal, nonprogressive experience of time. Douglass cannot say that he "lived" with Mr. Covey, because, within the ideology of time that his narratives take as their framework, "living" entails measured change and subjective development: an abstraction of identity, or progress, that time left to its own devices is assumed to effect. Rather than having been deprived of time, though, it is more the case that Douglass has been forced to live the kind of time slave labor produces, or laboring time. This laboring time does not function as an obvious medium of progress, and so Douglass writes, "The thought of only being a creature of the *present* and the *past*, troubled me, and I longed to have a *future*—a future with hope in it. To be shut up entirely to the past and present, is abhorrent to the human mind; it is to the soul—whose life and happiness is unceasing progress—what the prison is to the body; a blight and mildew, a hell of horror."[23] A "hell of horror" it is, but the world Douglass inhabits is not a temporal desert. Rather, slaveholders try to deprive Douglass of linear progressive time and replace it with laboring time. In doing so, they introduce a compound experience of time that marries a "premodern" to a "modern" formation.

Solomon Northup's *Twelve Years a Slave* of 1853, the narrative of a free man of color kidnapped and sold into twelve years of slavery, both resembles and illuminates by comparison Douglass's *Narrative*. The "twelve years" in the title of Northup's narrative would seek to emphasize the linear chronology of Northup's life, and much of the body of Northup's narrative takes precisely that approach.[24] Two chapters stand out as different: those that describe the labor required to produce the slave economy's two major crops, cotton and sugar. Where the majority of Northup's narrative takes great pains to document his progress in time, these two chapters figure a faceted system of labor that transforms time itself. In the opening passage from the chapter that describes the production of sugar, Northup remarks, "In consequence of my inability in cotton-picking, [my master] was in the habit of hiring me out on sugar plantations during the season of cane-cutting and sugar-making. He received for my services a dollar a day, with the money supplying my place on his cotton plantation. Cutting cane was an employment that suited me, and for three successive years I held the lead row at [the sugar plantation], leading a gang of from fifty to an hundred hands."[25] This passage emphasizes the habitual character of these duties—the established fact of Northup's being hired out, the unremarkable succession of years, his repeated leadership of work gangs. Northup next outlines more specifically the cycle of repetition that defines his labor: "The ground is prepared in beds, the same as it is prepared for the reception of the cotton seed, except it is ploughed deeper. Drills are made in the same manner. Planting commences in January, and continues until April. It is necessary to plant a sugar field only once in three years. Three crops are taken before the seed or plant is exhausted."[26] Importantly, this is an experience of labor under slavery structured both by the calendar of capital accumulation and by the strength of the seed. Here time is not the transparent medium of progress. After describing sugar production in all its regularity, the narrator explains further that "[t]he only respite from constant labor the slave has through the whole year, is during the Christmas holidays": "It is the custom for one planter to give a 'Christmas supper,' inviting the slaves from neighboring plantations to join his own on the occasion. . . . Usually from three to five hundred are assembled, coming together on foot, in carts, on horseback, on mules. . . . Uncle Abram astride a mule, with Aunt Phebe and Patsey behind him, trotting towards a Christmas supper, would be no uncommon sight on Bayou Boeuf."[27] Northup's narrative concludes its somewhat unconvincingly cheerful account of the enjoyments of life in the holiday season: "Such is 'southern life as it is,' *three days in the year*, as I found it—the other three hundred and sixty-two being days of weariness, and fear, and suffering, and unremitting labor."[28]

In these passages, this narrative describes the experience of time under slavery as an experience of superimposition. On the one hand, it gives us premodern cycles of seasonal labor and Christmas delights; on the other hand, it depicts a slavery organized by the "unremitting labor" of modern industrial labor. There is a sense of repetition and cycle here, in the attention to what is "custom," what "usually" happens, what is "no uncommon sight," and these passages link these commonly repeated, virtually indistinguishable events to one of the most ritualistic of holidays. This version of change entertains only the changing same. It is instructive, however, to read this description against a similar scene in Thompson's time and work-discipline essay. There Thompson glosses a similar scene in his discussion of a 1736 poem by Stephen Duck, "The Thresher's Labour." Although Thompson describes Duck's poem as an "obligatory set-piece in eighteenth-century farming poetry," he also cautions against seeing the harvest celebration the poem describes as a "direct respons[e]" to new economic stimuli—notwithstanding that celebration's dependence on the laborer's harvest wages. The harvest celebration is, Thompson argues, "a moment at which the older collective rhythms break through the new, and a weight of folklore and of rural custom could be called as supporting evidence as the psychic satisfaction and ritual functions . . . of the harvest-home."[29] In this telling moment, Thompson makes recourse to literature—as he does throughout his essay—to exemplify the temporally conflicted nature of modernity. In this context, it becomes clear that what Northup's narrative retells is an experience of labor in which even the seasons do not interrupt the unremitting labor of the slaves, due to the capacity of slaveholders to require their workers to inhabit different and competing modes of time simultaneously. Just before his discussion of the Christmas season, for example, Northup recalls, "During the three seasons I labored on Hawkins' plantation, I was employed a considerable portion of the time in the sugar-house."[30] In a passage that distinctly recalls descriptions of factories and other modes of mass production, Northup continues:

The mill is an immense brick building, standing on the shore of the bayou. Running out from the building is an open shed, at least an hundred feet in length and forty or fifty feet in width. The boiler in which the steam is generated is situated outside the main building; the machinery and engine rest on a brick pier, fifteen feet above the floor, within the body of the building. The machinery turns two great iron rollers, between two and three feet in diameter and six or eight feet in length. They are elevated above the brick pier, and roll in towards each other. An endless carrier, made of chain and wood, like leathern belts used in small mills, extends from the iron rollers out of the main building and through the entire length of the open shed. The carts in which the cane is brought from the field as fast as it is cut, are unloaded at the sides of the shed. All along the endless carrier are ranged slave children, whose business it is to place the cane upon it, when it is conveyed through the shed into the main building, where it falls between the rollers, is crushed, and drops upon another carrier that conveys it out of the main building in an opposite direction, depositing it in the top of a chimney upon a fire beneath, which consumes it.[31]

In this long and detailed passage, the fine line—or rather, the radical rupture—separating premodern from modern modes of production, as well as premodern and modern ways of being in time, collapses, and we find ourselves in a terrain indistinguishable in its most basic outlines from that of the Lowell mills. It is clearly inaccurate, then, to count either Northup's chapters on cotton and sugar production or Douglass's account of his time spent at Covey's plantation as witnessing or reproducing the "deprivation of time in the life of the slave." Nor is it right to say that these narratives palliate this (nonexistent) deprivation by supplying African American readers with a reorganized sense of time in the life of the slave structured around progress.

Rather, these passages suggest that both *Twelve Years* and Douglass's life narratives require the reader to immerse herself in a world where she must be in time in more than one way. *Twelve Years* shows how time can take the form we recognize as progress, but it also indicates that progress is only one of time's declensions. From the difference between the time of linear progress and laboring time in its compounded form, we learn that "time" always requires a modifier. Yet these observations about *Twelve Years* do validate in an odd way the distrust of temporal variety pervading African American life writing and its criticism. If one hopes, as Douglass obviously does, to be viewed as the beneficiary of, and standard-bearer for, progress, then a frank and forthright account of his having been constituted out of this peculiar order of time would amount to a risk perhaps not worth taking. To publicly own an experience of temporal variety is to undermine one's claims to a coherent identity. In this sense, the life narrative's tendency to downplay its temporal variety in its addresses to the reader bespeaks a certain sensitivity to the politics of time. That act of repression suggests that the African American life narrative recognizes but does not willingly admit that there is no unmediated version of time. When we reconsider Frederick Douglass's metaleptic valuation of progressive time and its extension in the criticism on African American life writing, this genre comes more clearly into focus. Although Douglass's manifest project is to reassert the slave's experience of time as an experience of progress, and although this project neither accommodates nor even recognizes laboring time, going so far as to obscure it, laboring time in its curiously compounded form nevertheless interlaces both Northup's and Douglass's narratives. Douglass's long shadow may have in this way prevented laboring time from figuring in our understanding of African American life writing, except as the absence that this literature redresses, but Douglass's (failed) attempt to figure time exclusively as progress had considerable force. His emphasis on representing time as progress reminds us that at this moment, the rights and privileges of the "capitalist citizen" flowed to those who successfully represented their lives as if they were structured by homogeneous progress toward universal humanity.[32]

Time outside of Time in the Spiritual Autobiography

Jarena Lee's 1836 spiritual autobiography, *The Life and Experience of Jarena Lee*, expands our knowledge of the temporalities of African American literature even farther, for this narrative limns a temporality different from those considered so far. Like the historical romance's revolutionary messianic time, which also figures in the life narrative, Lee's "spirit time" involves an experience of communion that is best described as time outside of time, or spirit time, and thus as neither progress nor repetition. This may sound to secular ears suspiciously supernatural, but to the extent that this version of time figures prominently in Lee's narrative and therefore lives on as an experience of narrative, it must also figure in the calculus that we use to explain the relationship between time and social identity in the early and antebellum nation: to gainsay this narrative's conceptualization of a time outside of time is to follow Douglass in suggesting that, properly speaking, time is always experienced as progress. Conceding that time itself is subject to transformation, in other words, entails accepting that the pluralization of time has extended beyond its simple division into progress and repetition.[33]

According to William Andrews's account of this subgenre of the African American life narrative, the spiritual autobiography was popular in the first half of the nineteenth century, both during and after the Second Great Awakening.[34] The title of Lee's account indicates that these narratives tend to review the linear progress of one person during a journey through the sins and degradations of the world, a journey that eventually sees the autobiographer spiritually converted, sanctified, and called to preach. Those texts indebted, like Lee's, to the precepts of Holiness Methodism usually narrate the life of the spiritual autobiographer in chronological order, dividing it into three distinct stages. Lee describes them as follows: "First, conviction for sin. Second, justification from sin. Third, the entire sanctification of the soul to God."[35] Katherine Clay Bassard, following Hayden White, suggests that the spiritual autobiographer of Holiness Methodism in this way "writ[es] autobiography as chronicle."[36] The details of the spiritual autobiographer's three-stage journey are framed, as Jean M. Humez explains, in the following terms:

Conversion and sanctification were the two primary experiences of spiritual rebirth officially sanctioned by Holiness Methodism. Usually preceded by an extended period of anguish, self-condemnation, and guilty feelings ("conviction for sin"), Methodist conversion [or "justification"] brought about instantaneous positive change in one's whole self-image and orientation toward ultimate reality, leaving one with the joyful sense of being a completely "new creature." "Sanctification" was a kind of redoubling of one's assurance of transformation by grace. This controversial second blessing signaled entrance into a state of Christian perfection, purity, holiness, or perfect love, in which one felt permanently beyond the reach of committing further intentional sin.[37]

Holiness Methodism imagines, then, a generally forward movement through the three stages of conversion—conviction, justification, sanctification—and (at least doctrinally) conceives spiritual growth as a version of progress that even Douglass would endorse.[38]

Lee's narrative opens, for example, with a description of her misfortune at having been sent at the young age of seven to live as a maid to a white family. Even as a youth, Lee finds herself inclined toward matters of the spirit but to her dismay discovers that the family employing her does not share her disposition. After growing increasingly distant from these people, Lee eventually lies to the mistress of the house, claiming that she has completed an assigned chore when in fact she has not. It is at this point that Lee first finds herself "moved" by "the spirit of God" and worried that she is a "wretched sinner."[39] She immediately resolves to mend her ways but finds she can do nothing to prevent her "heart" from growing "harder" to her mistress and her mistress's family. Even in the face of this failure to reform, however, the "spirit of the Lord never entirely for[sakes]" her "but continue[s] striving with [her], until gracious power convert[s] [her] soul."[40] Lee first acknowledges her sin at an early age, but a period of waxing and waning self-knowledge immediately follows. Lee's conviction, or full admission and acceptance of her sin, eventually comes at a Presbyterian revival. After hearing the minister read a Psalm about humanity's characteristic relationship to sin, Lee is "made . . . to feel in some measure, the weight of [her] sins, and sinful nature" and is in this moment convicted.[41] Not yet justified and thus relieved of the burden of her sin, Lee despairs of her future, eventually attempting suicide. This act results in a protracted illness and her exile to live with a family of irreligious Catholics. Even under the careful watch that attends her stay with this family, her "anxiety still continue[s] respecting [her] soul," and she tries to steal opportunities to "read in the Bible."[42] Yet, "observing this," the lady of the house "took the Bible . . . and hid it, giving . . . a novel in its stead—which when [she] perceived, [Lee] refused to read."[43]

One might argue on the one hand that Lee's narrative so far represents her experience as defined by the temporal desert we recognize from Gates's description. Her struggles with sin net her little more than suicidal thoughts and continued servitude with white families. Perhaps unsurprisingly, this is not the unassailable representation of progress Douglass desires from the African American life narrative, although it does confirm, in an oblique way, the idea that even free African Americans suffered under the kind of temporal deprivation Gates finds in the slave narrative. On the other hand, a kind of progress here mitigates the bleak prospect of Lee's life, most tellingly in the passages already referred to wherein Lee suggests that even in the midst of her apparently time-barren suffering, the "spirit of the Lord never entirely for[sakes] her, but continue[s] striving with [her], until gracious power convert[s] [her] soul." It would not be too much of a stretch to suggest that the language of striving and eventual conversion gestures to the eschatological prospect of time as progress. In this sense, we can argue that Lee vacillates between, in Douglass's (and Gates's) terms, both no experience of time and an experience of time as progress. However, Lee reveals a different vacillation between two kinds of time in her comments on her mistress's offer of a novel. Her account of refusing novel reading stages an explicit contrast between the worldly time of progress symbolized by the novel and the experience of time outside of time afforded by Bible reading. Where Douglass valorizes reading and writing of any kind, a valorization that has led to literacy being figured as one of the prime objects of nineteenth-century African American political desire, Lee paints a very different picture. For Lee, there is reading and writing, and then there is the Word. Lee's refusal suggests that where Bible reading facilitates an achronic communion with God, the novel represents a worldly experience of time as *mere* progress. Lee thus obliquely confirms that the novel may have been understood to provide an experience of time as progress, but Lee's preference for Bible reading also indicates that other kinds of reading facilitated other experiences of time. In this sense, simultaneity, as well as social identity and community, may have been more difficult to accomplish than generally imagined. According to Lee, the most popular artifact of Western print capitalism, the Bible, articulates a time of the spirit hostile to earthly imagined communities and their narrative instantiation.

Lee is finally justified, or forgiven of her sin, when, after casting about for a religious ministration that suits her character, she eventually discovers a group of like-minded people worshiping in what will shortly thereafter become an African Methodist Episcopal (AME) congregation. She explains that, while attending one of their meetings, "there appeared to *my* view, in the center of [my] heart *one* sin; and this was *malice*, against one particular individual, who had strove deeply to injure me, which I resented. At this discovery I said, *Lord* I forgive *every* creature. That instant, it appeared to me, as if a garment, which had entirely clothed my whole person, even to my fingers ends, split at the crown of my head, and was stripped away from me, passing like a shadow, from my sight—when the glory of God seemed to cover me in its stead."[44] Up until this point Lee's narrative primarily figures either "temporal deprivation" or, when it focuses on God's striving with Lee's soul, time as progress. But when this promised moment of conversion actually arrives, we find an experience of divine repetition through rebirth. Both Humez and Bassard read this, and other similar accounts of feeling stripped, for what they say about the racial politics of the period. Humez argues, for example, that the "new skin" accompanying conversion functions as a protective layer against white prejudice.[45] Bassard similarly claims that Lee's growing a new skin is not "a whitening of Lee but a reassigning of the meaning of her blackness. Having been 'clothed' in God's 'salvation,' Lee's (still) black skin is transformed from a sinful taint to a sign of God's glory."[46] These readings are suggestive, but when Lee states that she was "stripped" and then covered with the "glory of God," she seems very clearly to assert that she has been reborn into a prelapsarian state. Humez indicates in her description of the stages of Holiness Methodism that justification "leav[es] one with the joyful sense of being a completely 'new creature.'" But a "completely 'new creature'" in this tradition is, in fact, she who has been returned to an original perfection absent sin. Lee's narrative here should, then, not only be conceived as facilitating a secular experience of race. Equally important are its revelations about the impact of divine communion as understood by Lee: Lee frames her experience as an experience of return rather than as either the progress Douglass values or exclusively the experience of racialization that Bassard perceives. And she assumes that the spiritual autobiography amounts to a useful genre for transmitting that experience to others.

Keeping in mind the importance of the religious framework that shaded Lee's experience of time, we can see that in its account of the third and final stage of her spiritual journey, sanctification, Lee's narrative shows her experiencing her life as structured by neither progress nor repetition. Eventually realizing that the third and final stage of her journey awaits her, Lee remarks, "I began to feel now that my heart was not clean in [God's] sight; that there yet remained the roots of bitterness, which if not destroyed, would ere long sprout up from these roots, and overwhelm me in a new growth of the branches and brushwood of sin."[47] Here we find Lee threatened by the possibility that she might backslide in time, yet this is an experience wherein she would be "overwhelm[ed] in a new growth of the branches and brushwood of sin" developing out of the "roots of bitterness" remaining even after her justification. Lee commits herself to intensive prayer and eventually visits a local church. After a prolonged delay, sanctification finally arrives: "During this, I stood perfectly still, the tears rolling down in a flood from my eyes. So great was the joy, that it is past description. There is no language that can describe it, except that which was heard by St. Paul, when he was caught up to the third heaven, and heard words which it was not lawful to utter."[48] Lee emphasizes the fact that the language she hears, the communion she experiences, the place she visits cannot be represented, making her experience of time as progress appear irrelevant by comparison. In the end, Lee's unrepresentable experience of absolute communion with God in a time outside of time actually supplants her narrative of progress. Lee also indicates that writing cannot relay her experience of spiritual communion, of time outside of time. Any experience of textual inscription and decoding, save the Bible, involves a worldly experience of time as progress: thus her own experience, like St. Paul's, is "not lawful to utter," even in the book she presents as a faithful account of her spiritual journey.

The fact that progressive time no longer dominates Lee's experience of her life after this moment of sanctification—that progress from this point has indeed become undesirable—is reinforced when she recounts her decision to preach despite an AME ban on female ministers. Given the church's policy, Lee questions her calling and even considers that her inclination to preach might represent a departure from God's wishes. She is, however, reassured in her faith, and in her evangelical mission, by a vision:

[W]hile I wrestled with [the Lord] for the victory over this disposition to doubt whether I should persevere, there appeared a form of fire, about the size of a man's hand, as I was on my knees; at the same moment, there appeared to the eye of faith, a man robed in a white garment, from the shoulders down to the feet; from him a voice proceeded, saying: "Thou shalt never return from the cross." Since that time I have never doubted, but believe that god will keep me until the day of redemption. Now I could adopt the very language of St. Paul, and say nothing could have separated my soul from the love of god, which is in Christ Jesus. . . . From that time, 1807, until the present, 1833, I have not yet doubted the power and goodness of God to keep me from falling, through sanctification of the spirit and belief of the truth.[49]

Struggling with the fear that her calling to preach represents her fall from sanctification, Lee becomes convinced that the opposite is true. Once sanctified, Lee will "never return from the cross," never again succumb to the worldly experience of time as progress. Sanctification "signaled entrance into a state of Christian perfection, purity, holiness, or perfect love, in which one felt permanently beyond the reach of committing further intentional sin."[50] Rather than focusing, as Gates might, on the dates in this passage as signs of Lee's progress in time, we should, then, read Lee as suggesting that time as progress essentially stopped when she was sanctified. Her experience of time outside of time is permanent; the time of the unsanctified has, for her, ceased.

Although in this sense sanctification factors as the definitive moment of Lee's experience of time outside of time, we are given previews of it even earlier in her narrative. There are, of course, those moments when Lee gestures to the Bible as offering a privileged, direct link to God unmediated by the worldly experience of progressive time entailed in novel reading. Prior to her justification, moreover, a vision of Satan comes to Lee in the form of a dog, prompting her to reflect on the fate of those who are condemned to hell, a place that she fears she will visit if she continues to succumb to worldly temptation. Lee claims even at this early point that the "language" she might use to describe the fate of the damned is "too strong and expressive to be applied to any state of suffering in *time*. Were it to be thus applied, the reality could no where be found in human life; the consequence would be, that *this* scripture [i.e., the Biblical scripture relating the structure of hell] would be found a false testimony. But when made to apply to an *endless* state of perdition, in *eternity*, beyond the bounds of human life, then this language is found not to exceed our views of a state of *eternal* damnation."[51] Until this point in the narrative, representations of time as progress have dominated, as they will again shortly hereafter. But this passage interrupts these figurations of progress with an attempt to represent through elision an experience of time without change. Although language cannot capture the enormity and the paradox of this experience, Lee remains certain of its truth, a certainty that will be echoed later when she is sanctified. And although she explains that the fate of the damned cannot be represented "in time," she is really suggesting that it cannot be represented in a framework that conceives time as progress.[52]

In one of the more compelling readings of Lee's spiritual autobiography, Bassard acknowledges these periodic interruptions of time as progress, interruptions she claims look like interruptions only because they depart from the Anglo-Protestant tradition of structuring spiritual autobiographies as narratives of one individual's linear progress. For Bassard, these departures signal Lee's constant striving after religious and racial community. She argues that "Lee reinvents the traditional Anglo-Christian morphology of conversion by representing her conversion story as a search for religious community, culturally inscribed, even as the representations of the search for religious community transgress these narrative boundaries."[53] Lee stood at the "beginnings of the formation of African American community consciousness in the North following gradual emancipation."[54] Thus to view her journey as a strictly individualist undertaking in the tradition of white Protestants is to miss the point. Lee's peripatetic wanderings represent not only the urgings of the spirit but also her effort to find a secular home—a social identity, a community. Bassard, for example, offers her own reading of the moment that finds Lee justified and blessed with a new skin. She focuses on the fact that this transformation, this rebirth into a new skin is occasioned by Lee's finally finding her "people," a community whom she trusts. As Bassard reminds us, Lee introduces her account of her conviction by remarking that an African American cook in the house where she worked recommended that she attend a service at an AME church. Reluctant to visit because of this church's strict rules, Lee nevertheless decides to attend one of its services: "The man who was to speak in the afternoon of that day, was the Rev. Richard Allen, since bishop of the African Methodist Episcopals in America. During the labors of this man that afternoon, I had come to the conclusion, that this is the people to which my heart unites, and it so happened, that as soon as the service closed he invited such as felt a desire to flee the wrath to come, to unite on trial with them—I embraced the opportunity."[55] The emphasis here is, Bassard argues, at least as much on communion with one's fellow humans as it is on communion with the divine. Indeed, the communion with the divine that immediately follows, when Lee is born into her new skin, could not have happened without the support provided by Lee's "people."[56] Joycelyn Moody's reading of Lee's 1849 expanded spiritual autobiography, as well as that of Zilpha Elaw, adopts a similar stance. Moody distinguishes Lee's and Elaw's autobiographies from other spiritual writings in the Protestant tradition, which, she suggests, tend to emphasize the spiritual emergence of the individual and the sense that to inhabit the place of the sanctified soul is actually to break with family and community. Moody connects these nineteenth-century African American women instead to the early Puritans: "In their attention to race, gender, and nation, Lee's and Elaw's respective narratives depart from traditional early American spiritual autobiographies. Reflecting the Puritan resistance to individuality, each narrator resists distinguishing themselves from other members of the religious community, the African American community, and the women's community to which she belongs, to assert instead a collective identity."[57] Here the spiritual autobiography, an ontogenetic narrative, is reframed as a story of the emergence of a communal identity, or a narrative of phylogenesis.

In Bassard's and Moody's readings, this historical moment is rewritten in what should by now be a recognizable fashion—that is, as the moment when supralocal identity came to dominate. Thus Bassard suggests that "[t]he search for religious instruction and a church 'home' . . . becomes a search for community, for a 'people.'"[58] This perspective underplays the fact that Lee's ostensible "search for community, for a 'people,'" is accompanied by a series of deeply anticommunitarian experiences of time outside of time. While Bassard may be correct in stating that Lee's spiritual autobiography differs in its representation of chronology from similar white American texts, her perspective minimizes some important points of resemblance. In both traditions, the moment of communion with the divine, of time outside of time, actually severs the spiritual autobiographer's connection to other humans. Simultaneity with others is periodically impossible; so too are secular community and social identity. Lee's *Life* is, then, not (or at least not only) a story of social identity, and to read it as if it were such a story is to focus on a kind of identity formation Lee ultimately devalues. It is, in other words, to overwrite Lee's narrative and accommodate it to the contemporary critical preoccupation with the emergence of generic identity in progressive time. The extent to which Lee's spiritual autobiography confounds such an emphasis on community and identity is indicated by the fact that women preachers such as Lee encountered intense resistance to their ministries, specifically because they relied so much on divine communion, or time outside of time, for their own authority. As Humez explains, the AME male hierarchy was suspicious of preachers such as Lee, and not only because they were women. Against the growing trend in the AME church, these women preachers defended the integrity and authority of direct spiritual communion with the divine, perhaps because they had limited access to literacy and scriptural training. These women "stood staunchly on the claim of direct inspiration by the Holy Spirit as the primary, if not the *only*, credentials that ought to be required for spiritual leadership."[59] They undertook this in the face of a church "attempt[ing] to restrain or eliminate altogether those ecstatic or spirit-inspired practices from informal Afro-American religion that they saw as 'extravagant,' 'heathenish,' and mere 'baptized superstition.'"[60]

Lee's references to St. Paul make explicit the fact that the experience and authority these women value is an anti-identitarian, anticommunitarian experience of divine as opposed to secular time. Recall, for example, that when Lee describes her experience of sanctification, she writes, "During this, I stood perfectly still, the tears rolling down in a flood from my eyes. So great was the joy, that it is past description. There is no language that can describe it, except that which was heard by St. Paul, when he was caught up to the third heaven, and heard words which it was not lawful to utter."[61] As Frances Smith Foster suggests, "In all essential features, *The Life and Religious Experience of Jarena Lee* . . . conform[s] to the basic patterns of American spiritual autobiography as derived from the New Testament example of Saul of Tarsus."[62] Foster explains this story as follows: "During a journey to Damascus, Saul, the persecutor of Christians, is metamorphosed into Paul, the principal founder of Christian theology. . . . Though traveling with a large entourage, all of whom heard the judging question: 'why persecutest thou me?' Saul alone saw the 'blinding light.' From this experience Saul temporarily lost his sight, his authority, and his direction only to emerge with a new vision, a new name, and a new mission."[63] In her discussion of one of the earliest African American autobiographies, *A Narrative of the Lord's Wonderful Dealings with John Marrant, a Black* (1788), Foster also explains that during Marrant's spiritual communion, his "companions, like Saul's, witnessed the effects of his encounter with God but did not experience it themselves."[64] If the stories of Saul/Paul and Marrant serve as any guide to Lee's narrative, and Foster suggests that they should, then Lee's narrative will look much less like a story of the search for, and discovery of, community than Bassard might hope. In both cases, spiritual communion marks these men's difference from, rather than their resemblance to or identification with, their traveling companions. The experience of time outside of time described in the New Testament story of Saul/Paul, in John Marrant's *Narrative*, and in Lee's narrative represents one of the strongest barriers to secular community and to social identity conceivable.

Looking back over Lee's *Life*, then, we can see its important departures from what Douglass and Gates might ask us to expect from the African American life narrative. Its early stages appear to figure an experience of time as either progress or repetition, but when we turn to the third stage of Lee's journey, "sanctification," we find something entirely different: an experience of time outside of time. Even the first two stages of Lee's narrative can be parsed to reveal a variegated experience of time that incorporates all three of these possibilities: although these two earlier stages form a composite picture of progress on the road to sanctification, this apparent progress is itself shot through with a series of elliptical gestures that represent moments when Lee comprehends an eternity she is nevertheless unable to represent in writing. As William Andrews suggests, "Ample evidence in the Afro-American spiritual autobiography tradition testifies to the fact that . . . visionary experiences [arose] from intervals when God str[uck] the sinner 'dead' to all but heavenly revelations."[65] Much like sanctification, then, the early stages of trials, struggles, and visitations from God remove the spiritual autobiographer from a primary experience of time as progress. Given this variability, it is not precise enough to say that the spiritual auto-biography represents an experience of time as progress that culminates in spiritual communion in a time outside of time. As with Douglass's and Northup's narratives, we see not the deprivation of time, but rather an ex-cess of coextensive times.

Fictions of the Messiah

Like his other life narratives, Frederick Douglass's biographical long fiction about the life of Madison Washington, "The Heroic Slave" (1853), belies the notions that time has a natural state and that the slave was deprived of time. This fictional account of the leader of a real shipboard slave revolt frames Washington's struggle as an American struggle and borrows heavily from the language of American nationalism. Literary history would suggest that as a result "The Heroic Slave" contributed to the growth of the same na-tional community it sought to indict. In this reading, "The Heroic Slave" is tragically ironic. It invites African American and white readers alike to inhabit an identity category—the "American"—constituted through racist disidentification with black people. Douglass's story certainly looks like a tribute to Madison Washington's struggle against slavery and the nation it-self. However, American history would argue that the "trope of revolution-ary struggle" at the center of "The Heroic Slave" actually serves to trap Af-rican Americans in an identity based on the exclusion of blackness.[66] In at least one important respect, this argument resembles the Gatesian reading of Douglass's autobiographical writing. It suggests that this particular fic-tional life narrative contributed to the transformation of identity in the an-tebellum United States by precipitating identification with the American national community and a concurrent disidentification with local commu-nities. In other words, it reads Douglass's critique of American slavery as if it actually strengthens American identity by encouraging African Americans to route their equity claims through (white American) nationalistic rheto-ric. American literary history sees no space "outside" America in Douglass's text. This reading of "The Heroic Slave" ignores the "deprivation of time in the life of the slave," but it nevertheless reinforces intractable assump-tions about the offerings of progress, which, as we have seen, follow from equally tenacious ideas about homogeneous empty time and its relationship to identity.

Yet Douglass actually reforms the rhetoric of American nationalism in "The Heroic Slave" by linking the trope of revolutionary struggle endemic to American nationalism with the claim that revolution brings a kind of messianic time. In so doing, "The Heroic Slave" interrupts the logic that imagines for everyone everywhere a destiny of abstract social identity. "The Heroic Slave" contends that revolutionary social upheaval transforms time in such a way that progress is both impossible and undesirable; it figures a revolutionary messianic time that commingles past, present, and future and conceives a certain "solidarity of those born later with those who have preceded them, with all those whose bodily or personal integrity has been violated at the hands of other human beings."[67] Douglass's fiction thus articulates a socially produced time that is in no way empty, as we will see—a time that, like laboring time, undermines the notion of identity based in temporal simultaneity. Here, as in Walter Benjamin's discussion of messianic time, "[t]he profane illumination caused by shock, like the mystical union with the appearance of the Messiah, forces a cessation, crystallization, of the momentary event."[68] As Svetlana Boym describes it, in this Benjaminian version of messianic time, "Past, Present, and Future [are] superimposing" events: "[E]very epoch dreams the next one and in doing so revives the one before it."[69]

Douglass's tale opens by framing its protagonist, Madison Washington, as the heir to a specifically American tradition of political action and revolutionary commitment:

The State of Virginia is famous in American annals for the multitudinous array of her statesmen and heroes. She has been dignified by some the mother of statesmen. History has not been sparing in recording their names, or in blazoning their deeds. . . . By some strange neglect, *one* of the truest, manliest, and bravest of her children,—one who, in after years, will, I think, command the pen of genius to set his merits forth, holds now no higher place in the records of that grand old Commonwealth than is held by a horse or an ox. Let those account for it who can, but there stands the fact, that a man who loved liberty as well as did Patrick Henry,—who deserved it as much as Thomas Jefferson,—and who fought for it with a valor as high, an arm as strong, and against odds as great, as he who led all the armies of the American colonies through the great war for freedom and independence, lives now only in the chattel records of his native State.[70]

Reinserting Madison Washington, an African American, in a carefully chosen line of white American forefathers, Douglass highlights the unequal fortunes of African Americans and white Americans when it comes to national history. This gesture recalls Douglass's objection elsewhere to the absence of birth dates in slave culture, criticizing as it does the historiography of the United States for obscuring African American revolutionaries, such as Washington, and their place in time.

"The Heroic Slave" introduces a more radical perspective on time and history, however, when it later represents Tom Grant, the white first mate aboard the slave ship *Creole*, describing Washington's part in the shipboard slave revolt for which he was known. Sitting with several friends, Grant explains how it was that the white crew was overpowered: " 'The leader of the mutiny in question was just as shrewd a fellow as ever I met in my life, and was as well fitted to lead in a dangerous enterprise as any one white man in ten thousand. The name of this man, strange to say, (ominous of greatness,) was MADISON WASHINGTON. In the short time he had been on board, he had secured the confidence of every officer. The negroes fairly worshiped him. His manner and bearing were such, that no one could suspect him of a murderous purpose.' "[71] Grant next recounts that after using a hidden file to free the slaves on board from their chains, Washington led a revolt against the white captain and crew of the ship, some of whom the slaves killed in the first few minutes of the uprising. With the captain nearly dead and the remaining white crew lodged out of reach in the rigging of the *Creole*, Grant proceeded to order his crewmen to leave their nests and continue to fight the slaves. Grant next recalls that after addressing Washington as a " 'murderous villain,' " Grant advanced to attack him. Washington responded both physically and rhetorically, replying to the specific charge of murder: " 'You call me a *black murderer*. I am not a murderer. God is my witness that LIBERTY, not *malice*, is the motive for this night's work. I have done no more to those dead men yonder, than they would have done to me in like circumstances. We have struck for our freedom, and if a true man's heart be in you, you will honor us for the deed. We have done that which you applaud your fathers for doing, and if we are murderers, *so were they*.' "[72] At this point, Grant remarks to his listeners: " 'I felt little disposition to reply to this impudent speech. By heaven, it disarmed me. The fellow loomed up before me. I forgot his blackness in the dignity of his manner, and the eloquence of his speech. It seemed as if the souls of both the great dead (whose names he bore) had entered him.' "[73] On the one hand, this passage reports both Washington's eloquence and Grant's failure to comprehend this revolutionary's humanity. Even as Grant obliquely compliments Washington, he does so with the racist suggestion that he "forgot [Washington's] blackness in the dignity of his manner, and the eloquence of his speech." In this context, it appears that for Tom Grant, at least, those "great dead (whose names he bore)" have supplanted Madison Washington and obscured his heroism. At the same time, Washington's closing invocation of "your fathers" imagines a very different relationship between him and those "great dead." Washington's reply proposes that in the moment of revolutionary action, he radically bridged the gap between him and the Revolutionary forefathers whose names he carries; Washington nominates himself the contemporary and equal of these "great dead," not their legatee or vessel. When Washington remarks that "if we are murderers, *so were they*," the contrasting verb tenses detract from their proximity, but this passage effectively positions the white revolutionaries of 1776 and the revolutionary African American slave of 1841 as contemporaries. "The Heroic Slave" suggests that these men's shared desire for "LIBERTY" and willingness to be revolutionaries for it dissolves all temporal barriers: all revolutionaries for liberty are contemporaries. Thus it appears that "the souls of both the great dead (whose names he bore) had entered" Washington. In this aspect, Maggie Sale is right to claim that by "imagining a life history and creating a subject-position for the rebel leader, Madison Washington," Douglass "challenge[s] U.S. Americans to imagine the action of the *Creole* rebels, especially Madison Washington, as like that of the founding fathers."[74] But her contention that this story "assert[s] the equivalence of the struggle of the enslaved and that of the Revolution" is only partially correct.[75] These two struggles are more than equivalent. Under revolutionary messianic time, they are one and the same. When Sale claims that Douglass "figure[s] Madison Washington and his fellow rebels as within a tradition established by the founders," the dislocation implied in "tradition" distracts from the fact that revolutionary messianic time renders all just struggles contemporaneous. In Douglass's representation of revolutionary time, "tradition" is condensed into a single point of revolutionary change.

Paul Gilroy understands the apparent death drive marking Madison Washington's revolutionary resistance aboard the *Creole* as the product of a specific "revolutionary eschatology" unaccounted for in Sale's focus on the "trope of revolutionary struggle." Gilroy claims that like other aspects of black Atlantic culture, "The Heroic Slave" records a desire for "freedom through death" that appears to capitulate to Christianity's emphasis on the afterlife. But Gilroy also explains that we might do better to view this death-drive as a secular phenomenon of revolutionary consciousness. Illuminating Washington's revolutionary act, Gilroy explains:

This inclination towards death and away from bondage is fundamental. It reminds us that in the revolutionary eschatology which helps to define this primal history of modernity, whether apocalyptic or redemptive, it is the moment of jubilee that has the upper hand over the pursuit of utopia by rational means. The discourse of black spirituality which legitimises these moments of violence possesses a utopian truth content that projects beyond the limits of the present. The repeated choice of death rather than bondage articulates a principle of negativity that is opposed to the formal logic and rational calculation characteristic of modern western thinking.[76]

In Gilroy's estimation, although slaves failed to pursue "utopia by rational means" in the nineteenth century, they correctly identified a version of freedom to be delivered in a "jubilee" that follows from revolutionary actions such as those depicted in "The Heroic Slave." Read in this light, the freedom Madison Washington secures in his revolution against slavery flows not only to those who live in the present moment but also to those who inhabit the past. In this "revolutionary eschatology," revolution precipitates jubilee—a radical experience of time that does not segregate the past and future. "The Heroic Slave" argues that revolution collapses those temporal distinctions—past, present, and future—emblematic of Western thinking. If "jubilee" is the product of Madison Washington's act of overpowering his legal masters, then revolutionary resistance has forced time itself to change. Just as white men's desire to accumulate capital produces laboring time, so, too, can revolution produce messianic time. Walter Benjamin's comments on "Judgment Day" also place the kind of time Douglass here imagines in a larger context. In his "Theses on the Philosophy of History," Benjamin writes, "To be sure, only a redeemed mankind receives the fullness of its past—which is to say, only for a redeemed mankind has its past become citable in all its moments. Each moment it has lived becomes a *citation à l'ordre du jour*—and that day is Judgment Day."[77] The moment of revolution that Douglass describes in "The Heroic Slave" precipitates a kind of "Judgment Day," not only freeing those who are in bondage in the present but also condemning those who currently enslave them. Douglass and Benjamin indicate that true revolution brings the past into the present in order to effect an unbending, universal justice for all times. The moment of true revolution is in no way homogeneous or empty but unimaginably full; the moment of revolution conjures all moments at once and distributes universal justice. Douglass figures this collapse of progressive time and the advent of revolutionary messianic time most forcefully in his comments on Madison Washington and his "great dead" contemporaries. But he also portrays related transformations of time throughout "The Heroic Slave."

At one point, for example, Douglass describes the conditions that attend his own effort to reclaim Washington from obscurity. As he considers the work that he hopes "The Heroic Slave" will accomplish, Douglass writes the following of Madison Washington: "Glimpses of this great character are all that can now be presented. He is brought to view only by a few transient incidents, and these afford but partial satisfaction. Like a guiding star on a stormy night, he is seen through the parted clouds and the howling tempests; or, like the gray peak of a menacing rock on a perilous coast, he is seen by the quivering flash of angry lightning, and he again disappears covered with mystery."[78] Under such conditions, Douglass's efforts at historical documentation strike him as almost futile: "Curiously, earnestly, anxiously we peer into the dark, and wish even for the blinding flash, or the light of northern skies to reveal him. But alas! he is still enveloped in darkness, and we return from the pursuit like a wearied and disheartened mother, (after a tedious and unsuccessful search for a lost child,) who returns weighed down with disappointment and sorrow. Speaking of marks, traces, possibles, and probabilities, we come before our readers."[79] The first paragraph finds Douglass yearning for the clarity of historical vision that only revolution affords. Given that "clouds" and "howling tempests" obscure the past and the future, Douglass seeks a force that will part those clouds and bring an illuminating flash of lightning. Madison Washington's revolutionary action serves as the "blinding flash" that closes the distance between Washington and his revolutionary forbears. In a similar moment, "The Heroic Slave" depicts Washington in the South before his attempts to escape slavery caused him to be sold and sent to sea on the *Creole*, a ship servicing the internal slave trade. At this point in the narrative, Washington is still hatching his plans to escape from plantation slavery. As he delivers an open-air soliloquy on his predicament, the narrator describes Washington nearing the brink of desperation only to become reinvigorated as he glimpses the future: "The hope of freedom seemed to sweeten, for a season, the bitter cup of slavery, and to make it, for a time, tolerable; for when in the very whirlwind of anguish,—when his heart's cord seemed screwed up to snapping tension, hope sprung up and soothed his troubled spirit."[80] Douglass imagines a future capable of rescuing Washington from dejection. Indeed, Washington recovers as that future intrudes on the present, transforming his present under slavery.

A later scene finds Mr. Listwell, a friendly white Quaker who serves as the ubiquitous witness to Washington's plight, resting at home on a stormy evening. This evening comes "[f]ive years after the . . . singular occurrence" of Mr. Listwell's having secretly witnessed Washington deliver his private soliloquy on his escape plans.[81] Describing the tempestuous night outside, the narrator muses, "A whole wilderness of thought might pass through one's mind during such an evening. The smouldering embers, partaking of the spirit and the restless night, became fruitful of varied and fantastic pictures, and revived many bygone scenes and old impressions."[82] Mr. Listwell's barking dog interrupts these "varied and fantastic pictures" and signals the arrival of Madison Washington at the Listwell home. Not realizing that Mr. Listwell knows he is a fugitive, Washington requests shelter. Upon Washington's arrival, Mr. Listwell reveals his peculiar state of mind that evening, commenting to his wife, "'I am glad we did not go to bed earlier,—I have felt all the evening as if somebody would be here to-night.'"[83] After welcoming Washington to his home, Mr. Listwell tells Washington how he had overheard his soliloquy on freedom. He closes with the following: "'Ever since that morning,' said Mr. Listwell, 'you have seldom been absent from my mind, and though now I did not dare to hope that I should ever see you again, I have often wished that such might be my fortune; for, from that hour, your face seemed to be daguerreotyped on my memory.'"[84] In the context of this work's larger claims, these passing comments on foreknowledge and memory resonate as the revolutionary messianic time consciousness we have been considering. A passage appearing only a few paragraphs after Mr. Listwell's reference to Washington's having been "daguerreotyped on [his] memory" secures this point. First describing his escape from slavery, Washington eventually tells of the fire that drove him from his hiding place in the woods and prompted his journey to the Listwell home: "'I will not harrow up your feelings by portraying the terrific scene of this awful conflagration. There is nothing to which I can liken it. It was horribly and indescribably grand. The whole world seemed on fire, and it appeared to me that the day of judgment had come; that the burning bowels of the earth had burst forth, and that the end of all things was at hand.'"[85] Washington is a witness to "jubilee," or in New Testament terms, "Judgment Day," because his decision to break for freedom places him in a unique position: "the end of all things" follows, here, from Washington's revolutionary activity.[86] In this sense, "The Heroic Slave" joins Gilroy's "revolutionary eschatology" to Sale's "trope of revolutionary struggle" in a way that offers an uncommon but essential take on the mechanics of time and identity in the nineteenth century. Where tradition considers messianic faith a passive waiting for the moment when the Messiah shifts power from one quarter to another, Douglass suggests that revolutionary action creates a temporality that ensures power will be justly redistributed by bringing all moments into the present. Revolution brings messianic time, or "jubilee," and so allows for a total view of history that underwrites innately reasonable judgments. If considered in relation to the "awful conflagration" that Madison Washington describes, then Washington's unexpected resurgence of hope, the return of "bygone scenes" at the Listwell home, and Mr. Listwell's premonition about Washington's arrival all read as articulations of the messianic time that defines revolutionary action in Douglass's account.

The presence of revolutionary messianic time in Douglass's "The Heroic Slave," as well as its presence in other life narratives, should be read in two ways. This messianic temporality offered hope in a time of bleak prospects for African Americans. Slaveholders and the racist state sought to deny African Americans access to the past and the future, making them "creatures of the present." Yet this literature conceives of an experience of time, precipitated by revolutionary action, that has the potential to reconnect African Americans to their ancestors and descendants in diaspora—not through an imagined experience of simultaneity but rather through a much more significant moment of shared justice. In an interesting way, this way of conceptualizing time also expands the list of potential candidates for inclusion in the genealogy of African Americans so as to include figures typically thought of as white. Perhaps most important, this experience of time envisions the advent of just and reasonable social structures at a moment when that possibility seemed at best a remote one. At the same time, revolutionary messianic time's copresence with the other modalities of time found in the life narrative returns us to what we continuously encounter in this period's literature: the failure of fraternity that such a conflict of time impels. This literature suggests that, rather than simply alternating among different modalities of time, African Americans lived a conflict of time, one in which they experienced time as simultaneously progressive and recursive; one in which the past and present were both the same and different. The simultaneity of experience that was required for a holistic sense of community was absent. This literature suggests, in other words, that antebellum African America had both more and less in terms of time than we thought.

In the light of Madison Washington's fight for liberty, Irving's and Hawthorne's allusions to the historical afterimage attain new significance. Here a surplus of time yields a political subject who at his moment of greatest visibility grows suddenly indistinct: Madison Washington's heroic actions and his heroic names collaborate to forestall the consolidation of his social identity. To a degree, Tom Grant's racialism explains this obfuscation of Washington by those names that he bears. As Hawthorne's and Irving's images would suggest, however, the image of a composite human figure constituted out of several discordant orders of time haunts this period's literature. In this respect, Douglass's Washington—a product of several different orders of time who never quite rises to legibility—signifies the heroic possibility of those who are torn and divided by modernity's unequal times.

Epilogue
The Spatial Turn and the Scale of Freedom

> *[T]he challenge of the global is also that of rethinking time.*
> —Ian Baucom, *"Globalit, Inc.; Or, the Cultural Logic of Global Literary Studies"*

It has been intriguing to watch the spatial turn barnstorm the academy, but perhaps it is time to ask why the embrace has been so quick and eager. Why is it that the accommodation of old modes of humanistic study to this new one has proceeded so smoothly? What makes it possible for new curricular programs at the undergraduate and graduate levels to have such remarkable traction? In these final pages, I suggest very briefly that the answer might lie with the particular logic of social becoming that the spatial turn permits. I also propose a short list of questions that will need to be asked as we find our way through the spatial turn. As curricula and departments are restructured according to its demands, it might be worth asking: How will postcolonial studies fit into the new spatial scales overtaking literary studies? What does the term "print culture" signify in the context of the new spatial scales? What role will genre criticism play in our research and our teaching of them? Most significantly, does shifting the axis or scale of an analysis necessarily displace the logic of cultural national-ism? On this last issue, most advocates of the spatial turn would answer in the affirmative. Yet I offer the cautionary suggestion that if the spatial turn ignores Ian Baucom's injunction to integrate a "rethinking [of] time" into its basic premises, then it might turn out that shifting the scale and axis of the humanities effectively restabilizes the identitarian logic of nationalism. Why worry about nationalism if we're not talking about nations? Because it just might happen that the spatial turn winds up being national identity's new island in the stream.

The Human in Time

Much of the recent work encouraging the adoption of new spatial scales for the study of literature claims to move the field forward in two ways. According to these arguments, the spatial turn offers both an empirical improvement on and an ideological rupture with the traditional nation-based study of literature and the humanities. On the issue of the empirical, the assumption is that the national frame is simply inadequate to the task of understanding the global flows that define modernity and even the premodern. In terms of ideology, the spatial turn proposes to break with the nationalism of past intellectual formations. And as Pheng Cheah succinctly puts it, "We live in an era when nationalism seems to be out of favor in academia."[1] In a recent special issue of *PMLA* titled "Globalizing Literary Studies," Paul Jay touches on both of these issues. On the one hand, Jay indicates that the long-standing cultural nationalism of literary study obscures a long history of global intercultural engagement. He calls for a less rigid boundary separating the present as an era of globalization from the assumed national integrity of the past. Echoing Wai Chee Dimock's arguments in *Through Other Continents*, he writes, "We need to bring [the] transnational perspective to how we present the history of literature in the West, moving away from a traditional division of discrete national literatures into ossified literary-historical periods and giving the history of global expansion, trade, and intercultural exchange precedence in our curriculum over the mapping of an essentially aestheticized national character."[2] In a familiar refrain, he also offers that "the structure of American literary studies in United States universities has always been informed by a broadly nationalist ideal."[3] Jay dates globalization to the early modern period, suggesting that the very idea of a national literature is and always has been bankrupt, and he also proposes that we "ought to focus less on identifying what seems inherently English or American in the literatures we teach and write about and more on understanding the functional relation between literature and the nation-state, how literary writing has been theorized and politicized in efforts to define and empower nation-states, especially from the Enlightenment onward."[4] The spatial turn—realized here as a global literary studies—presents itself as a fresh alternative to these problems of nation-based thinking and as a passageway to a broader scale of freedom. There is some wiggle room here on one of the major issues introduced by this imperative: Were these merely "efforts" to empower nation-states, or did these efforts succeed? As is often the case in such arguments, that specific question is left for another day. Yet the primary message seems clear. A global literary studies will produce a kind of empirical clarity that will, in turn, give the lie to nationalisms past and present. If the nation ever was, then it will no longer be if global studies has its way. These figments of our collective imagination will dissolve when faced with the empirical fact of globality. If I exaggerate the extent of the claims being made for the spatial turn, then I do not do so by much.

The particular rhetoric of global humanism endorsed by such views is strong enough to motivate Pheng Cheah to attempt to countercheck its cosmopolitanist intent. In *Inhuman Conditions*, Cheah argues that the new emphasis on global studies revives a transcendental imaginary inhospitable to the very work of identifying specific conflicts and conjunctures that a more politically engaged version of the spatial turn would seek to enact. The political-economic formation of globalization and the academic formation of global studies, Cheah argues, complement each other. Together, they figure the nation as the particular and provincial site of antihumanism in contrast to the universal humanism of the category of the global. The most sophisticated accounts of the global seek to avoid this trap by presenting literary and other forms of culture as registering intercultural flow, contact, and exchange. (To the credit of those Americanists working in border and hemispheric studies, it is this more sophisticated approach that has so far predominated in this particular subfield. Here literature and other forms of culture witness the nation's failure to draw firm boundaries around itself.) As Cheah explains, culture is in this analytic an unbounded force; it does not respect national boundaries. This is fine and good, but as Cheah also argues, this interest in cross-border analysis has the potential to reframe these global flows as sites of liberation that engender and endorse human fellow feeling and a cosmopolitan political consciousness. Freed of the specifying constraints of the national, that is, literature and culture can be repositioned as the vehicle of a global political consciousness facilitative of a revival of unselfconscious humanism. This latter inclination mirrors the rhetoric of economic globalization's sponsors: both the process and its study carry a promise of emancipation. Although American literary studies has for the most part resisted the surging interest in a reconstructed political cosmopolitanism, favoring instead sites of conflict and contrast, there is a common intellectual watershed connecting contemporary Americanists to the cosmopolitanists. That connection is the idea of transcending the local.

As Cheah argues, the desire for an emancipating global humanism has deep roots. They extend back to Kant's desire to achieve a human culture and a study of the humanities capable of supporting a global human empathy based on the transcendence of particular local cultural features and the articulation of a universally shared culture of the human.[5] Although Kant's notion of a cosmopolitan human culture has been revived in recent years, Cheah suggests that its investment in transcendence misunderstands the real possibilities for a truly human culture. He emphasizes that Kant's framework for cosmopolitan humanism is not only ahistorical; it is antihistorical. Rather than the salutary interest in contrasts and conflicts that a vigorous study of global culture would bring forward, the Kantian view would encourage a cosmopolitan humanism that hinges on experiences that transcend space and time. This particular version of the human can be achieved only through a transcendence of the given conditions of a specific spatiotemporal location and by coming to recognize those common qualities of human intellection that exist across time and space in all locations— conditions that provide for the exercise of a socially binding form of judgment that Kant names the *sensus communis*. For Cheah, the preferred alternative to the Kantian framework should be clear. Rather than making transcendence of the local into a condition for achieving a cosmopolitan humanism, we should identify the finite historical conditions of a given moment as "the inhuman conditions of humanity."[6] In other words, rather than focus on human culture as an arena for achieving the transcendence of our given conditions, Cheah calls for an immanent humanism in which what is best for all humanity can only emerge from what *already is*—from the complex of *what is given*. Here the human emerges from an engagement with the full conditions of difference that define a given moment. For Cheah, then, the scale of human freedom always has finite determinate coordinates; the merely conjectural free space of the transcendental has no role in his version of humanism. There is no liberation from the nation into a larger scale of freedom associated with (but irreducible to) the globe; for Cheah, freedom is achieved in and through the given conditions that define the human condition.

I would add one significant point to Cheah's otherwise convincing critique. As this book's readings argue, an expanded sense of what constitutes the inhuman conditions of humanity in the era of modernity will have to contend with the fact that those conditions do not emerge from a single now. This is another way of saying that if the "given conditions" of humanity are immanent rather than transcendent—in rather than out of time— then any proper understanding of the human will have to contend with the fact that among the constituting conditions of the human is a time that is out of joint. Moreover, if under these circumstances the human is the sum of all that is and has been, as Cheah argues, then it will in some respects amount to a sum of different ways of being in time. For this and other reasons, Baucom's "Globalit, Inc." is one of the more cautious contributions to the *PMLA* special issue on globalization in which his and Paul Jay's essays appear. Unlike most of the other contributors, Baucom lingers over the question of whether "globalization does and will entail the liberation or the erasure of difference."[7] As he explains, this question emerges from one of the most resilient critiques of globalization as economic practice. The perceived threat of globalization figured in references to the growth of transnational capital and the outsourcing of jobs to the global South is that globalization will level the cultural and economic playing field in more bad ways than good ones. However, Baucom approaches the question of globalization's relationship to difference from a slightly altered angle. For him, the difference that matters—the difference whose character scholars must protect from erasure by the rhetoric of globalization—is the difference that is "the brokenness of time, the heterochronic disturbances that perturb the synchronized tickings of global time."[8] Against similitude, universal equivalency, and simultaneity, which both economic globalization and global studies fetishize, Baucom poses the disjointed nature of time in modernity, and he calls for a scholarship of the humanities that elaborates Cheah's inhuman conditions of humanity as defined in large part by the "heterochronic disturbances . . . of time." This is exactly right.

The Atlantic Promise

If a cosmopolitical global studies has made few inroads into American literary studies, then the same cannot be said of the transatlantic turn. It seems so obvious, after all, and it seems to illuminate so much about literatures in English. It is also here, perhaps, that the particular logic of social becoming I would identify with nationalism has most successfully staked its claim. One sees the signs of this success in a growing sentiment articulated on the first page of an important recent book by Christopher L. Miller, *The French Atlantic Triangle: Literature and Culture of the Slave Trade*: "As a subject of inquiry," Miller writes, "the slave trade cannot help but cast a horrific, negative light on the vogue in postcolonial studies for the celebration of encounter, movement, and hybridity."[9] Here Miller names what seems to be a broad and growing consensus: postcolonial studies is (and always was) a problem. Although the precise objects of scrutiny are unidentified, one can surmise the targets: Homi Bhabha, Gayatri Spivak, and Paul Gilroy are the most likely candidates. The accusation against the mode of scholarship that these names have come to symbolize goes something like this: Postcolonial studies ignores the unequal nature of power, preferring instead to "celebrate" minor infractions against the rule of law, economic deprivation, and other forms of injustice. It overinvests in trivial modes of resistance that obscure the pain, death, and deprivation visited upon subaltern subjects. It tells us nothing about the real lives of the people who endured these forms of deprivation, and it distracts us from the work of specifying the discursive frameworks that maintain those conditions. It holds out the promise of freedom where there is none. Worst of all, perhaps, it is insufficiently historical. These standard complaints represent some of the unfinished business of literary studies, and they need to be addressed directly in the context of the spatial turn. I hazard the suggestion that a little more attention to hybridity and postcoloniality might be just what the spatial turn needs. I also propose that a rethinking of certain assumptions about time that underlie the spatial turn will go a long way toward bringing that needed attention to bear.

Consider, for example, Laura Doyle's recent magnum opus, *Freedom's Empire: Race and the Rise of the Novel in Atlantic Modernity, 1640–1940*, which opens by locating the origins of modern racial thought in the seventeenth-century English Civil Wars. According to Doyle, this moment saw the emergence of a print-based discourse of Anglo-Saxonism that encouraged a broad sense that whites had rights. To the extent that Doyle figures race as a compensatory replacement for modernity's dislocations and identitarian losses, her account mirrors the structure of other similar studies placing the origins of Atlantic racialism much later—Dana Nelson's *National Manhood*, for example, or Ezra Tawil's *The Making of Racial Sentiment*. Starting in the early 1600s, Doyle argues, Parliament began to encourage an institutionalized antiquarianism that it hoped would establish its rights vis-à-vis the king by demonstrating the importance of councils to Saxon governance and the priority of self-sovereignty to the formation of the English people as a whole. As the Puritan Revolution gathered force in England, the rhetoric of liberty fashioned out of this Anglo-Saxonist antiquarianism began to work its way downward to the lower reaches of society. According to Doyle, "Because the Long Parliament had not immediately replaced the Star Chamber with any equivalent censorship organ, there circulated increasing numbers of polemical newspapers, pamphlets, and petitions that eventually made it impossible for Cromwell or Parliament or the new merchants to maintain control of the liberty discourse."[10] This spread of a radical liberty-seeking print culture encouraged not only dissenting men but also elite women and the lower orders to take up "the same Saxonist rhetoric of liberty that the Parliamentarians . . . had come to use."[11] This rise of a liberty-seeking print culture eventuated in the still resonant idea that print culture is a natural agent of liberty—a view that historians of the book increasingly (and rightly) associate with technological determinism. As Doyle has it, moreover, the Putney debaters "stumbled on" the pressing questions that haunt all such modern discourses of liberty: Just what is it that grounds the claim to individual sovereignty? By what order of authority is it determined that the self-sovereign individual is so? According to Doyle, the answer lay more or less ready to hand: race. The previous fifty years of cumulative Anglo-Saxonism had nurtured the idea that the English share a common historical heritage. The English heart is a white heart that manifests itself in a love of liberty—a love that in turn entitles the English to their liberty.

That white English heart—my term, not Doyle's—turns out to be extraordinarily important. As such hearts are wont to do, it just cannot let its body stay at home. The English love of liberty licenses and even compels the English to do liberty's work. Some people call that work genocide; the English called it liberation. Because of their propulsive liberty-loving hearts, the English were required to be constantly in motion. Imperial (mis)adventure gets rewritten here as moral mission; modernity's forces of displacement—the rise of mercantilism, the economic decimation of the rural counties—are the necessary consequence of freedom's march. Those displacements involving an Atlantic crossing turn out to be perhaps the most important, because they get figured in the novel of Atlantic modernity as precipitants of a racial self-possession: these are incidents wherein itinerant selves are "reborn" into their racial birthright. Doyle, calling this the "Atlantic swoon," describes it in this way: "the self in an Atlantic swoon moment faces an abyss, losing its old social identity as it faints—only to reawaken, uprooted and yet newly racialized, 'born again' from its own ashes, as Rousseau and Hegel say of the state."[12] Over the life of the novel genre, Doyle argues, the Atlantic swoon plays a central role in what it means to write a novel and what the novel accomplishes by way of subject formation. Again and again, we encounter characters displaced from their home environment who lose their old encasement of identity and are reborn into a new racialized self after a confrontation with the sublime, rape, an Atlantic

storm, or some other occasion of radical self-dismemberment. The protocols of racialism are the price of free agency—not only for the fictional
characters in these novels, but also for all novel readers. In Doyle's account,
moreover, potential threats to the order of English liberty—from women,
from slaves—are always recuperated. This is to say that by various means—
the interposition of a fraternity of white men who guard each other's interests in law and in practice, the persistence of legalized racial slavery, the
spread of the idea that race is the only ground for freedom—the threat that
women and slaves would seem to represent is always neutralized. As Doyle
tells the story, "a contractual society positions everyone as a lone outsider
who *must join a race* if he or she wants security."[13] Put quite simply, in the
Atlantic world, there is no escape from race, and race is predicated on the
idea that only some people deserve freedom. Indeed, Doyle specifically rejects the idea that there is any way to live outside of race, and she questions
the motives and methods of those who claim that capacity for themselves
or for others—now or in the past. She writes in her introduction, "These
writers offer neither exit from nor hope for race as a freeing embrace."[14] As
Doyle readily admits, neither does she.

I have summarized this book at some length because in many senses
it encapsulates the major issues that have preoccupied Americanists for the
last decade or so—the formation of national identity and nations, the relationship of both of these to racialism, the role of literature in these formations—while introducing the new context of the Atlantic spatial scale. I
have also turned to Doyle's book because its arguments rehearse (much
more convincingly than many others have) several of the major positions
about literature's relationship to simultaneity that I have been at pains to
question in this book. And it also does so in the context of an analysis more
attentive to matters of form than most. In Doyle's considered analysis,
however, a reoriented and amplified spatial scale does not lead to a revised
sense of identity as under duress in the modern era. It instead leads to the
unveiling of a (racialized) Atlantic subjectivity from which there is neither
escape nor shelter. This subjectivity hinges on the presence of what Doyle
repeatedly describes as "print culture." A (racialized) Atlantic subjectivity
emerges from an experience of print-based simultaneity that "bind[s] modern communities" and offers coherence to the individuals who inhabit
those communities.[15] In a discussion of eighteenth-century historiography
and its serial publication, for example, Doyle writes, "The combination of
diachronic longevity and synchronic reach in the readership would enforce
the experience of group suspense and group identification at the same time

it countered readers' geographical distension and economic isolation. . . . Readers could experience their dispersed independence from each other *together*."[16] Here the figure of print returns to span the Atlantic. Although this is not humanist harmony of the sort that Cheah fears plagues cosmopolitanism, it does imagine the emergence of a racialized modern subject tied to print culture's capacity to "bind" in a way that transcends the local. In this sense, it imagines a "print culture" whose main significance is its ability to encourage the " 'lifting out' of social relations from local contexts of interaction and their restructuring across indefinite spans of timespace."[17] In other words, this altogether erudite and compendious study based on a spatial turn extends rather than interrupts the critical preoccupation with modernity's dialectic of social dislocation and translocal reembedding.

In this sense, it not only ignores but implicitly rejects some of the central tenets of postcolonial literary studies. There would seem to be a clear difference between doing what a nation-based study of literature might do (i.e., describe how Americans came to be Americans) and the spatial turn represented in Doyle's book. Yet from the perspective of a still relevant postcolonial studies, this seemingly clear difference just might amount to a splitting of hairs that do not exist. Postcolonial studies made clear that the problem with the classic forms of nationalism is not that they are associated with the nation per se. The problem is that they assume a model of identity formation that ignores those incomplete identifications—the failure to "bind"—engendered by modernity's conflict of times. Postcolonial studies also acknowledged how ignoring issues of formal and temporal hybridity reifies—which is to say abstracts and naturalizes—the idea of absolute mastery and absolute oppression. In his discussion of the slave trade, Christopher Miller writes, "The contemporary vogue for in-betweenness and hybridity in cultural studies has had little to say about this experience of inelegant horror and Manichaean difference."[18] In fact, what a discussion of hybridity might offer here, should it be permitted to join the conversation on equal terms, is an observation along these lines: the "inelegant horror" that was slavery relied upon ideas of Manichean difference as its structuring principle. To the extent that we insist that race was (or is) an actually existing structure of Manichean difference, we do no more than reproduce slavery's foundational terms.

Overlooked in offhand dismissals of postcolonial studies is the extent to which it coherently challenged received notions about the work of literature—or, as the phrasing tends to go when these received notions are aired in public, the work of print culture. As I suggest in my introduction, the most compelling early discussions of hybridity and postcoloniality often turn on a critique of Benedict Anderson's idea of print capitalism and its contribution to the temporality of nation formation. By considering the form of the novel in depth, these studies rewrote our understanding of what the realist novel might mean to the study of social identity. They challenged Anderson's overhasty reading of the novel as being about "homogeneous empty time" (a reading Anderson himself would move beyond), and they showed how a more attentive account of the novel form tells a very different story about modern subjectivity. In this still convincing story, formal and (consequently) temporal hybridity is a feature of the novel itself, and the novel's hybridity has a constitutive force in relationship to its readers. The novel is not one. Neither are the subjects who emerge from it—not just postcolonial subjects, or brown people, or the subaltern, either. One of the central (if often forgotten) points of postcolonial studies was that the dominant—the white man, the Anglo-Atlantic subject, the Englishman, the American—is hybrid too. In other words, nothing grounds the dominant subject's claim to a killing authority based on his racial purity. Anglo-Saxonism is bunk, and so is the imperial stance that it supports. The problem with this and other nationalist discourses is that they underwrite bunk-based fantasies of an absolute community possessing inherent and unchanging rights by focusing on purity rather than mutually implicating hybridity—by focusing on life outside of rather than in time. No self-respecting scholar of postcolonial studies would deny the facts of oppression. But he or she might attempt to render untenable the relevant discourses of purity and Manichean opposition so as to foreclose the positions of safety that those discourses seek to construct for the dominant in law, economy, and culture. That is to say, in real life. The question to be asked here is whether the spatial turn has the capacity to do the same.

Our Backs Turned to the Future

What might a reckoning with time and the global look like? I approach this question by way of a final reading of a painting by the Gilded Age artist Edward Lamson Henry. Henry's historical genre painting is known for its attachment to nostalgic backward glances—the way it turns to earlier moments in the history of the United States and restages them as the prehistory of Gilded Age America. Henry is exactly the kind of bourgeois antimodernist that T. Jackson Lears describes, and his work invites us to cast our thoughts back to the Rip Van Winkle paintings with which we began. With the Mexican-American War, the Civil War, slavery, and the economic upheavals of the mid-nineteenth century behind them, Henry's American contemporaries were much less likely than they might have been one hundred or even fifty years earlier to tell stories that explicitly envisioned the rising glory of America as a process destined to eventuate in humans transcending the parochialism of national difference in the way that John L. O'Sullivan imagined. Yet Henry's paintings work hard to extend O'Sullivan's rhetoric into the nineteenth century's final decades. Henry was especially fond of recalling the early promise associated with the expansion of the rail system in the United States, and a number of his pictures seek to capture the optimism associated with these vehicles. In paintings such as *The First Railroad Train on the Mohawk and Hudson Road* (1892–93; Figure 6), Henry restages the moment in the 1830s when new rails were being laid and the nation's interior was being opened to travel. He harkens back, in other words, to a moment that historians typically identify with the advent of modernity and the homogenization of time. In this and other respects, Henry's painting echoes the Rip Van Winkle paintings: as in those images, the subject of Henry's painting is the advent of a modernity made visible by its contrast with the antiquated forms of the premodern. The horse-drawn carriages whose passengers have gathered to watch the train depart stand in distinct contrast to the machine-driven train. Where the carriages are limited only by the quality of the roads they travel—roads that the signpost at the center of the image represents as multiple and moving in several directions at once—the railroad train moves in only one direction. Its future is in this sense already known; the character of the modern is that of the unidirectional line. The railroad train's nose is pointed toward a future imaginatively cleared of the democratic chaos gathered around its tail. As in the Rip Van Winkle story, a president's portrait hanging in front of a village inn occupies the center of the frame; here that president is Andrew Jackson. The democratic populism associated with Jackson figures in this scene as the promiscuous assembly of human types scattered throughout the image. On the far side of the train are African American laborers fresh from—and some still in—the fields. In the foreground are well-heeled white citizens wearing top hats and bonnets. A child runs in one direction; what appears to be the conductor races in another. A motley assemblage of Huck Finn types gaze at the train's mechanism in the company of a well-dressed boy who recalls Tom Sawyer. In the foreground, discarded trees,

Figure 6. *The First Railroad Train on the Mohawk and Hudson Road* (1892–93). Edward Lamson Henry. Oil on canvas, 42 3/4 × 110 in. Albany Institute of History & Art. Gift of the Friends of the Institute through Catherine Gansvoort (Mrs. Abraham) Lansing, x 1940.600.57.

railroad ties, and railroad tracks confuse the scene even further. Yet the railroad train seems poised to take us away from all of this chaos: the direction in which its smoke travels suggests that the wind is at its back; indeed, that smoke would indicate that not only the ingenuity of man but also the force of nature itself enables this escape from the confusion of the democratically local. In this reading, Henry's painting retroactively integrates this moment into an unfolding narrative of national self-realization whose transcendental future is clear to all.

Yet the approach of this book would be to notice other details in this image that tell against the notion of a neat divide separating the premodern from the modern. Do the horse-drawn carriages waiting at the crossing really differ so much from the carriages lined up behind the "iron horse"? Although the literal engine of movement has changed, the vehicle of conveyance has altered very little. The railroad track attempts to point a straight line into the future, but the converging sight lines created by the extra rail lengths, the cleared and fallen trees, and the unused bedrock scattered in the foreground do not point in only one direction. When they finally meet at this painting's center, they focus our attention on a figure whose back is turned to us. Although the scene does not lack for motion, a certain directional focus is absent. In contrast to the smoke trailing from the engine's chimney, the sky itself is a scene of concentrated energy pointing nowhere: the gathering storm clouds neither depart to nor arrive from any particular direction, and the organizing presence of the sun's location in the sky is obscured. All of this is to say that it takes a great deal of work to imagine that this painting represents the definitive passing of the old and the arrival of the new. It is more faithful to the image to say that it represents forces moving in several directions at once: in the painting's formal composition we read the heterochronic time of modernity. We read the conjuncture. If Henry's reference to the "firstness" of this railroad asks us to believe that this scene allegorizes something about the American past, then what we see here is a past with a future not yet known. This book has been less interested than others might be in the singular future that Henry asks us to envision waiting just off the painting's edge at stage left. It has directed our attention instead to that figure standing near the center of the frame: the curious man with his back turned to the future.

Notes

Introduction

1. One dedicated member whose name is lost to history copied each composition into a logbook that is now at the Nantucket Historical Association. The letter from which I quote is reprinted in Lloyd P. Pratt, "Literate Culture and Community in Antebellum Nantucket," *Historic Nantucket* 49, no. 3 (2000): 6.

2. Anthony Giddens, *The Consequences of Modernity* (Stanford, Calif.: Stanford University Press, 1990), 178.

3. Svetlana Boym, *The Future of Nostalgia* (New York: Basic Books, 2001), 9.

4. Ibid., 30.

5. Stuart Sherman, *Telling Time: Clocks, Diaries, and English Diurnal Form, 1660–1785* (Chicago: University of Chicago Press, 1996), x.

6. I use the term "chronotype" rather than Bakhtin's "chronotope" to indicate how modernity involves ways of being in time that follow from what Giddens calls the "distanciation of space-time." See my discussion of Giddens in Chapters 1 and 3. For Bakhtin on the chronotope, see M. M. Bakhtin, *The Dialogic Imagination: Four Essays*, trans. Caryl Emerson and Michael Holquist (Austin: University of Texas Press, 1981), 84–258.

7. In this respect, I take up Wai Chee Dimock's and Gayatri Spivak's recent suggestion that literary history must proceed at a level of detail different from what Franco Moretti has called "reading at a distance." See Franco Moretti, *Graphs, Maps, Trees: Abstract Models for a Literary History* (London: Verso, 2005). For Dimock's and Spivak's responses, see Wai Chee Dimock, "Genre as World System: Epic and Novel on Four Continents," *Narrative* 14, no. 1 (2006): 85–101; Gayatri Chakravorty Spivak, "World Systems and the Creole," *Narrative* 14, no. 1 (2006): 102–12.

8. Boym, *Future of Nostalgia*, 22.

9. See Arjun Appadurai, "The Production of Locality," in *Modernity at Large: Cultural Dimensions of Globalization* (Minneapolis: University of Minnesota Press, 1996).

10. D. H. Lawrence, *Studies in Classic American Literature* (Garden City, N.Y.: Doubleday, 1953), 62. To suggest that this subject escapes determination by his social context would be to suggest something similar to what post–World War II critics argued about the way the modern American "sacrificed" his "relation" to reality. See Richard Chase, *The American Novel and Its Tradition* (Baltimore: Johns Hopkins University Press, 1980). This position was convincingly put to rest by works such as Donald Pease's *Visionary Compacts*, as well as much of the writing

associated with the New Americanists, which sought to reconnect ideology critique to the study of American literature.

11. For an account of how Darwin's theory of natural selection actually favors differentiation over similitude across time, see Elizabeth Grosz, *The Nick of Time: Politics, Evolution, and the Untimely* (Sydney: Allen & Unwin, 2004).

12. For Giddens, the counterfactual work of utopian thought is important to the extent that it allows us to recognize more of the possibilities immanent in any particular moment. Although Giddens emphasizes a utopian realism of the present, I suggest that we might think in similar terms in relation to the past. Thus the critical work being described here is a kind of utopian realism of the past. See Giddens, *Consequences of Modernity*, 177–78.

13. Roberto Mangabeira Unger, *False Necessity: Anti-Necessitarian Social Theory in the Service of Radical Democracy; From Politics, a Work in Constructive Social Theory* (London: Verso, 2001), 1–40.

14. It is worth noting that Anderson has objected to the wholesale importation of his imagined communities thesis into the U.S. national context. Indeed, he proposes that the particular cultural history of the United States should warn against applying his work to the U.S. national environment. See his introduction to Benedict Anderson, *The Spectre of Comparisons: Nationalism, Southeast Asia, and the World* (London: Verso, 1998), 1–28.

15. Wai Chee Dimock, *Through Other Continents: American Literature across Deep Time* (Princeton, N.J.: Princeton University Press, 2006), 74.

16. Ibid., 129.

17. Rufus W. Griswold, *The Prose Writers of America: With a Survey of the Intellectual History, Condition, and Prospects of the Country* (Philadelphia: Carey and Hart, 1845), 49–50.

18. George Dekker, *The American Historical Romance* (New York: Cambridge University Press, 1987), 67.

19. Pascale Casanova, *The World Republic of Letters* (Cambridge, Mass.: Harvard University Press, 2004), 9–81.

20. Stephen Owen, "Genres in Motion," *PMLA* 122, no. 5 (2007): 1390.

21. Ibid.

22. Amy Kaplan, " 'Left Alone with America': The Absence of Empire in the Study of American Culture," in *Cultures of United States Imperialism*, ed. Amy Kaplan and Donald Pease (Durham, N.C.: Duke University Press, 1994); Edward W. Said, *Culture and Imperialism* (New York: Knopf, 1993).

23. Griswold, *Prose Writers of America*, 50.

24. Bruce Burgett, "American Nationalism—R.I.P.," *American Literary History* 13, no. 2 (2001): 317–28.

25. Much work has been done on the sentimental novel's transatlantic qualities. See, for example, Nancy Armstrong and Leonard Tennenhouse, *The Imaginary Puritan: Literature, Intellectual Labor, and the Origins of Personal Life* (Berkeley: University of California Press, 1992). See also Cathy N. Davidson, *Revolution and the Word: The Rise of the Novel in America* (New York: Oxford University Press, 1986); Amanda Claybaugh, *The Novel of Purpose: Literature and Social Reform in the Anglo-American World* (Ithaca, N.Y.: Cornell University Press, 2007). On lyric, see

Sharon Cameron, *Lyric Time: Dickinson and the Limits of Genre* (Baltimore: Johns Hopkins University Press, 1979); Virginia Walker Jackson, *Dickinson's Misery: A Theory of Lyric Reading* (Princeton, N.J.: Princeton University Press, 2005); Susan Stewart, *Poetry and the Fate of the Senses* (Chicago: University of Chicago Press, 2002).

26. Gregg D. Crane, *The Cambridge Introduction to the Nineteenth-Century American Novel* (New York: Cambridge University Press, 2007), 1.

27. See Nina Baym, *Novels, Readers, and Reviewers: Responses to Fiction in Antebellum America* (Ithaca, N.Y.: Cornell University Press, 1984), 196–223.

28. Dimock, *Through Other Continents*, 73–74.

29. John Frow, *Genre* (New York: Routledge, 2006), 10.

30. Fredric Jameson, *The Political Unconscious: Narrative as a Socially Symbolic Act* (Ithaca, N.Y.: Cornell University Press, 1981), 141.

31. Dimock, *Through Other Continents*, 91.

32. Sherman, *Telling Time*, x.

33. See Fredric Jameson, "Nostalgia for the Present," *South Atlantic Quarterly* 88, no. 2 (1989): 517–37.

34. Pratt, "Literate Culture and Community in Antebellum Nantucket," 6.

35. Leon Jackson, *The Business of Letters: Authorial Economies in Antebellum America* (Stanford, Calif.: Stanford University Press, 2008), 187.

36. According to Jackson, "Susan Warner, Edgar Allan Poe, Nathaniel P. Willis, Henry Wadsworth Longfellow, Lydia Sigourney, Sarah Hale, William Cullen Bryant, Sarah Helen Whitman, and Harriet Beecher Stowe were all competition winners." Ibid., 187–88.

37. Ibid., 187.

38. Pratt, "Literate Culture and Community in Antebellum Nantucket," 6.

39. See Janet Gurkin Altman, *Epistolarity: Approaches to a Form* (Columbus: Ohio State University Press, 1982).

40. I discuss these two forms of simultaneity at greater length in my analysis of *The House of the Seven Gables* in Chapter 2.

41. For a discussion of the American embrace of history writing, see Nina Baym, *American Women Writers and the Work of History, 1790–1860* (New Brunswick, N.J.: Rutgers University Press, 1995).

42. For a discussion of the reign of historicism in American literary studies, see Jennifer Fleissner, "When the Symptom Becomes a Resource," *American Literary History* 20, no. 3 (2008): 640–55.

Chapter 1

1. For a consideration of how the visual arts have represented the scene of reading, as well as certain other figures of print, see Garrett Stewart, *The Look of Reading: Book, Painting, Text* (Chicago: University of Chicago Press, 2006). Stewart terms such scenes "reverse *ekphrasis*."

2. In Ernest Lee Tuveson, *Redeemer Nation: The Idea of America's Millennial Role* (Chicago: University of Chicago Press, 1968), 73.

3. Jürgen Habermas, *The Philosophical Discourse of Modernity: Twelve Lectures*, trans. Frederick Lawrence (Cambridge, Mass.: MIT Press, 1987), 2.

4. Washington Irving, *The Sketch-Book of Geoffrey Crayon, Gent.* (New York: Oxford University Press, 1996), 54.

5. Giddens, *Consequences of Modernity*, 4.

6. Arjun Appadurai, *Modernity at Large: Cultural Dimensions of Globalization* (Minneapolis: University of Minnesota Press, 1996), 3.

7. In Boym, *Future of Nostalgia*, 19.

8. Ibid., 30.

9. Walter Benjamin, *Selected Writings*, ed. Howard Eiland and Michael William Jennings, trans. Marcus Paul Bullock, Howard Eiland, and Gary Smith, vol. 3, 1935–38 (Cambridge, Mass.: Belknap Press, 2002), 146.

10. See Ian Baucom, "Globalit, Inc.: Or, the Cultural Logic of Global Literary Studies," *PMLA* 116, no. 1 (2001): 158–72.

11. Daniel Bensaïd, *Marx for Our Times: Adventures and Misadventures of a Critique* (London: Verso, 2002), 10.

12. Peter Osborne, *The Politics of Time: Modernity and Avant-Garde* (London: Verso, 1995), 14.

13. Irving, *Sketch-Book of Geoffrey Crayon*, 34.

14. Ibid., 37.

15. Ibid., 38.

16. Ibid., 36.

17. Ibid., 37.

18. Ibid.

19. Ibid., 44.

20. Ibid., 45.

21. Ibid., 43.

22. See Donald E. Pease, *Visionary Compacts: American Renaissance Writings in Cultural Context* (Madison: University of Wisconsin Press, 1987).

23. For an account of Newton's impact, see Wai Chee Dimock, "Non-Newtonian Time: Robert Lowell, Roman History, Vietnam War," *American Literature: A Journal of Literary History, Criticism, and Bibliography* 74, no. 4 (2002): 911–31. For Darwin's influence on theories of historical time and on literature, see Grosz, *Nick of Time.*

24. Reinhart Koselleck, *Futures Past: On the Semantics of Historical Time* (Cambridge, Mass.: MIT Press, 1985), 6.

25. Ibid., 12.

26. Ibid., 32.

27. Ibid., 23.

28. Ibid., 30.

29. Dimock, "Non-Newtonian Time," 911. Koselleck has been criticized for neglecting to address imperialism's role in the advent of modern approaches to time. See Rey Chow, "The Interruption of Referentiality: Poststructuralism and the Conundrum of Critical Multiculturalism," *South Atlantic Quarterly* 101, no. 1 (2002): 171–86; Johannes Fabian, *Time and the Other: How Anthropology Makes Its Object* (New York: Columbia University Press, 2002); Osborne, *Politics of Time;*

Mary Louise Pratt, *Imperial Eyes: Travel Writing and Transculturation* (New York: Routledge, 1992). I address this issue at length in my discussion of literary regionalism.

30. Giddens, *Consequences of Modernity*, 16–17.

31. Ibid., 20.

32. Ibid., 21.

33. John Demos, *Circles and Lines: The Shape of Life in Early America* (Cambridge, Mass.: Harvard University Press, 2004), 22.

34. Ibid., 77.

35. Ibid., 39.

36. Ibid., 45.

37. For the history of Manifest Destiny, see Reginald Horsman, *Race and Manifest Destiny: The Origins of American Racial Anglo-Saxonism* (Cambridge, Mass.: Harvard University Press, 1981); Robert Walter Johannsen, Sam W. Haynes, and Christopher Morris, *Manifest Destiny and Empire: American Antebellum Expansionism* (College Station: Texas A & M University Press, 1997); Frederick Merk and Lois Bannister Merk, *Manifest Destiny and Mission in American History: A Reinterpretation* (Cambridge, Mass.: Harvard University Press, 1995); Alexander Saxton, *The Rise and Fall of the White Republic: Class Politics and Mass Culture in Nineteenth Century America* (London: Verso, 1990); Tuveson, *Redeemer Nation*; Albert Katz Weinberg, *Manifest Destiny: A Study of Nationalist Expansionism in American History* (New York: AMS Press, 1979). For Manifest Destiny's literary import, see Jenine Abboushi Dallal, "American Imperialism Unmanifest: Emerson's 'Inquest' and Cultural Regeneration," *American Literature: A Journal of Literary History, Criticism, and Bibliography* 73, no. 1 (2001): 47–83; Wai Chee Dimock, *Empire for Liberty: Melville and the Poetics of Individualism* (Princeton, N.J.: Princeton University Press, 1988); Amy Kaplan, "Manifest Domesticity," *American Literature: A Journal of Literary History, Criticism, and Bibliography* 70, no. 3 (1998): 581–606.

38. It is worth remembering that Habermas rejects Koselleck's claim that European modernity was open ended. According to Habermas, modern teleological constructions of history, including certain versions of Marxism, "closed off the future as a *source* of disruption in the present." Habermas, *Philosophical Discourse of Modernity*, 12. Habermas's comments suggest an ongoing need to contend with the several ways the future was imagined in European modernity. See also Harry Harootunian, "Remembering the Historical Present," *Critical Inquiry* 33, no. 3 (2007): 471–94.

39. As Tuveson explains, the Augustinianism that dominated the Christian world prior to the Reformation posited two realms—one earthly, the other heavenly—kept separate and unrelated until the Last Judgment. In this framework, earthly concerns remain secondary to the moment of Christ's Second Coming, when the earthly realm and its unredeemed inhabitants will fall away, and the redeemed will ascend to their rightful place in the company of God: "Those holding the Augustinian view that secular history is of no lasting importance could accept with equanimity the prospect that Satan's primacy will endure until the end. The wise man will concentrate on this lasting, this only truly valid fact." Tuveson argues,

however, that the Puritans "rejected the Augustinian attitude toward history" and in doing so effected a "momentous change." Tuveson, *Redeemer Nation*, 28, 98.

40. Ibid., 25.

41. In Merk and Merk, *Manifest Destiny and Mission in American History*, 34.

42. Ibid., 64.

43. Ibid., 51.

44. O'Sullivan's words reverberate even into the present. Introducing a volume on the relationship between Manifest Destiny and imperialism, Robert W. Johannsen writes, "In the United States, a publication explosion made possible by steam-powered rotary presses and other technological advances, the development of a common public school system, and one of the highest literacy rates in the world brought [antebellum America's political, social, and economic changes] within the reach of most Americans, adding credibility to even the most extravagant claims of Manifest Destiny's spokesmen." Johannsen, Haynes, and Morris, *Manifest Destiny and Empire*, 14. Just as O'Sullivan imagines the geographically dispersed peoples of the United States sharing a national "moment" enabled by technologies of print communication, Johannsen depicts a nation where America's new dynamism—its progress—is accessible to all through print.

45. John L. O'Sullivan, "The Great Nation of Futurity," *United States Magazine and Democratic Review* 6, no. 23 (1839): 427.

46. Ibid.

47. Irving, *Sketch-Book of Geoffrey Crayon*, 12.

48. O'Sullivan, "Great Nation of Futurity," 427.

49. Ibid., 430.

50. In Merk and Merk, *Manifest Destiny and Mission in American History*, 34.

51. Lauren Gail Berlant, *The Anatomy of National Fantasy: Hawthorne, Utopia, and Everyday Life* (Chicago: University of Chicago Press, 1991), 49.

52. See also Russ Castronovo, *Necro Citizenship: Death, Eroticism, and the Public Sphere in the Nineteenth-Century United States* (Durham, N.C.: Duke University Press, 2001).

53. Habermas, *Philosophical Discourse of Modernity*, 2.

54. Mark M. Smith, *Mastered by the Clock: Time, Slavery, and Freedom in the American South* (Chapel Hill: University of North Carolina Press, 1997), 42. Smith also suggests that "[o]ne reason for this intimacy was that all three notions of time embraced both cyclical and linear conceptions of how time moved." Ibid. See also Thomas M. Allen, *A Republic in Time: Temporality & Social Imagination in Nineteenth-Century America* (Chapel Hill: University of North Carolina Press, 2008); Dana Luciano, *Arranging Grief: Sacred Time and the Body in Nineteenth-Century America* (New York: New York University Press, 2007).

55. Mary Ann Doane, *The Emergence of Cinematic Time: Modernity, Contingency, the Archive* (Cambridge, Mass.: Harvard University Press, 2002), 45.

56. Ibid., 68.

57. Osborne, *Politics of Time*, 1.

58. Giddens, *Consequences of Modernity*, 45.

59. Doane's summary of the scholarship on time-work discipline is succinct and comprehensive. See Doane, *Emergence of Cinematic Time*, 4–9.

60. Michael O'Malley, *Keeping Watch: A History of American Time* (New York: Viking, 1990), 9.

61. Ibid., 12.

62. See also Adam Rothman's discussion of "Commerce and Slavery in Lower Louisiana." Rothman describes how local plantation practices "bel[ie] the idea that slavery and technological progress are incompatible." Adam Rothman, *Slave Country: American Expansion and the Origins of the Deep South* (Cambridge, Mass.: Harvard University Press, 2005), 76.

63. Smith, *Mastered by the Clock*, 11.

64. Ibid., 40.

65. Fredric Jameson, "The End of Temporality," *Critical Inquiry* 29, no. 4 (2003): 699.

66. Homi K. Bhabha, "DissemiNation: Time, Narrative, and the Margins of the Modern Nation," in *Nation and Narration*, ed. Homi K. Bhabha (New York: Routledge, 1990), 297.

67. For the debate over whether the United States is a postcolonial nation, see Joanna Brooks, "Colonial Flashpoints," *American Quarterly* 56, no. 4 (2004): 1107–13; Lawrence Buell, "American Literary Emergence as a Postcolonial Phenomenon," *American Literary History* 4, no. 3 (1992): 411–42; Roland Greene, "Colonial Becomes Postcolonial," *Modern Language Quarterly: A Journal of Literary History* 65, no. 3 (2004): 423–41; Kaplan, "'Left Alone with America'"; David Kazanjian, *The Colonizing Trick: National Culture and Imperial Citizenship in Early America* (Minneapolis: University of Minnesota Press, 2003); Jenny Sharpe, "Is the United States Postcolonial? Transnationalism, Immigration, and Race," in *Postcolonial America* (Urbana: University of Illinois Press, 2000), 103–21; Michael Warner, "What's Colonial about Colonial America?" in *Possible Pasts: Becoming Colonial in Early America*, ed. Robert Blair St. George (Ithaca, N.Y.: Cornell University Press, 2000), 49–72.

68. Bhabha, "DissemiNation," 313.

69. Ibid., 294. Bhabha has been criticized for overemphasizing the indeterminacy of identity. For a critique of Bhabha's account of postcolonial modernity, see Aijaz Ahmad, *In Theory: Classes, Nations, Literatures* (London: Verso, 1992).

70. Louis Althusser, "The Errors of Classical Economics: Outline for a Concept of Historical Time," in *Reading Capital* (London: Verso, 1990), 94.

71. Ibid., 106.

72. See also Appadurai's "Consumption, Duration, and History," in Appadurai, *Modernity at Large*, 66–85. Peter Osborne offers a useful critique of the Althusserian conjuncture in *Politics of Time*, 23–29.

73. Althusser, "Errors of Classical Economics," 101.

74. Ibid.

75. Ibid., 100.

76. In a rebuke to Althusser, Daniel Bensaïd argues that Marx's political economy forbids "harmonization," despite the desire of his interpreters to smooth the conflicts Marx describes and reframe them as a harmonious extractive system. See Bensaïd, *Marx for Our Times*, 40–69.

77. For an analysis of the fait accompli stories of postbellum literary regional-

ism, see Jacqueline Shea Murphy, "Replacing Regionalism: Abenaki Tales and 'Jewett's' Coastal Maine," *American Literary History* 10, no. 4 (1998): 664–90.

78. Habermas, *Philosophical Discourse of Modernity*, 12.

79. Irving, *Sketch-Book of Geoffrey Crayon*, 43.

80. Ibid.

81. Burgett, "American Nationalism—R.I.P.," 317–18. Donald Pease similarly suggests that Irving's image articulates an early nineteenth-century desire to bridge the cultural gap between the pre- and post-Revolutionary generations. See Pease, *Visionary Compacts*, 13–18.

82. Doane, *Emergence of Cinematic Time*, 71.

83. Ibid., 74, 77.

84. Irving, *Sketch-Book of Geoffrey Crayon*, 47.

85. Ibid.

86. Karl E. Beckson and Arthur F. Ganz, *Literary Terms: A Dictionary* (New York: Farrar, Straus and Giroux, 1975), 37.

87. *Oxford English Dictionary*, 2nd ed., s.v. "Chronicle."

88. Irving, *Sketch-Book of Geoffrey Crayon*, 47.

89. Benjamin, *Selected Writings*, 145.

90. Irving, *Sketch-Book of Geoffrey Crayon*, 35.

91. Benjamin, *Selected Writings*, 143.

92. Ibid., 146.

93. Ibid.

94. Ibid.

95. Ibid.

96. Irving, *Sketch-Book of Geoffrey Crayon*, 113.

97. Ibid., 114.

98. Ibid., 32.

99. See Peter Bain and Paul Shaw, eds., *Blackletter: Type and National Identity* (New York: Princeton Architectural Press, 1998); Bernhard Bischoff, *Latin Palaeography: Antiquity and the Middle Ages* (New York: Cambridge University Press, 1990).

100. Michael D. Bell, "Conditions of Literary Vocation," in *The Cambridge History of American Literature*, ed. Sacvan Bercovitch (New York: Cambridge University Press, 1995), 20.

101. W. J. Thomas Mitchell, *Picture Theory: Essays on Verbal and Visual Representation* (Chicago: University of Chicago Press, 1994), 152.

102. Murray Krieger and Joan Krieger, *Ekphrasis: The Illusion of the Natural Sign* (Baltimore: Johns Hopkins University Press, 1992), 11, 10, 11.

103. Ibid., 7.

104. Ibid., xvi.

105. One explanation for this continuing investment in the emergence of a coherent self, whatever name it might take, lies in the strong association of the fortunes of the individual self with the fortunes of the larger commonwealth in American culture. As Sacvan Bercovitch has argued, American Puritan rhetoric not only preserved a millennialist impulse quickly dissolving in England but also sutured that impulse to an argument about the meaning of America. Puritan ideology pow-

erfully synthesized two modes of historical narration—Christology and soteriology—traditionally held separate, combining them with a claim about national election that initiated an enduring vision of the inevitable future on America's horizon.
Christology traditionally read the lives of Christian saints in terms of the signal
events of Christ's life, while at the same time cautiously acknowledging the specific
actions that characterized those saints as individual human beings. Reform Christology, from which American Puritan rhetoric evolved, focused more intensely on
the course of life common to all and read what might otherwise appear to be local
and particular occurrences through the lens of Christological experience. The life of
the individual was in this manner subordinated to a Christological life model, so
much so that all experience could be recuperated to it. This version of Christology
emphasized that, although the unfolding events of an individual life might appear
novel, they were the antitype of a known past and adumbrated a known future.
Soteriology traditionally read the broader events of history—war, famine, civil
strife—as moments in the course of the prophesied redemption of man. Like
Christology, then, soteriology reads every event in terms of a redemptive history
already known in advance. Like Christology, soteriology assumes an inevitable and
defining future visible on the horizon. Historically, these hermeneutic practices
were adjuncts, even in the English versions of Protestantism. The American Puritans merged the two while simultaneously identifying the course of the individual
redeemed life and the history of redemption with the American colonial and theocratic project. American Puritans in this way assigned the continent and its Puritan
colonizers a mutually implicating known eschatological future. For Bercovitch, Cotton Mather's "Life of Winthrop," which comes near the end of the Massachusetts
Bay colony's experiment in theocracy, represents the culmination of this Puritan
rhetoric. It simultaneously prophesies a certain future for America, as the site of
God's greatest work of redemption; argues that this redemption can only occur in
America; and does both through its account of the life of a single man, Winthrop,
as a "representative American." Puritan rhetoric anthropomorphized America and
told the history of the Massachusetts Bay colony as a Christological narrative whose
outcome was already known. It "personified the New World as America micro-
christa": "Thus [Puritans] also combined the genres of political and spiritual exhor-
tation, and equated public with personal welfare. In effect, they invented a colony
in the image of a saint." Sacvan Bercovitch, *The Puritan Origins of the American Self*
(New Haven, Conn.: Yale University Press, 1975), 114. In the new form of "federal
hagiography," Puritan jeremiads and histories "recast colonial progress into the
journey of the latter-day saint." Bercovitch, *Puritan Origins of the American Self*, 115,
116. Simultaneously, Puritans "inverted the process of personal redemption into a
mode of historical expression" in their sermons and treatises, so that individuals
understood their own tribulations in terms of a corporate destiny being played out
locally in their own experience. Puritan rhetoric also emphasized that America was
the site of the larger world-historical redemption predicted in Revelations. Unlike
English Puritans, who perceived the events leading up to the Protestant revolution
as indicating a temporary and serendipitous conjunction hospitable to the coming
of the chiliad, American Puritans viewed their own locale as uniquely suited and
prophetically designated to be the source of a worldly theocratic redemption that

would presage the Apocalypse. This potent merging of soteriology and Christology was unprecedented, and, as Bercovitch argues, it would define the way Americans conceptualized the course of historical time, of the individual life, and of the practice of imperialism through the nineteenth century. It would also ensure that any attempt to suggest that no coherent form of identity emerged from the nineteenth century's efforts at national *cum* self-realization would be read as a direct attack on the integrity of the U.S. nation.

106. Lawrence, *Studies in Classic American Literature*, 62.

107. Ibid.

108. Ibid., 62, 8. My argument here resembles Walter Benn Michaels's contention that most American identity claims emerge from a problematic, early twentieth-century American nativism. See Walter Benn Michaels, *Our America: Nativism, Modernism, and Pluralism* (Durham, N.C.: Duke University Press, 1995). My position also differs from Michaels's claims: in addition to locating the identity project of American writing much earlier than does Michaels, I seek out both the sources and the political meaning of what Ross Posnock names "nonidentity" rather than suggesting that it is an ontological given. See Ross Posnock, "The Politics of Nonidentity: A Geneology," in *National Identities and Post-Americanist Narratives*, ed. Donald E. Pease (Durham, N.C.: Duke University Press, 1994), 34–68. For responses to Michaels's thesis, see "*Our America* and Nativist Modernism: A Panel," *Modernism/Modernity* 3, no. 3 (1995): 97–126.

109. See Arjun Appadurai, "The Production of Locality," in *Modernity at Large: Cultural Dimensions of Globalization* (Minneapolis: University of Minnesota Press, 1996), 178–200.

110. Althusser, "Errors of Classical Economics," 94.

111. Benedict Anderson, *Imagined Communities: Reflections on the Origin and Spread of Nationalism* (London: Verso, 1983), 26.

112. Ibid., 22–36.

113. Philip Gould, *Covenant and Republic: Historical Romance and the Politics of Puritanism* (New York: Cambridge University Press, 1996), 14.

114. Dana D. Nelson, *National Manhood: Capitalist Citizenship and the Imagined Fraternity of White Men* (Durham, N.C.: Duke University Press, 1998). In *Inhuman Conditions*, Pheng Cheah suggests that this overweening emphasis on the deleterious effects of nationalism misunderstands Anderson's claims and nationalism's historical role in winning a certain kind of civic justice. Pheng Cheah, *Inhuman Conditions: On Cosmopolitanism and Human Rights* (Cambridge, Mass.: Harvard University Press, 2006), 45–79.

115. Burgett, "American Nationalism—R.I.P.," 321–22. Burgett makes these comments in the context of a review of several studies published in the late 1990s, which in his estimation offer a more nuanced account of "imaginary form[s] of belonging" than is typical of such studies. According to Burgett, for example, David Waldstreicher's *In the Midst of Perpetual Fetes: The Making of American Nationalism, 1776–1820* attends to the fact that such "imaginings" take place in local contexts with "unpredictable" results. Hence the title of Burgett's review: "American Nationalism—R.I.P." For Burgett, "[p]art of the appeal of [Irving's] simple tale—and one of the reasons for its canonical status—results from the ways in which it fore-

grounds the dialectic of revolutionary change and historical continuity in the context of postrevolutionary US nationalism." Burgett, "American Nationalism—R.I.P.," 317–18.

116. Nelson, *National Manhood*, xi.

Chapter 2

1. Gould, *Covenant and Republic*, 13–14.

2. See Baym, *American Women Writers*. See also Baym, *Novels, Readers, and Reviewers*, 63–81.

3. On "The Republican Tradition and the Radical Specter," see T. Jackson Lears, *No Place of Grace: Antimodernism and the Transformation of American Culture, 1880–1920* (Chicago: University of Chicago Press, 1994), 26–32.

4. Philip Gould has suggested that the "long shadow" of Hawthorne and his prefaces has obscured the larger significance of the American historical romance as a genre. See Gould, *Covenant and Republic*, 2.

5. Nathaniel Hawthorne, *The House of the Seven Gables* (New York: Penguin, 1981), 1, 2.

6. Ibid., 2.

7. Baym warns that Hawthorne's use of the term "romance" is both internally inconsistent and out of step with broader usage. See Nina Baym, "Concepts of the Romance in Hawthorne's America," *Nineteenth-Century Fiction* 38, no. 4 (1984): 426–43. See also Baym, *Novels, Readers, and Reviewers*, 63–81.

8. Susan L. Mizruchi, *The Power of Historical Knowledge: Narrating the Past in Hawthorne, James, and Dreiser* (Princeton, N.J.: Princeton University Press, 1988), 105.

9. Edwin Percy Whipple, Review in *The House of the Seven Gables: Authoritative Text, Contexts, Criticism*, ed. Robert S. Levine (New York: W. W. Norton and Company, 2006), 325.

10. Anthony Trollope, "The Genius of Nathaniel Hawthorne," in *The House of the Seven Gables: Authoritative Text, Contexts, Criticism*, ed. Robert S. Levine (New York: W. W. Norton and Company, 2006), 332.

11. Meredith L. McGill, *American Literature and the Culture of Reprinting, 1834–1853* (Philadelphia: University of Pennsylvania Press, 2003), 239.

12. Lawrence Buell, *New England Literary Culture from Revolution through Renaissance* (Cambridge: Cambridge University Press, 1986), 245.

13. Gould, *Covenant and Republic*, 60.

14. György Lukács, *The Historical Novel* (Lincoln: University of Nebraska Press, 1983), 62.

15. Ibid., 85.

16. Boym, *Future of Nostalgia*, 50.

17. Gould, *Covenant and Republic*, 5.

18. McGill, *American Literature and the Culture of Reprinting*, 240.

19. Jeffrey Insko, "Anachronistic Imaginings: Hope Leslie's Challenge to Historicism," *American Literary History* 16, no. 2 (2004): 183.

20. Lukács suggests as much when he argues that there is no real difference between the novel of social realism and the historical fiction that concerns him. See Lukács, *Historical Novel*, 166–70.

21. In Robert S. Levine, ed., *The House of the Seven Gables: Authoritative Text, Contexts, Criticism* (New York: W. W. Norton and Company, 2006), 337.

22. Frank Kermode, "Hawthorne's Modernity," *Partisan Review* 41 (1974): 429.

23. In Levine, *House of the Seven Gables*, 337.

24. See Christopher Clark, *The Roots of Rural Capitalism: Western Massachusetts, 1780–1860* (Ithaca, N.Y.: Cornell University Press, 1990); Paul A. Gilje, *Wages of Independence: Capitalism in the Early American Republic* (Madison, Wis.: Madison House, 1997); Steven Hahn and Jonathan Prude, eds., *The Countryside in the Age of Capitalist Transformation: Essays in the Social History of Rural America* (Chapel Hill: University of North Carolina Press, 1985); Jeffrey P. Sklansky, *The Soul's Economy: Market Society and Selfhood in American Thought, 1820–1920* (Chapel Hill: University of North Carolina Press, 2002).

25. Gillian Brown, *Domestic Individualism: Imagining Self in Nineteenth-Century America* (Berkeley: University of California Press, 1990), 69.

26. Ibid., 70. On this issue, Jonathan Arac writes the following: "The key to redemption in *The House of the Seven Gables* is the replacing of all human action . . . with the beneficent process of nature—in particular, a nature that has been domesticated, in keeping with the book's intense household focus. The dreadful pattern of stasis in the house and repetition in the crimes of its inhabitants is undone by the natural development of Phoebe at her moment of transition from girl to woman." Jonathan Arac, "Narrative Forms," in *The Cambridge History of American Literature*, ed. Sacvan Bercovitch (New York: Cambridge University Press, 1995), 714.

27. Walter Benn Michaels, "Romance and Real Estate," in *The American Renaissance Reconsidered*, ed. Walter Benn Michaels and Donald E. Pease (Baltimore: Johns Hopkins University Press, 1985), 164.

28. Hawthorne, *House of the Seven Gables*, 2.

29. In Levine, *House of the Seven Gables*, 337.

30. In ibid., 344.

31. Michael T. Gilmore, "The Artist and the Marketplace in *The House of the Seven Gables*," *ELH* 48, no. 1 (1981): 176.

32. Michaels, "Romance and Real Estate," 160.

33. Arac, "Narrative Forms," 648.

34. Ibid.

35. Hawthorne, *House of the Seven Gables*, 6.

36. Ibid., 38.

37. Ibid., 40.

38. Ibid., 264.

39. Ibid., 2.

40. Anderson, *Imagined Communities*, 24.

41. Ibid.

42. Ibid.

43. Hawthorne, *House of the Seven Gables*, 19.

44. Ibid., 20.

45. Ibid.

46. Ibid., 59.

47. Ibid., 120.

48. Ibid., 232.

49. Ibid., 240.

50. Ibid., 151.

51. Ibid.

52. Partha Chatterjee, "Anderson's Utopia," *Diacritics: A Review of Contemporary Criticism* 29, no. 4 (1999): 128–34.

53. See Chapter 1 of this volume.

54. Chatterjee, "Anderson's Utopia," 131–32.

55. Significant recent studies of this epic include Alf Hiltebeitel, *Rethinking the Mahabharata: A Reader's Guide to the Education of the Dharma King* (Chicago: University of Chicago Press, 2001); Julian F. Woods, *Destiny and Human Initiative in the Mahabharata* (Albany, N.Y.: SUNY Press, 2001).

56. On the epic versus novel distinction, see György Lukács, *The Theory of the Novel: A Historico-Philosophical Essay on the Forms of Great Epic Literature* (Cambridge, Mass.: MIT Press, 1971). Svetlana Boym summarizes Lukács's argument as follows: "The novel, a modern substitute for the ancient epic, is a sort of 'half-art' that has come to reflect the 'bad infinity' of the modern world and the loss of a transcendental home." Boym, *Future of Nostalgia*, 25.

57. Crane, *Cambridge Introduction to the Nineteenth-Century American Novel*, 26.

58. McGill, *American Literature and the Culture of Reprinting*, 224.

59. Ibid., 220.

60. Ibid.

61. Ibid.

62. Richard H. Brodhead, *Hawthorne, Melville, and the Novel* (Chicago: University of Chicago Press, 1976), 22.

63. McGill, *American Literature and the Culture of Reprinting*, 231.

64. Ibid., 233.

65. In Levine, *House of the Seven Gables*, 335.

66. In ibid., 327.

67. In John L. Idol and Buford Jones, eds., *Nathaniel Hawthorne: The Contemporary Reviews* (New York: Cambridge University Press, 1994), 133.

68. In Levine, *House of the Seven Gables*, 410.

69. Nathaniel Hawthorne, *The Scarlet Letter* (New York: Penguin, 1983), 62.

70. Ibid., 40–41.

71. Ibid., 41–42.

72. Ibid., 47.

73. Ibid., 49–50.

74. Ibid., 63.

75. Insko, "Anachronistic Imaginings," 179.

76. Hawthorne, *Scarlet Letter*, 40–41.

77. Hawthorne, *House of the Seven Gables*, 35–36.

78. Ibid., 36.

79. Ibid., 257.

80. In Levine, *House of the Seven Gables*, 313.

81. See Wolfgang Schivelbusch, *The Railway Journey: The Industrialization of Time and Space in the Nineteenth Century* (Berkeley: University of California Press, 1986).

82. In Levine, *House of the Seven Gables*, 313.

83. Ibid.

84. Arac, "Narrative Forms," 648.

85. Hawthorne, *House of the Seven Gables*, 187. Although the Penguin edition uses "nigger," the first America edition uses "nigga." See Nathaniel Hawthorne, *The House of the Seven Gables* (Boston: Ticknor, Reed, and Fields, 1851).

86. In Idol and Jones, *Nathaniel Hawthorne*, 164.

87. Richard H. Brodhead, *Cultures of Letters: Scenes of Reading and Writing in Nineteenth-Century America* (Chicago: University of Chicago Press, 1993), 136.

88. For dialect writing in African American literature, see Barbara Johnson, "Metaphor, Metonymy, and Voice in *Their Eyes*," in *Black Literature and Literary Theory*, ed. Henry Louis Gates Jr. (New York: Methuen, 1984); Houston A. Baker, *The Journey Back: Issues in Black Literature and Criticism* (Chicago: University of Chicago Press, 1980); Henry Louis Gates Jr., "Zora Neale Hurston: 'A Negro Way of Saying,'" afterword to *Their Eyes Were Watching God*, by Zora Neale Hurston (New York: Harper & Row, 1990), 195–205; Karla F. C. Holloway, *The Character of the Word: The Texts of Zora Neale Hurston* (New York: Greenway Press, 1987); Barbara Johnson, "Thresholds of Difference: Structures of Address in Zora Neale Hurston," *Critical Inquiry* 12, no. 1 (1985): 278–89. On dialect writing in literary regionalism, see Brodhead, *Cultures of Letters*; Marjorie Pryse, "Sex, Class, and 'Category Crisis': Reading Jewett's Transitivity," in *Jewett and Her Contemporaries: Reshaping the Canon*, ed. Karen L. Kilcup and Thomas S. Edwards (Gainesville: University Press of Florida, 1999); Sandra A. Zagarell, "Troubling Regionalism: Rural Life and the Cosmopolitan Eye in Jewett's *Deephaven*," *American Literary History* 10, no. 4 (1998): 639–63; Sandra A. Zagarell, "Response to Jacqueline Shea Murphy's 'Replacing Regionalism,'" *American Literary History* 10, no. 4 (1998): 691–97. On dialect writing in Anglo-American modernism, see Michael North, *The Dialect of Modernism: Race, Language, and Twentieth-Century Literature* (New York: Oxford University Press, 1994). For its place in the writing of Gilded Age America, see Gavin Roger Jones, *Strange Talk: The Politics of Dialect Literature in Gilded Age America* (Berkeley: University of California Press, 1999).

89. Hawthorne, *House of the Seven Gables*, 186.

90. See my discussion of Southwestern humor in Chapter 3.

91. Hawthorne, *House of the Seven Gables*, 186.

92. Ibid., 187–88.

93. Augustus Baldwin Longstreet, *Georgia Scenes* (Nashville, Tenn.: J. J. Sanders and Co., 1992), xxiv.

94. In ibid., viii.

95. In ibid., ix.

96. In ibid., xii–xiii (Kibler's ellipsis, first emphasis added).

97. Ibid., xxiv.

98. Ibid., 47.

99. This account borrows from de Man's description of allegory: "[I]n the world of allegory, time is the originary constitutive category. . . . [I]t remains necessary, if there is to be allegory, that the allegorical sign refer to another sign that precedes it. The meaning constituted by the allegorical sign can then consist only in the *repetition* . . . of a previous sign with which it can never coincide, since it is of the essence of this previous sign to be pure anteriority." Paul de Man, "The Rhetoric of Temporality," in *Blindness and Insight: Essays in the Rhetoric of Contemporary Criticism* (Minneapolis: University of Minnesota Press, 1983), 207. In de Man's view, we must be able to conceive that an allegorical sign departs from a sign that precedes it. In this way, allegory and irony share a similar structure: "[I]n both cases, the relationship between sign and meaning is discontinuous, involving an extraneous principle that determines the point and the manner at and in which the relationship is articulated. In both cases, the sign points to something that differs from its literal meaning and has for its function the thematization of this difference." Ibid., 209. With both allegory and irony, the full figurative meaning of a statement is the total of (a) the literal meaning of the combined signs, (b) that thing outside of itself to which these combined signs gesture, and (c) the thematized distance between (a) and (b).

100. For arguments distinguishing Sedgwick's romance from Hawthorne's writing, see Baym, *American Women Writers*; Gould, *Covenant and Republic*; Carolyn L. Karcher, "Catharine Maria Sedgwick in Literary History," in *Catharine Maria Sedgwick: Critical Perspectives*, ed. Lucinda L. Damon-Bach and Victoria Clements (Boston: Northeastern University Press, 2003), 5–15. For an account of Sedgwick's "progressive" racialism, see Ezra F. Tawil, "Domestic Frontier Romance, or, How the Sentimental Heroine Became White," *Novel: A Forum on Fiction* 32, no. 1 (1998): 99–124.

101. Catharine Maria Sedgwick, *Hope Leslie, or, Early Times in the Massachusetts* (New Brunswick, N.J.: Rutgers University Press, 1987), xx.

102. Dekker, *American Historical Romance*, 45.

103. E. Miller Budick, *Fiction and Historical Consciousness: The American Romance Tradition* (New Haven, Conn.: Yale University Press, 1989), xiii.

104. Mary Kelley, Introduction to *Hope Leslie, or, Early Times in the Massachusetts*, ed. Mary Kelley (New Brunswick, N.J.: Rutgers University Press, 1987), x.

105. In Lucinda L. Damon-Bach and Victoria Clements, eds., *Catharine Maria Sedgwick: Critical Perspectives* (Boston: Northeastern University Press, 2003), 77.

106. Kelley, Introduction, xx–xxi.

107. Judith Fetterley, " 'My Sister! My Sister!': The Rhetoric of Catharine Sedgwick's Hope Leslie," in *Catharine Maria Sedgwick: Critical Perspectives*, ed. Lucinda L. Damon-Bach and Victoria Clements (Boston: Northeastern University Press, 2003), 78.

108. Ibid., 81.

109. Tawil, "Domestic Frontier Romance," 100.

110. Sedgwick, *Hope Leslie*, 5.

111. Ibid., 6.
112. Ibid.
113. Ibid., 15.
114. Ibid., 16.
115. Ibid., 17.
116. Ibid.
117. Ibid., 225.
118. O'Malley, *Keeping Watch*, 9.
119. Ibid., 5.
120. Sedgwick, *Hope Leslie*, 30.
121. Ibid., 34.
122. Ibid., 61, 60.
123. Ibid., 60.
124. Ibid., 164.
125. Kelley, introduction in ibid., xiii.
126. Sedgwick, *Hope Leslie*, 27.
127. Ibid., 29.
128. Ibid., 64.
129. Ibid., 91.
130. Ibid., 123.
131. Ibid., 132.
132. Ibid., 343.
133. Ibid., 295.
134. Anderson, *Imagined Communities*, 35.
135. Sedgwick, *Hope Leslie*, 295–96.
136. In Damon-Bach and Clements, *Catharine Maria Sedgwick*, 75.
137. Michael D. Bell, "History and Romance Convention in Catharine Sedgwick's Hope Leslie," *American Quarterly* 22 (1970): 213–14.
138. Ibid., 221.
139. Ibid., 216, 20, 19.
140. Insko, "Anachronistic Imaginings," 182.
141. Sedgwick, *Hope Leslie*, 145.
142. Ibid., 159.
143. Ibid., 196.
144. Ibid., 304.
145. Ibid., 17.
146. Ibid., 29.
147. Ibid., 73.
148. Ibid., 157.
149. Ibid.
150. Ibid., 159.
151. Ibid., 259–60.
152. Ibid., 35.
153. Ibid., 47.
154. Ibid.
155. Ibid., 66.

156. Ibid.

157. Ibid., 67.

158. Ibid.

159. Ibid.

160. Ibid., 75.

161. Ibid.

162. Ibid.

163. Ibid.

164. Ibid., 145.

165. Ibid., 85.

166. Ibid., 100.

167. Joseph C. Hart, *Miriam Coffin, or the Whale-Fishermen* (Nantucket, Mass.: Mill Hill Press, 1995), xxxiv–xxxv.

168. Ibid., xliv.

169. Ibid., xliv–xlv.

170. Ibid., 18.

171. Ibid., 82.

172. Ibid., 83.

173. Gould, *Covenant and Republic*, 13.

174. Ibid., 2.

175. See Pease's account of the influence of Cold War critics in his introduction to *Visionary Compacts* and Gould's analysis of the liberal canonization of Hawthorne in his introduction to *Covenant and Republic*. Arac's description of the debate over the meaning of the romance in European circles usefully recalls a broader international genealogy of the term: "In calling such a work 'a romance,' Poe recalls the debates over the 'romantic' in German literary theory around 1800, where the mixture of modes, the breakdown of 'classical' genres helped to define the modern, 'Romantic' product of verbal art. The 'novel' (*Roman* in German, *roman* in French) was the name given to this genre to end genre." Arac, "Narrative Forms," 697.

176. Ibid., 608.

177. E. Miller Budick, *Nineteenth-Century American Romance: Genre and the Construction of Democratic Culture* (New York: Twayne, 1996), 15.

178. Ibid., 17.

179. Tawil, "Domestic Frontier Romance," 107.

180. Dana D. Nelson, *The Word in Black and White: Reading "Race" in American Literature, 1638–1867* (New York: Oxford University Press, 1992), 39.

181. Ibid., 55. Gustavus Stadler's account of Sedgwick's *Hope Leslie* is primarily dedicated to understanding the work of national and racial identification enacted by Sedgwick's romance. It does, however, conclude with the claim that the "legacy of *Hope Leslie*'s Magawisca should be to question the degree to which [national and racial] identifications took place neatly and uncritically." Gustavus Stadler, "Magawisca's Body of Knowledge: Nation-Building in *Hope Leslie*," *Yale Journal of Criticism: Interpretation in the Humanities* 12, no. 1 (1999): 54.

182. Brodhead, *Hawthorne, Melville, and the Novel*, 11.

183. Arac, "Narrative Forms," 717, 623.

184. Gould, *Covenant and Republic*, 14.

185. Tawil, "Domestic Frontier Romance," 119.
186. Chase, *American Novel and Its Tradition*, x.
187. Ibid., xi.
188. Ibid., 1.
189. Ibid., 2, 5, 7, 10. In *Hawthorne, Melville, and the Novel*, Richard Brodhead contests Chase's overzealous distinction of American romance from British novel, but even Brodhead describes the romance as a "confliction of fictions" that exploits "the differences of imaginative potential of disparate genres of fiction." Brodhead, *Hawthorne, Melville, and the Novel*, 20, 22. He also suggests that the romance's "epiphanic moments . . . lead us abruptly from . . . a temporal to an atemporal vision." Ibid., 11. Recalling David van Leer's work on Hawthornean anachronism, Lauren Berlant proposes that Hawthorne's fictions "demonstrate the paradoxically non-synchronic nature of any present tense or horizon of experience." Berlant, *Anatomy of National Fantasy*, 11. For Arac, Hawthorne's romances in particular "[break] up the national narrative into minutely examined local units," engaging a protomodernist technique of interruption. Arac, "Narrative Forms," 648. George Dekker comments that "there is an oddity and even paradox in the coupling of 'historical' and 'romance'—since the latter is normally associated with things archetypal and atemporal—so there is an apparent contradiction implicit in the novel's subsuming romance (any sort of romance), because each has so long been used as each other's foil and ideal opposite." Dekker, *American Historical Romance*, 15. And Philip Gould identifies a "syncretic" mix of "biblical prophecy and liberal ideology" manifested as two different versions of historical time that combine in the "early republic's synchronicity of cyclical and progressive time." Gould, *Covenant and Republic*, 57.
190. Berlant, *Anatomy of National Fantasy*, 24–25.
191. Nathaniel Hawthorne, *Selected Tales and Sketches* (New York: Penguin Books, 1987), 105.
192. Hawthorne, *House of the Seven Gables*, 34.
193. Benjamin, *Selected Writings*, 146.

Chapter 3

1. Boym, *Future of Nostalgia*, 6.
2. Lears, *No Place of Grace*, xv.
3. Ibid., 28.
4. Brodhead, *Cultures of Letters*, 133, 25.
5. William Porter, ed., *The Big Bear of Arkansas and Other Sketches, Illustrative of Characters and Incidents in the South and South-West* (New York: AMS Press, 1973), 149.
6. Although Southwestern humor has not directly figured in the growing body of critical writing on whiteness, masculinity, and middle- and working-class identity, an argument seems imminent that will extend the work of Bruce Burgett, *Sentimental Bodies: Sex, Gender, and Citizenship in the Early Republic* (Princeton,

N.J.: Princeton University Press, 1998); Eric Lott, *Love and Theft: Blackface Minstrelsy and the American Working Class* (New York: Oxford University Press, 1993); Nelson, *Word in Black and White*; Nelson, *National Manhood*; David R. Roediger, *The Wages of Whiteness: Race and the Making of the American Working Class* (London: Verso, 1999). For a sense of the long-term impact of Southwestern humor's particular version of racialism, see Edward J. Piacentino, ed., *The Enduring Legacy of Old Southwest Humor* (Baton Rouge: Louisiana State University Press, 2006).

    7. Arac, "Narrative Forms," 630–31.

    8. Ibid., 631.

    9. Giddens, *Consequences of Modernity*, 17.

    10. Ibid., 20.

    11. Ibid., 142.

    12. Ibid., 143.

    13. Ibid., 142.

    14. Ibid., 103.

    15. Nelson, *National Manhood*, 1–28.

    16. Thomas Bangs Thorpe, "The Big Bear of Arkansas," in *The Big Bear of Arkansas and Other Sketches, Illustrative of Characters and Incidents in the South and South-West*, ed. William Porter (New York: AMS Press, 1973), 14.

    17. Giddens represents the current predominating view when he writes, "The primacy of place in pre-modern settings has been largely destroyed by disembedding and time-space distanciation. Place has become phantasmagoric because the structures by means of which it is constituted are no longer locally organised. The local and the global, in other words, have become inextricably intertwined. Feelings of close attachment to our identification with places still persist. But these are themselves disembedded: they do not just express locally based practices and involvements but are shot through with much more distant influences." Giddens, *Consequences of Modernity*, 108–9.

    18. Appadurai, *Modernity at Large*, 179.

    19. The standard accounts of Southwestern humor's practice of social sorting are Walter Blair and Hamlin Lewis Hill, *America's Humor: From Poor Richard to Doonesbury* (New York: Oxford University Press, 1978); Walter Blair and Raven Ioor McDavid, eds., *The Mirth of a Nation: America's Great Dialect Humor* (Minneapolis: University of Minnesota Press, 1983); Pascal Covici, "Mark Twain and the Humor of the Old Southwest," in *The Frontier Humorists: Critical Views*, ed. M. Thomas Inge (Hamden, Conn.: Archon Books, 1975), 233–58; Kenneth Schuyler Lynn, ed., *The Comic Tradition in America: An Anthology* (Garden City, N.Y.: Doubleday, 1958); Franklin J. Meine, "Tall Tales of the Old Southwest," in *The Frontier Humorists: Critical Views*, ed. M. Thomas Inge (Hamden, Conn.: Archon Books, 1975), 15–31. For a more recent recasting of this discussion vis-à-vis the idea of narrative community, see Scott Romine, *The Narrative Forms of Southern Community* (Baton Rouge: Louisiana State University Press, 1999). See also Richard J. Gray, *Writing the South: Ideas of an American Region* (Baton Rouge: Louisiana State University Press, 1997).

    20. Thomas Bangs Thorpe, *The Hive of "The Bee-Hunter," A Repository of*

Sketches, Including Peculiar American Character, Scenery, and Rural Sports (New York: D. Appleton and Company, 1854), 5–6.

21. See Blair and McDavid, *Mirth of a Nation*; Meine, "Tall Tales of the Old Southwest."

22. Thorpe, "Big Bear of Arkansas," 14.

23. Notwithstanding the geographic and other particularities that define these authors, Cohen and Dillingham determine that "a composite portrait is possible." Some of the features they describe seem more the expression of this literature's imagination than the truth of a common historical class:

> The typical Old Southwestern humorist smiled easily but was no clown. He was a man of education and breeding who felt deeply and spoke with conviction. Usually he wanted to talk about politics. Often a devoted Whig, he was convinced that if the nation was to be saved from chaos and degradation, only the honor, resonableness, and sense of responsibility of gentlemen—Whig gentlemen—could save it. Usually he was a lawyer and often also a judge, a state legislator, a congressman, or even a governor, but he might have been a physician, a planter, or, rarely, an actor, artist, or army officer. Frequently he was also a newspaper editor. For the South he felt a protective and defensive love, although he might have been born elsewhere. He was greatly angered by the North, which seemed to show little understanding of the South and its institutions. He defended slavery and, when the time came, secession, with passion. He was a relatively young man, but already he had known frustration, and he was to know a good deal more of it before his life was over. Ambitious and hot-tempered, he endured defeat only with personal pain.

Hennig Cohen and William B. Dillingham, Introduction to *Humor of the Old Southwest*, ed. Hennig Cohen and William B. Dillingham (Athens: University of Georgia Press, 1994), xx.

24. Ibid., xxxix.

25. Mary Louise Pratt, *Imperial Eyes: Travel Writing and Transculturation*, 2nd ed. (New York: Routledge, 2008), 41.

26. James E. Kibler, Introduction to *Georgia Scenes*, by Augustus Baldwin Longstreet (Nashville, Tenn.: J. J. Sanders and Company, 1992), xv.

27. Covici, "Mark Twain and the Humor of the Old Southwest," 233.

28. Longstreet, *Georgia Scenes*, 9.

29. Ibid., 12.

30. Ibid., 12–13.

31. Ibid., 14.

32. Fabian, *Time and the Other*, 1–35.

33. Cohen and Dillingham, Introduction, xxiv.

34. Osborne, *Politics of Time*, 16.

35. Ibid., 16–17.

36. Fabian's account of the anthropological traveler is illuminating in this context: "It was [J. M.] Degérando who [in 1800] expressed the temporalizing ethos of an emerging anthropology in this concise and programmatic formula: 'The philosophical traveler, sailing to the ends of the earth, is in fact traveling in time; he is exploring the past; every step he makes is the passage of an age.' . . . It is in this sense

of a vehicle for the self-realization of man that the topos of travel signals achieved secularization of Time. A new discourse is built on an enormous literature of travelogues, collections, and syntheses of travel accounts." Fabian, *Time and the Other*, 6–7.

37. Walter Blair, "Humor of the Old Southwest," in *The Frontier Humorists: Critical Views*, ed. M. Thomas Inge (Hamden, Conn.: Archon Press, 1975), 65.

38. My discussion of the production of locality here derives from Arjun Appadurai's account of locality. Appadurai indicates that "[i]t is one of the grand clichés of social theory (going back to Toennies, Weber, and Durkheim) that locality as a property or diacritic of social life comes under siege in modern societies." By contrast, he suggests that "locality is an inherently fragile social achievement. Even in the most intimate, spatially confined, geographically isolated situations, locality must be maintained against various kinds of odds." Appadurai, "Production of Locality," 179. He describes the work of social interaction—often called rituals—that goes into producing locality. In other words, he proposes that even before the advent of modernity, locality was a positive outcome rather than simply an inert condition. This view allows him to suggest that even after the advent of modernity, the production of locality continues. Here I offer a rather different version, in which locality is equally modern and equally an effect. This version of locality is not, however, consequent upon the deliberate or considered labor of specific "local" actors.

39. Porter, *Big Bear of Arkansas*, 106.

40. Ibid. (brackets in original).

41. Ibid., 107.

42. Ibid.

43. Ibid., 108.

44. Ibid., 109.

45. Ibid., 111.

46. Ibid., 112.

47. Joseph M. Field, "Stopping to Wood," in *Humor of the Old Southwest*, ed. Hennig Cohen and William B. Dillingham (Athens: University of Georgia Press, 1994), 106.

48. Ibid.

49. On the issue of Indian hauntings, see Renée L. Bergland, *The National Uncanny: Indian Ghosts and American Subjects* (Hanover, N.H.: University Press of New England, 2000).

50. Field, "Stopping to Wood," 106.

51. Ibid., 107.

52. Ibid.

53. Ibid., 108.

54. William Tappan Thompson, "The Coon-Hunt; or, a Fency Country," in *Humor of the Old Southwest*, ed. Hennig Cohen and William B. Dillingham (Athens: University of Georgia Press, 1994), 167.

55. Ibid., 166.

56. E. P. Thompson, "Time, Work-Discipline, and Industrial Capitalism," *Past and Present* 38, no. 1 (1967): 78.

57. Porter, *Big Bear of Arkansas*, viii.

58. Johnson Jones Hooper, *Adventures of Captain Simon Suggs, Late of the Tallapoosa Volunteers; Together with "Taking the Census" and Other Alabama Sketches* (Tuscaloosa: University of Alabama Press, 1993), 12.

59. Brodhead, *Cultures of Letters*, 120.

60. Ibid., 132.

61. Ibid., 125.

62. Zagarell, "Troubling Regionalism," 655.

63. Ibid.

64. Ibid., 656.

65. Murphy, "Replacing Regionalism."

66. Johanna Nicol Shields, Introduction to *Adventures of Captain Simon Suggs, Late of the Tallapoosa Volunteers; Together With "Taking the Census" And Other Alabama Sketches* (Tuscaloosa: University of Alabama Press, 1993), xxii.

67. Hooper, *Adventures of Captain Simon Suggs*, 149.

68. Ibid.

69. Ibid., 152.

70. Ibid.

71. Ibid., 152–53.

72. Zagarell, "Troubling Regionalism," 655.

73. Augustus Baldwin Longstreet, "The Fight," in *Humor of the Old Southwest*, ed. Hennig Cohen and William B. Dillingham (Athens: University of Georgia Press, 1994), 36.

74. Ibid. (emphasis added).

75. Solomon Smith, "Interview with an Editor," in *Humor of the Old Southwest*, ed. Hennig Cohen and William B. Dillingham (Athens: University of Georgia Press, 1994), 79.

76. Ibid.

77. Cohen and Dillingham, Introduction, xxxiv.

Chapter 4

1. Joycelyn Moody traces this burdensome requirement to address white readers, and to do so in rhetorically complex ways, as far back as the petition of "Belinda" in 1783 to the Massachusetts State Legislature, which requested compensation for the time of Belinda's enslavement. Moody argues the following about the six spiritual autobiographies by black women she studies: "While none of the six narratives is a formal legal document like Belinda's, each similarly petitions its hegemonic readership (of which the 1783 Massachusetts state legislature is a microcosmic analogue) to regard its poor, black, and formerly enslaved female subject as both 'a free moral agent, accountable for her own actions' and as one due 'that freedom, which the Almighty Father intended for all the human race.'" Joycelyn Moody, *Sentimental Confessions: Spiritual Narratives of Nineteenth-Century African American Women* (Athens: University of Georgia Press, 2001), 2.

2. Katherine Clay Bassard, *Spiritual Interrogations: Culture, Gender, and Com-*

munity in Early African American Women's Writing (Princeton, N.J.: Princeton University Press, 1999), 92.

3. Saidiya V. Hartman, *Scenes of Subjection: Terror, Slavery, and Self-Making in Nineteenth-Century America* (New York: Oxford University Press, 1997), 24.

4. Giddens, *Consequences of Modernity*, 4.

5. Appadurai, *Modernity at Large*, 3.

6. Christopher L. Miller, *The French Atlantic Triangle: Literature and Culture of the Slave Trade* (Durham, N.C.: Duke University Press, 2008), 49.

7. Ibid.

8. Paul Gilroy, *The Black Atlantic: Modernity and Double Consciousness* (Cambridge, Mass.: Harvard University Press, 1993), 41–71.

9. Frederick Douglass, *Autobiographies* (New York: Library of America, 1994), 15.

10. It is worth noting that when Douglass says that he has never "seen any authentic record containing his age," this does not amount to proof that those records do not exist. As Mark Smith writes, "The deaths of slaves, like their births, were . . . brought within th[e] purview of the clock." Smith, *Mastered by the Clock*, 51. This point would seem to be confirmed by J. Dickson Preston's investigation of plantation records confirming Douglass's date of birth. See William S. McFeely, *Frederick Douglass* (New York: Norton, 1991), 294.

11. Orlando Patterson, *Slavery and Social Death: A Comparative Study* (Cambridge, Mass.: Harvard University Press, 1982), 5.

12. Ibid.

13. Ibid., 7.

14. Henry Louis Gates Jr., "The Literature of the Slave," in *Figures in Black* (New York: Oxford University Press, 1986), 100–101.

15. Ibid., 90.

16. Douglass, *Autobiographies*, 140.

17. Ibid., 264.

18. Ibid., 267.

19. Thompson, "Time, Work-Discipline, and Industrial Capitalism," 73.

20. Ibid., 76. It bears mentioning that Thompson saw fit to accommodate the idea of anachronistic forms of time-work discipline. He writes, for example, "The farm-servant, or the regular wage-earning field labourer, who worked, unremittingly, the full statute hours or longer, who had no common rights or land, and who (if not living-in) lived in a tied cottage, was undoubtedly subject to an intense labour discipline, whether in the seventeenth or the nineteenth century." Ibid., 77. Speaking of "modern mothers," moreover, he writes that, "despite school times and television times, the rhythms of women's work in the home are not wholly attuned to the measurement of the clock. The mother of young children has an imperfect sense of time and attends to other human tides. She has not altogether moved out of 'pre-industrial society.'" Ibid., 79. And near the end of his famous essay, Thompson writes, "[W]e may doubt how far [the imposition of a new time-discipline] was ever fully accomplished: irregular labour rhythms were perpetuated . . . into the present century." Ibid., 90.

21. Ibid., 85–86.

22. Smith, *Mastered by the Clock*, 15.

23. Douglass, *Autobiographies*, 304–5.

24. The slave narrative's use of chronological detail has received a great deal of critical attention. Andrews and Sekora argue, for example, that the white abolitionist sponsors of many African American life writers thought that a convincing slave narrative would be detailed, realistic, and chronological. Emphasizing these constraints, literary history has read these strategies as the trace of white interference. See William L. Andrews, "The Novelization of Voice in Early African American Narrative," *PMLA* 105, no. 1 (1990): 23–34; Wilson J. Moses, "Writing Freely? Frederick Douglass and the Constraints of Racialized Writing," in *Frederick Douglass: New Literary and Historical Essays*, ed. Eric J. Sundquist (New York: Cambridge University Press, 1991); John Sekora, "Black Message/White Envelope: Genre, Authenticity, and Authority in the Antebellum Slave Narrative," *Callaloo: A Journal of African American and African Arts and Letters* 10, no. 3 (1987): 482–515. Moody offers a rereading of this notion of white interference in chapter 4 of her *Sentimental Confessions*. For a discussion of a later version of this methodological issue, see Saidiya Hartman's caveat regarding her use of the WPA testimony of formerly enslaved African Americans. Hartman, *Scenes of Subjection*, 10–14.

25. Solomon Northup, *Twelve Years a Slave* (Baton Rouge: Louisiana State University Press, 1968), 159.

26. Ibid.

27. Ibid., 163.

28. Ibid., 169.

29. Thompson, "Time, Work-Discipline, and Industrial Capitalism," 63.

30. Northup, *Twelve Years a Slave*, 161.

31. Ibid., 161–62.

32. For a more elaborated discussion of capitalist citizenship, see Nelson, *National Manhood*, 46.

33. Joycelyn Moody makes a similar point in *Sentimental Confessions*, where she writes that "to 'read around' the spiritual dimensions present in these books is to neglect an essential and vital aspect of them." Moody, *Sentimental Confessions*, xi.

34. See William L. Andrews, ed., *Sisters of the Spirit: Three Black Women's Autobiographies of the Nineteenth Century*, Religion in North America (Bloomington: Indiana University Press, 1986), 1–22.

35. Ibid., 33.

36. Bassard, *Spiritual Interrogations*, 92. Bassard makes this comment in the context of her discussion of Lee's later, and more detailed, *Religious Experience and Journal of Mrs. Jarena Lee, Giving an Account of Her Call to Preach the Gospel* (1849). Bassard argues for an "intertextual" understanding of Lee's better-known *Life and Experience*. Her characterization of the *Journal*, however, applies to *Life and Experience* as well: "[T]he focus in the journal is precisely on the movement of Lee's body/text as she chronicles an exhausting list of dates, times, locations, audiences, and scriptural texts. From time to time, Lee pauses long enough to relate a brief scene or memorable event, but the bulk of the journal is tightly compressed. . . . Lee is, then, writing autobiography as chronicle." Ibid., 91–92.

37. Jean M. Humez, "'My Spirit Eye': Some Functions of Spiritual and Visionary Experience in the Lives of Five Black Women Preachers, 1810–1880," in *Women and the Structure of Society: Selected Research from the Fifth Berkshire Conference on the History of Women*, ed. Barbara J. Harris and Jo Ann McNamara (Durham, N.C.: Duke University Press, 1984), 133.

38. This is true notwithstanding Frances Smith Foster's comment in *Written by Herself* that "[t]he spiritual narrator's secular or personal experiences are given as means of contrast, as points from which to identify the difference between corporeal and spiritual, and are not allowed to obscure the primary intentions of the narrative." Frances Smith Foster, *Written by Herself: Literary Production by African American Women, 1746–1892* (Bloomington: Indiana University Press, 1993), 60. While it may be true that the spiritual and corporeal development of the narrator are represented as occurring at different registers, this makes it no less true that both journeys look like progress.

39. Andrews, *Sisters of the Spirit*, 27.

40. Ibid.

41. Ibid.

42. Ibid., 28.

43. Ibid.

44. Ibid., 29.

45. Humez, "'My Spirit Eye,'" 134–35.

46. Bassard, *Spiritual Interrogations*, 101.

47. Andrews, *Sisters of the Spirit*, 33.

48. Ibid., 34.

49. Ibid., 37–38.

50. Humez, "'My Spirit Eye,'" 133.

51. Andrews, *Sisters of the Spirit*, 31 (first two emphases in original; others added).

52. For a similar account of the way that the "linearity of chronological time is disrupted from the beginning" of Lee's *Life*, see Carla L. Peterson, *Doers of the Word: African-American Women Speakers and Writers in the North, 1830–1880* (New York: Oxford University Press, 1995), 83–87.

53. Bassard, *Spiritual Interrogations*, 95.

54. Ibid., 93.

55. Andrews, *Sisters of the Spirit*, 29.

56. Peterson, following Victor Turner, similarly argues that itinerant women preachers such as Lee entered the "liminal" spaces opened up by the Second Great Awakening, such as camp meetings, which allowed for the creation of *communitas*. Peterson briefly acknowledges the anticommunitarian nature of these women's liminality when she notes, "[T]hese women often entered the liminal space of *communitas* alone and could remain isolated within it despite the fact that their activities were designed to enhance community welfare. Indeed, these women did not always become part of the *communitas* but rather held an ambiguous insider/outsider status in relation to it." Peterson, *"Doers of the Word,"* 18. She does not pursue this observation, however, but rather immediately consolidates it into a dominant

narrative of extralocal identification and community by framing these liminal spaces as a crucial moment of African American "nation building." Ibid., 19.

57. Moody, *Sentimental Confessions*, 54.

58. Bassard, *Spiritual Interrogations*, 97.

59. Humez, "'My Spirit Eye,'" 138.

60. Ibid., 140.

61. Andrews, *Sisters of the Spirit*, 34.

62. Foster, *Written by Herself*, 63.

63. Ibid., 62.

64. Ibid., 64.

65. Andrews, *Sisters of the Spirit*, 11.

66. In her introduction to *The Slumbering Volcano*, Maggie Montesinos Sale traces the origins of this notion that American national rhetoric is infinitely elastic and thus fully encompassing. For influential readings of "The Heroic Slave," see William L. Andrews, *To Tell a Free Story: The First Century of Afro-American Autobiography, 1760–1865* (Urbana: University of Illinois Press, 1986), 185–88; Gilroy, *The Black Atlantic*, 187–223; Maggie Sale, "Critiques from Within: Antebellum Projects of Resistance," *American Literature: A Journal of Literary History, Criticism, and Bibliography* 64, no. 4 (1992): 695–718; Maggie Montesinos Sale, *The Slumbering Volcano: American Slave Ship Revolts and the Production of Rebellious Masculinity* (Durham, N.C.: Duke University Press, 1997), 173–97; Robert B. Stepto, "Storytelling in Early Afro-American Fiction: Frederick Douglass' 'The Heroic Slave,'" *Georgia Review* 36, no. 2 (1982): 355–68; Richard Yarborough, "Race, Violence, and Manhood: The Masculine Ideal in Frederick Douglass's 'The Heroic Slave,'" in *Frederick Douglass: New Literary and Historical Essays*, ed. Eric J. Sundquist (Cambridge: Cambridge University Press, 1991), 166–88. On nonnational uses of American nationalism, see David Waldstreicher, *In the Midst of Perpetual Fetes: The Making of American Nationalism, 1776–1820* (Chapel Hill: University of North Carolina Press, 1997).

67. Habermas, *Philosophical Discourse of Modernity*, 14–15.

68. Ibid., 11.

69. Boym, *Future of Nostalgia*, 27.

70. Frederick Douglass, *The Oxford Frederick Douglass Reader* (New York: Oxford University Press, 1996), 132.

71. Ibid., 160.

72. Ibid., 161.

73. Ibid.

74. Sale, *Slumbering Volcano*, 173.

75. Ibid., 176.

76. Gilroy, *Black Atlantic*, 68.

77. Walter Benjamin, *Illuminations*, trans. Hannah Arendt (New York: Harcourt, 1968), 254.

78. Douglass, *Oxford Frederick Douglass Reader*, 132.

79. Ibid.

80. Ibid., 135.

81. Ibid., 136.

82. Ibid.

83. Ibid., 137.

84. Ibid., 138.

85. Ibid., 141.

86. Gilroy and Douglass both refer to a tradition that understands "jubilee" as a time, in the Old Testament sense, when enslaved peoples are freed from bondage and an originally just distribution of goods is restored. The same tradition understands "Judgment Day" as the time when the coming of the Messiah accomplishes much the same thing.

Epilogue

1. Cheah, *Inhuman Conditions*, 17.

2. Paul Jay, "Beyond Discipline? Globalization and the Future of English," *PMLA* 116, no. 1 (2001): 43.

3. Ibid., 33.

4. Ibid., 42.

5. Cheah quotes Kant in the following passage: "The humanities (*humaniora*) cultivate our mental powers by instilling in us 'the universal feeling of sympathy, and the ability to engage universally in very intimate communication [*das Vermögen, sich innigst und allgemein mitteilen, zu können*]. When these two qualities are combined, they constitute the sociability [*Geselligkeit*] that befits humanity and distinguishes it from the limitation of animals.'" Cheah, *Inhuman Conditions*, 23.

6. Ibid., 10.

7. Baucom, "Globalit, Inc.," 158.

8. Ibid., 162.

9. Christopher L. Miller, *The French Atlantic Triangle: Literature and Culture of the Slave Trade* (Durham, N.C.: Duke University Press, 2008), ix.

10. Laura Doyle, *Freedom's Empire: Race and the Rise of the Novel in Atlantic Modernity, 1640–1940* (Durham, N.C.: Duke University Press, 2008), 38.

11. Ibid., 39–40.

12. Ibid., 7.

13. Ibid., 12.

14. Ibid., 23.

15. Ibid., 12.

16. Ibid., 68.

17. Giddens, *Consequences of Modernity*, 21.

18. Miller, *French Atlantic Triangle*, 50.

Bibliography

Ahmad, Aijaz. *In Theory: Classes, Nations, Literatures*. London: Verso, 1992.

Allen, Thomas M. *A Republic in Time: Temporality & Social Imagination in Nine-teenth-Century America*. Chapel Hill: University of North Carolina Press, 2008.

Althusser, Louis. "The Errors of Classical Economics: Outline for a Concept of His-torical Time." In *Reading Capital*, 91–118. London: Verso, 1990.

Altman, Janet Gurkin. *Epistolarity: Approaches to a Form*. Columbus: Ohio State University Press, 1982.

Anderson, Benedict. *Imagined Communities: Reflections on the Origin and Spread of Nationalism*. London: Verso, 1983.

———. *The Spectre of Comparisons: Nationalism, Southeast Asia, and the World*. London: Verso, 1998.

Andrews, William L. "The Novelization of Voice in Early African American Narra-tive." *PMLA* 105, no. 1 (1990): 23–34.

———. *To Tell a Free Story: The First Century of Afro-American Autobiography, 1760–1865*. Urbana: University of Illinois Press, 1986.

———, ed. *Sisters of the Spirit: Three Black Women's Autobiographies of the Nine-teenth Century*, Religion in North America. Bloomington: Indiana University Press, 1986.

Appadurai, Arjun. *Modernity at Large: Cultural Dimensions of Globalization*. Minne-apolis: University of Minnesota Press, 1996.

———. "The Production of Locality." In *Modernity at Large: Cultural Dimensions of Globalization*, 178–200. Minneapolis: University of Minnesota Press, 1996.

Arac, Jonathan. "Narrative Forms." In *The Cambridge History of American Litera-ture*, edited by Sacvan Bercovitch, 2:605–778. New York: Cambridge Univer-sity Press, 1995.

Armstrong, Nancy, and Leonard Tennenhouse. *The Imaginary Puritan: Literature, Intellectual Labor, and the Origins of Personal Life*. Berkeley: University of Cali-fornia Press, 1992.

Augst, Thomas. *The Clerk's Tale: Young Men and Moral Life in Nineteenth-Century America*. Chicago: University of Chicago Press, 2003.

Bain, Peter, and Paul Shaw, eds. *Blackletter: Type and National Identity*. New York: Princeton Architectural Press, 1998.

Baker, Houston A. *The Journey Back: Issues in Black Literature and Criticism*. Chi-cago: University of Chicago Press, 1980.

Bakhtin, M. M. *The Dialogic Imagination: Four Essays*. Translated by Caryl Emerson and Michael Holquist. Austin: University of Texas Press, 1981.

Bassard, Katherine Clay. *Spiritual Interrogations: Culture, Gender, and Community in Early African American Women's Writing*. Princeton, N.J.: Princeton University Press, 1999.

Baucom, Ian. "Globalit, Inc.: Or, the Cultural Logic of Global Literary Studies." *PMLA* 116, no. 1 (2001): 158–72.

Bauman, Zygmunt. *Liquid Modernity*. Cambridge, Mass.: Polity Press, 2000.

Baym, Nina. *American Women Writers and the Work of History, 1790–1860*. New Brunswick, N.J.: Rutgers University Press, 1995.

———. "Concepts of the Romance in Hawthorne's America." *Nineteenth-Century Fiction* 38, no. 4 (1984): 426–43.

———. *Novels, Readers, and Reviewers: Responses to Fiction in Antebellum America*. Ithaca, N.Y.: Cornell University Press, 1984.

Beckson, Karl E., and Arthur F. Ganz. *Literary Terms: A Dictionary*. New York: Farrar, Straus and Giroux, 1975.

Bell, Michael D. "Conditions of Literary Vocation." In *The Cambridge History of American Literature*, edited by Sacvan Bercovitch, 2:9–123. New York: Cambridge University Press, 1995.

———. "History and Romance Convention in Catharine Sedgwick's Hope Leslie." *American Quarterly* 22 (1970): 213–21.

Benjamin, Walter. *Illuminations*. Translated by Hannah Arendt. New York: Harcourt, 1968.

———. *Selected Writings*. Edited by Howard Eiland and Michael William Jennings. Translated by Marcus Paul Bullock, Howard Eiland, and Gary Smith. 4 vols. Cambridge, Mass.: Belknap Press, 2002.

Bensaïd, Daniel. *Marx for Our Times: Adventures and Misadventures of a Critique*. London: Verso, 2002.

Bercovitch, Sacvan. *The Puritan Origins of the American Self*. New Haven, Conn.: Yale University Press, 1975.

Bergland, Renée L. *The National Uncanny: Indian Ghosts and American Subjects*. Hanover, N.H.: University Press of New England, 2000.

Berlant, Lauren Gail. *The Anatomy of National Fantasy: Hawthorne, Utopia, and Everyday Life*. Chicago: University of Chicago Press, 1991.

Berman, Marshall. *All That Is Solid Melts into Air: The Experience of Modernity*. New York: Viking Penguin, 1988.

Bhabha, Homi K. "DissemiNation: Time, Narrative, and the Margins of the Modern Nation." In *Nation and Narration*, edited by Homi K. Bhabha, 291–322. New York: Routledge, 1990.

Bischoff, Bernhard. *Latin Palaeography: Antiquity and the Middle Ages*. New York: Cambridge University Press, 1990.

Blair, Walter. "Humor of the Old Southwest." In *The Frontier Humorists: Critical Views*, edited by M. Thomas Inge, 45–82. Hamden, Conn.: Archon Press, 1975.

Blair, Walter, and Hamlin Lewis Hill. *America's Humor: From Poor Richard to Doonesbury*. New York: Oxford University Press, 1978.

Blair, Walter, and Raven Ioor McDavid, eds. *The Mirth of a Nation: America's Great Dialect Humor*. Minneapolis: University of Minnesota Press, 1983.

Boym, Svetlana. *The Future of Nostalgia*. New York: Basic Books, 2001.

Brodhead, Richard H. *Cultures of Letters: Scenes of Reading and Writing in Nineteenth-Century America*. Chicago: University of Chicago Press, 1993.

———. *Hawthorne, Melville, and the Novel*. Chicago: University of Chicago Press, 1976.

Brooks, Joanna. "Colonial Flashpoints." *American Quarterly* 56, no. 4 (2004): 1107–13.

Brown, Gillian. *Domestic Individualism: Imagining Self in Nineteenth-Century America*. Berkeley: University of California Press, 1990.

Brown, Matthew P. *The Pilgrim and the Bee: Reading Rituals and Book Culture in Early New England*. Philadelphia: University of Pennsylvania Press, 2007.

Budick, E. Miller. *Fiction and Historical Consciousness: The American Romance Tradition*. New Haven, Conn.: Yale University Press, 1989.

———. *Nineteenth-Century American Romance: Genre and the Construction of Democratic Culture*. New York: Twayne, 1996.

Buell, Lawrence. "American Literary Emergence as a Postcolonial Phenomenon." *American Literary History* 4, no. 3 (1992): 411–42.

———. *New England Literary Culture from Revolution through Renaissance*. Cambridge: Cambridge University Press, 1986.

Burgett, Bruce. "American Nationalism—R.I.P." *American Literary History* 13, no. 2 (2001): 317–28.

———. *Sentimental Bodies: Sex, Gender, and Citizenship in the Early Republic*. Princeton, N.J.: Princeton University Press, 1998.

Cameron, Sharon. *Lyric Time: Dickinson and the Limits of Genre*. Baltimore: Johns Hopkins University Press, 1979.

Casanova, Pascale. *The World Republic of Letters*. Cambridge, Mass.: Harvard University Press, 2004.

Casper, Scott E., Jeffrey Groves, Stephen Nissenbaum, and Michael Winship, eds. *A History of the Book in America: The Industrial Book, 1840–1880*. Vol. 3. Chapel Hill: University of North Carolina Press, 2007.

Castronovo, Russ. *Necro Citizenship: Death, Eroticism, and the Public Sphere in the Nineteenth-Century United States*. Durham, N.C.: Duke University Press, 2001.

Chase, Richard. *The American Novel and Its Tradition*. Baltimore: Johns Hopkins University Press, 1980.

Chatterjee, Partha. "Anderson's Utopia." *Diacritics: A Review of Contemporary Criticism* 29, no. 4 (1999): 128–34.

Cheah, Pheng. *Inhuman Conditions: On Cosmopolitanism and Human Rights*. Cambridge, Mass.: Harvard University Press, 2006.

Chow, Rey. "The Interruption of Referentiality: Poststructuralism and the Conundrum of Critical Multiculturalism." *South Atlantic Quarterly* 101, no. 1 (2002): 171–86.

Clark, Christopher. *The Roots of Rural Capitalism: Western Massachusetts, 1780–1860*. Ithaca, N.Y.: Cornell University Press, 1990.

Claybaugh, Amanda. *The Novel of Purpose: Literature and Social Reform in the Anglo-American World*. Ithaca, N.Y.: Cornell University Press, 2007.

Cohen, Hennig, and William B. Dillingham. Introduction to *Humor of the Old*

Southwest, edited by Hennig Cohen and William B. Dillingham, xv–xl. Athens: University of Georgia Press, 1994.

Covici, Pascal. "Mark Twain and the Humor of the Old Southwest." In *The Frontier Humorists: Critical Views*, edited by M. Thomas Inge, 233–58. Hamden, Conn.: Archon Books, 1975.

Crane, Gregg D. *The Cambridge Introduction to the Nineteenth-Century American Novel*. New York: Cambridge University Press, 2007.

Dallal, Jenine Abboushi. "American Imperialism Unmanifest: Emerson's 'Inquest' and Cultural Regeneration." *American Literature: A Journal of Literary History, Criticism, and Bibliography* 73, no. 1 (2001): 47–83.

Damon-Bach, Lucinda L., and Victoria Clements, eds. *Catharine Maria Sedgwick: Critical Perspectives*. Boston: Northeastern University Press, 2003.

Davidson, Cathy N. *Revolution and the Word: The Rise of the Novel in America*. New York: Oxford University Press, 1986.

Dekker, George. *The American Historical Romance*. New York: Cambridge University Press, 1987.

De Man, Paul. "The Rhetoric of Temporality." In *Blindness and Insight: Essays in the Rhetoric of Contemporary Criticism*, 187–228. Minneapolis: University of Minnesota Press, 1983.

Demos, John. *Circles and Lines: The Shape of Life in Early America*. Cambridge, Mass.: Harvard University Press, 2004.

Dimock, Wai Chee. *Empire for Liberty: Melville and the Poetics of Individualism*. Princeton, N.J.: Princeton University Press, 1988.

———. "Genre as World System: Epic and Novel on Four Continents." *Narrative* 14, no. 1 (2006): 85–101.

———. "Non-Newtonian Time: Robert Lowell, Roman History, Vietnam War." *American Literature: A Journal of Literary History, Criticism, and Bibliography* 74, no. 4 (2002): 911–31.

———. *Through Other Continents: American Literature across Deep Time*. Princeton, N.J.: Princeton University Press, 2006.

Doane, Mary Ann. *The Emergence of Cinematic Time: Modernity, Contingency, the Archive*. Cambridge, Mass.: Harvard University Press, 2002.

Douglass, Frederick. *Autobiographies*. New York: Library of America, 1994.

———. *The Oxford Frederick Douglass Reader*. New York: Oxford University Press, 1996.

Doyle, Laura. *Freedom's Empire: Race and the Rise of the Novel in Atlantic Modernity, 1640–1940*. Durham, N.C.: Duke University Press, 2008.

Fabian, Johannes. *Time and the Other: How Anthropology Makes Its Object*. New York: Columbia University Press, 2002.

Fetterley, Judith. "'My Sister! My Sister!': The Rhetoric of Catharine Sedgwick's *Hope Leslie*." In *Catharine Maria Sedgwick: Critical Perspectives*, edited by Lucinda L. Damon-Bach and Victoria Clements, 78–103. Boston: Northeastern University Press, 2003.

Field, Joseph M. "Stopping to Wood." In *Humor of the Old Southwest*, edited by Hennig Cohen and William B. Dillingham, 106–9. Athens: University of Georgia Press, 1994.

Fleissner, Jennifer. "When the Symptom Becomes a Resource." *American Literary History* 20, no. 3 (2008): 640–55.

Foster, Frances Smith. *Written by Herself: Literary Production by African American Women, 1746–1892.* Bloomington: Indiana University Press, 1993.

Frow, John. *Genre.* New York: Routledge, 2006.

Gates, Henry Louis, Jr. "Zora Neale Hurston: 'A Negro Way of Saying.'" Afterword to *Their Eyes Were Watching God,* by Zora Neale Hurston, 195–205. New York: Harper & Row, 1990.

———. "The Literature of the Slave." In *Figures in Black,* 59–164. New York: Oxford University Press, 1986.

Giddens, Anthony. *The Consequences of Modernity.* Stanford, Calif.: Stanford University Press, 1990.

Gilje, Paul A. *Wages of Independence: Capitalism in the Early American Republic.* Madison, Wis.: Madison House, 1997.

Gilmore, Michael T. "The Artist and the Marketplace in *The House of the Seven Gables.*" *ELH* 48, no. 1 (1981): 172–89.

Gilroy, Paul. *The Black Atlantic: Modernity and Double Consciousness.* Cambridge, Mass.: Harvard University Press, 1993.

Gould, Philip. *Covenant and Republic: Historical Romance and the Politics of Puritanism.* New York: Cambridge University Press, 1996.

Gray, Richard J. *Writing the South: Ideas of an American Region.* Baton Rouge: Louisiana State University Press, 1997.

Greene, Roland. "Colonial Becomes Postcolonial." *Modern Language Quarterly: A Journal of Literary History* 65, no. 3 (2004): 423–41.

Griswold, Rufus W. *The Prose Writers of America: With a Survey of the Intellectual History, Condition, and Prospects of the Country.* Philadelphia: Carey and Hart, 1845.

Grosz, Elizabeth. *The Nick of Time: Politics, Evolution, and the Untimely.* Sydney: Allen & Unwin, 2004.

Habermas, Jürgen. *The Philosophical Discourse of Modernity: Twelve Lectures.* Translated by Frederick Lawrence. Cambridge, Mass.: MIT Press, 1987.

Hahn, Steven, and Jonathan Prude, eds. *The Countryside in the Age of Capitalist Transformation: Essays in the Social History of Rural America.* Chapel Hill: University of North Carolina Press, 1985.

Harootunian, Harry. "Remembering the Historical Present." *Critical Inquiry* 33, no. 3 (2007): 471–94.

Hart, Joseph C. *Miriam Coffin, or the Whale-Fishermen.* Nantucket, Mass.: Mill Hill Press, 1995.

Hartman, Saidiya V. *Scenes of Subjection: Terror, Slavery, and Self-Making in Nineteenth-Century America.* New York: Oxford University Press, 1997.

Hawthorne, Nathaniel. *The House of the Seven Gables.* Boston: Ticknor, Reed, and Fields, 1851.

———. *The House of the Seven Gables.* New York: Penguin, 1981.

———. *The Scarlet Letter.* New York: Penguin, 1983.

———. *Selected Tales and Sketches.* New York: Penguin Books, 1987.

Hiltebeitel, Alf. *Rethinking the Mahabharata: A Reader's Guide to the Education of the Dharma King.* Chicago: University of Chicago Press, 2001.

Holloway, Karla F. C. *The Character of the Word: The Texts of Zora Neale Hurston.* New York: Greenway Press, 1987.

Hooper, Johnson Jones. *Adventures of Captain Simon Suggs, Late of the Tallapoosa Volunteers; Together with "Taking the Census" and Other Alabama Sketches.* Tuscaloosa: University of Alabama Press, 1993.

Horsman, Reginald. *Race and Manifest Destiny: The Origins of American Racial Anglo-Saxonism.* Cambridge, Mass.: Harvard University Press, 1981.

Humez, Jean M. "'My Spirit Eye': Some Functions of Spiritual and Visionary Experience in the Lives of Five Black Women Preachers, 1810–1880." In *Women and the Structure of Society: Selected Research from the Fifth Berkshire Conference on the History of Women,* edited by Barbara J. Harris and Jo Ann McNamara, 129–46. Durham, N.C.: Duke University Press, 1984.

Idol, John L., and Buford Jones, eds. *Nathaniel Hawthorne: The Contemporary Reviews.* New York: Cambridge University Press, 1994.

Insko, Jeffrey. "Anachronistic Imaginings: Hope Leslie's Challenge to Historicism." *American Literary History* 16, no. 2 (2004): 179–207.

Irving, Washington. *The Sketch-Book of Geoffrey Crayon, Gent.* New York: Oxford University Press, 1996.

Jackson, Leon. *The Business of Letters: Authorial Economies in Antebellum America.* Stanford, Calif.: Stanford University Press, 2008.

Jackson, Virginia Walker. *Dickinson's Misery: A Theory of Lyric Reading.* Princeton, N.J.: Princeton University Press, 2005.

Jameson, Fredric. "The End of Temporality." *Critical Inquiry* 29, no. 4 (2003): 695–718.

———. "Nostalgia for the Present." *South Atlantic Quarterly* 88, no. 2 (1989): 517–37.

———. *The Political Unconscious: Narrative as a Socially Symbolic Act.* Ithaca, N.Y.: Cornell University Press, 1981.

Jay, Paul. "Beyond Discipline? Globalization and the Future of English." *PMLA* 116, no. 1 (2001): 32–47.

Haynes, Sam W., and Christopher Morris, eds. *Manifest Destiny and Empire: American Antebellum Expansionism.* College Station: Texas A & M University Press, 1997.

Johnson, Barbara. "Metaphor, Metonymy, and Voice in *Their Eyes.*" In *Black Literature and Literary Theory,* edited by Henry Louis Gates Jr., 205–21. New York: Methuen, 1984.

———. "Thresholds of Difference: Structures of Address in Zora Neale Hurston." *Critical Inquiry* 12, no. 1 (1985): 278–89.

Jones, Gavin Roger. *Strange Talk: The Politics of Dialect Literature in Gilded Age America.* Berkeley: University of California Press, 1999.

Kaplan, Amy. "'Left Alone with America': The Absence of Empire in the Study of American Culture." In *Cultures of United States Imperialism,* edited by Amy Kaplan and Donald Pease, 3–21. Durham, N.C.: Duke University Press, 1994.

————. "Manifest Domesticity." *American Literature: A Journal of Literary History, Criticism, and Bibliography* 70, no. 3 (1998): 581–606.

Karcher, Carolyn L. "Catharine Maria Sedgwick in Literary History." In *Catharine Maria Sedgwick: Critical Perspectives*, edited by Lucinda L. Damon-Bach and Victoria Clements, 5–15. Boston: Northeastern University Press, 2003.

Kazanjian, David. *The Colonizing Trick: National Culture and Imperial Citizenship in Early America*. Minneapolis: University of Minnesota Press, 2003.

Kelley, Mary. Introduction to *Hope Leslie, or, Early Times in the Massachusetts*, edited by Mary Kelley, ix–xxxvii. New Brunswick, N.J.: Rutgers University Press, 1987.

Kermode, Frank. "Hawthorne's Modernity." *Partisan Review* 41 (1974): 428–41.

Kibler, James E. Introduction to *Georgia Scenes*, by Augustus Baldwin Longstreet, vii–xxii. Nashville, Tenn.: J. J. Sanders and Company, 1992.

Koselleck, Reinhart. *Futures Past: On the Semantics of Historical Time*. Cambridge, Mass.: MIT Press, 1985.

Krieger, Murray. *Ekphrasis: The Illusion of the Natural Sign*. Baltimore: Johns Hopkins University Press, 1992.

Lawrence, D. H. *Studies in Classic American Literature*. Garden City, N.Y.: Doubleday, 1953.

Lears, T. Jackson. *No Place of Grace: Antimodernism and the Transformation of American Culture, 1880–1920*. Chicago: University of Chicago Press, 1994.

Levine, Robert S., ed. *The House of the Seven Gables: Authoritative Text, Contexts, Criticisms*. New York: W. W. Norton and Company, 2006.

Longstreet, Augustus Baldwin. "The Fight." In *Humor of the Old Southwest*, edited by Hennig Cohen and William B. Dillingham, 36–45. Athens: University of Georgia Press, 1994.

————. *Georgia Scenes*. Nashville, Tenn.: J. J. Sanders and Co., 1992.

Lott, Eric. *Love and Theft: Blackface Minstrelsy and the American Working Class*. New York: Oxford University Press, 1993.

Luciano, Dana. *Arranging Grief: Sacred Time and the Body in Nineteenth-Century America*. New York: New York University Press, 2007.

Lukács, György. *The Historical Novel*. Lincoln: University of Nebraska Press, 1983.

————. *The Theory of the Novel: A Historico-Philosophical Essay on the Forms of Great Epic Literature*. Cambridge, Mass.: MIT Press, 1971.

Lynn, Kenneth Schuyler. *The Comic Tradition in America: An Anthology*. Garden City, N.Y.: Doubleday, 1958.

McFeely, William S. *Frederick Douglass*. New York: Norton, 1991.

McGill, Meredith L. *American Literature and the Culture of Reprinting, 1834–1853*. Philadelphia: University of Pennsylvania Press, 2003.

Meine, Franklin J. "Tall Tales of the Old Southwest." In *The Frontier Humorists: Critical Views*, edited by M. Thomas Inge, 15–31. Hamden, Conn.: Archon Books, 1975.

Merk, Frederick, and Lois Bannister Merk. *Manifest Destiny and Mission in American History: A Reinterpretation*. Cambridge, Mass.: Harvard University Press, 1995.

Michaels, Walter Benn. *Our America: Nativism, Modernism, and Pluralism.* Durham, N.C.: Duke University Press, 1995.

———. "Romance and Real Estate." In *The American Renaissance Reconsidered*, edited by Walter Benn Michaels and Donald E. Pease, 156–82. Baltimore: Johns Hopkins University Press, 1985.

Mignolo, Walter. "The Enduring Enchantment: (Or the Epistemic Privilege of Modernity and Where to Go from Here)." *South Atlantic Quarterly* 101, no. 4 (2002): 927–54.

———. *Local Histories/Global Designs: Coloniality, Subaltern Knowledges, and Border Thinking.* Princeton, N.J.: Princeton University Press, 2000.

Miller, Christopher L. *The French Atlantic Triangle: Literature and Culture of the Slave Trade.* Durham, N.C.: Duke University Press, 2008.

Mitchell, W. J. Thomas. *Picture Theory: Essays on Verbal and Visual Representation.* Chicago: University of Chicago Press, 1994.

Mizruchi, Susan L. *The Power of Historical Knowledge: Narrating the Past in Hawthorne, James, and Dreiser.* Princeton, N.J.: Princeton University Press, 1988.

Moody, Joycelyn. *Sentimental Confessions: Spiritual Narratives of Nineteenth-Century African American Women.* Athens: University of Georgia Press, 2001.

Moretti, Franco. *Graphs, Maps, Trees: Abstract Models for a Literary History.* London: Verso, 2005.

Moses, Wilson J. "Writing Freely? Frederick Douglass and the Constraints of Racialized Writing." In *Frederick Douglass: New Literary and Historical Essays*, edited by Eric J. Sundquist, 66–83. New York: Cambridge University Press, 1991.

Murphy, Jacqueline Shea. "Replacing Regionalism: Abenaki Tales and 'Jewett's' Coastal Maine." *American Literary History* 10, no. 4 (1998): 664–90.

Nelson, Dana D. *National Manhood: Capitalist Citizenship and the Imagined Fraternity of White Men.* Durham, N.C.: Duke University Press, 1998.

———. *The Word in Black and White: Reading "Race" in American Literature, 1638–1867.* New York: Oxford University Press, 1992.

Nichols, Charles H. "The Slave Narrator and the Picaresque Mode: Archetypes for Modern Black Personae." In *The Slave's Narrative*, edited by Charles T. Davis and Henry Louis Gates Jr., 283–98. New York: Oxford University Press, 1985.

North, Michael. *The Dialect of Modernism: Race, Language, and Twentieth-Century Literature.* New York: Oxford University Press, 1994.

Northup, Solomon. *Twelve Years a Slave.* Baton Rouge: Louisiana State University Press, 1968.

O'Malley, Michael. *Keeping Watch: A History of American Time.* New York: Viking, 1990.

Osborne, Peter. *The Politics of Time: Modernity and Avant-Garde.* London: Verso, 1995.

O'Sullivan, John L. "The Great Nation of Futurity." *United States Magazine and Democratic Review* 6, no. 23 (1839): 426–30.

"*Our America* and Nativist Modernism: A Panel." *Modernism/Modernity* 3, no. 3 (1995): 97–126.

Owen, Stephen. "Genres in Motion." *PMLA* 122, no. 5 (2007): 1389–93.

Patterson, Orlando. *Slavery and Social Death: A Comparative Study.* Cambridge, Mass.: Harvard University Press, 1982.

Pease, Donald E. *Visionary Compacts: American Renaissance Writings in Cultural Context.* Madison: University of Wisconsin Press, 1987.

Peterson, Carla L. *"Doers of the Word": African-American Women Speakers and Writers in the North (1830–1880).* New York: Oxford University Press, 1995.

Piacentino, Edward J., ed. *The Enduring Legacy of Old Southwest Humor.* Baton Rouge: Louisiana State University Press, 2006.

Porter, William, ed. *The Big Bear of Arkansas and Other Sketches, Illustrative of Characters and Incidents in the South and South-West.* New York: AMS Press, 1973.

Posnock, Ross. "The Politics of Nonidentity: A Geneology." In *National Identities and Post-Americanist Narratives,* edited by Donald E. Pease, 34–68. Durham, N.C.: Duke University Press, 1994.

Pratt, Lloyd P. "Literate Culture and Community in Antebellum Nantucket." *Historic Nantucket* 49, no. 3 (2000): 5–10.

Pratt, Mary Louise. *Imperial Eyes: Travel Writing and Transculturation.* New York: Routledge, 1992.

———. *Imperial Eyes: Travel Writing and Transculturation.* 2nd ed. New York: Routledge, 2008.

Pryse, Marjorie. "Sex, Class, and 'Category Crisis': Reading Jewett's Transitivity." In *Jewett and Her Contemporaries: Reshaping the Canon,* edited by Karen L. Kilcup and Thomas S. Edwards, 31–62. Gainesville: University Press of Florida, 1999.

Roediger, David R. *The Wages of Whiteness: Race and the Making of the American Working Class.* London: Verso, 1999.

Romine, Scott. *The Narrative Forms of Southern Community.* Baton Rouge: Louisiana State University Press, 1999.

Rothman, Adam. *Slave Country: American Expansion and the Origins of the Deep South.* Cambridge, Mass.: Harvard University Press, 2005.

Said, Edward W. *Culture and Imperialism.* New York: Knopf, 1993.

Sale, Maggie. "Critiques from Within: Antebellum Projects of Resistance." *American Literature: A Journal of Literary History, Criticism, and Bibliography* 64, no. 4 (1992): 695–718.

Sale, Maggie Montesinos. *The Slumbering Volcano: American Slave Ship Revolts and the Production of Rebellious Masculinity.* Durham, N.C.: Duke University Press, 1997.

Saxton, Alexander. *The Rise and Fall of the White Republic: Class Politics and Mass Culture in Nineteenth-Century America.* London: Verso, 1990.

Schivelbusch, Wolfgang. *The Railway Journey: The Industrialization of Time and Space in the Nineteenth Century.* Berkeley: University of California Press, 1986.

Sedgwick, Catharine Maria. *Hope Leslie, or, Early Times in the Massachusetts.* New Brunswick, N.J.: Rutgers University Press, 1987.

Sekora, John. "Black Message/White Envelope: Genre, Authenticity, and Authority in the Antebellum Slave Narrative." *Callaloo: A Journal of African American and African Arts and Letters* 10, no. 3 (1987): 482–515.

Sharpe, Jenny. "Is the United States Postcolonial? Transnationalism, Immigration, and Race." In *Postcolonial America*, 103–21. Urbana: University of Illinois Press, 2000.

Sherman, Stuart. *Telling Time: Clocks, Diaries, and English Diurnal Form, 1660–1785.* Chicago: University of Chicago Press, 1996.

Shields, Johanna Nicol. Introduction to *Adventures of Captain Simon Suggs, Late of the Tallapoosa Volunteers; Together with "Taking the Census" and Other Alabama Sketches*, vii–lxix. Tuscaloosa: University of Alabama Press, 1993.

Sklansky, Jeffrey P. *The Soul's Economy: Market Society and Selfhood in American Thought, 1820–1920.* Chapel Hill: University of North Carolina Press, 2002.

Smith, Mark M. *Mastered by the Clock: Time, Slavery, and Freedom in the American South.* Chapel Hill: University of North Carolina Press, 1997.

Smith, Solomon. "Interview with an Editor." In *Humor of the Old Southwest*, edited by Hennig Cohen and William B. Dillingham, 77–79. Athens: University of Georgia Press, 1994.

Spivak, Gayatri Chakravorty. "World Systems and the Creole." *Narrative* 14, no. 1 (2006): 102–12.

Stadler, Gustavus. "Magawisca's Body of Knowledge: Nation-Building in *Hope Leslie*." *Yale Journal of Criticism: Interpretation in the Humanities* 12, no. 1 (1999): 41–56.

Stepto, Robert B. "Storytelling in Early Afro-American Fiction: Frederick Douglass' 'The Heroic Slave.'" *Georgia Review* 36, no. 2 (1982): 355–68.

Stewart, Garrett. *The Look of Reading: Book, Painting, Text.* Chicago: University of Chicago Press, 2006.

Stewart, Susan. *Poetry and the Fate of the Senses.* Chicago: University of Chicago Press, 2002.

Tawil, Ezra F. "Domestic Frontier Romance, or, How the Sentimental Heroine Became White." *Novel: A Forum on Fiction* 32, no. 1 (1998): 99–124.

———. *The Making of Racial Sentiment: Slavery and the Birth of the Frontier Romance.* New York: Cambridge University Press, 2006.

Thompson, E. P. "Time, Work-Discipline, and Industrial Capitalism." *Past and Present* 38, no. 1 (1967): 56–97.

Thompson, William Tappan. "The Coon-Hunt; or, a Fency Country." In *Humor of the Old Southwest*, edited by Hennig Cohen and William B. Dillingham, 165–68. Athens: University of Georgia Press, 1994.

Thorpe, Thomas Bangs. "The Big Bear of Arkansas." In *The Big Bear of Arkansas and Other Sketches, Illustrative of Characters and Incidents in the South and South-West*, edited by William Porter, 13–31. New York: AMS Press, 1973.

———. *The Hive of "The Bee-Hunter," A Repository of Sketches, Including Peculiar American Character, Scenery, and Rural Sports.* New York: D. Appleton and Company, 1854.

Trollope, Anthony. "The Genius of Nathaniel Hawthorne." In *The House of the Seven Gables: Authoritative Text, Contexts, Criticism*, edited by Robert S. Levine, 332–35. New York: W. W. Norton and Company, 2006.

Tuveson, Ernest Lee. *Redeemer Nation: The Idea of America's Millennial Role.* Chicago: University of Chicago Press, 1968.

Unger, Roberto Mangabeira. *False Necessity: Anti-Necessitarian Social Theory in the Service of Radical Democracy; From Politics, a Work in Constructive Social Theory*. London: Verso, 2001.

Van Leer, David. "Hester's Labyrinth: Transcendental Rhetoric in Puritan Boston." In *New Essays on* The Scarlet Letter, edited by Michael J. Colacurcio, 57–100. New York: Cambridge University Press, 1985.

Waldstreicher, David. *In the Midst of Perpetual Fetes: The Making of American Nationalism, 1776–1820*. Chapel Hill: University of North Carolina Press, 1997.

Warner, Michael. "What's Colonial about Colonial America?" In *Possible Pasts: Becoming Colonial in Early America*, edited by Robert Blair St. George, 49–72. Ithaca, N.Y.: Cornell University Press, 2000.

Weinberg, Albert Katz. *Manifest Destiny: A Study of Nationalist Expansionism in American History*. New York: AMS Press, 1979.

Whipple, Edwin Percy. In *The House of the Seven Gables: Authoritative Text, Contexts, Criticism*, edited by Robert S. Levine, 324–27. New York: W. W. Norton and Company, 2006.

Woods, Julian F. *Destiny and Human Initiative in the Mahabharata*. Albany: SUNY Press, 2001.

Yarborough, Richard. "Race, Violence, and Manhood: The Masculine Ideal in Frederick Douglass's 'The Heroic Slave.'" In *Frederick Douglass: New Literary and Historical Essays*, edited by Eric J. Sundquist, 166–88. Cambridge: Cambridge University Press, 1991.

Zagarell, Sandra A. "Response to Jacqueline Shea Murphy's 'Replacing Regionalism.'" *American Literary History* 10, no. 4 (1998): 691–97.

———. "Troubling Regionalism: Rural Life and the Cosmopolitan Eye in Jewett's *Deephaven*." *American Literary History* 10, no. 4 (1998): 639–63.

Index

Acknowledgments

I am grateful to the many people and several institutions that supported the writing of this book. The Nantucket Historical Association's (NHA) Verney Fellowship and the Massachusetts Foundation for the Humanities/Bay State Historical League Scholar-in-Residence Program funded my research on Nantucket. Betsy Lowenstein, Elizabeth Oldham, and Betsy Tyler made working at the NHA and the Nantucket Atheneum a delight. Yale University's Morse Fellowship in the Humanities and Michigan State University's Intramural Research Grants Program supplied me with time for writing. At MSU, Dean Karin Wurst also provided funds to support the book's indexing and illustrations. My thinking on the issue of time in America was significantly improved by commentary from audiences at Yale's Americanist Colloquium and at the Dartmouth Institute in American Studies. Early versions of the arguments included here appeared as "Progress, Labor, Revolution: The Modern Times of African American Life Writing," in *Novel: A Forum on Fiction* 34 (Fall 2000); "Dialect Writing and Simultaneity in the American Historical Romance," in *differences: A Journal of Feminist Cultural Studies* 13 (Winter 2002); and "*Magna Opera Atlantica*," in *Novel: A Forum on Fiction* 41 (Spring–Summer 2008). Brown University gave this book its questions. I trust Ellen Rooney to understand the depth of my gratitude if I say simply that she taught me how to read. Nancy Armstrong has been a characteristically incisive reader of my work and has been supportive beyond measure. Philip Gould knows everything there is worth knowing about American literature, and something more besides. I am glad to have benefited from that knowledge. Leonard Tennenhouse has supplied many different kinds of wisdom. I wrote much of this book in the company of a group whose members included Amanda Emerson, Elisa Glick, Wally Pansing, Gautam Premnath, Kasturi Ray, and Annette Van. I am deeply grateful for their generosity and their insight. Liz Barboza, Denise Davis, and Elizabeth Weed made Alumnae Hall a second home. Stephen Biel, Jeanne Follansbee Quinn, and my students in the History and Literature Program at Harvard made the time I spent there rewarding. At Yale I shared the halls with some remarkable colleagues. It was a particular honor to work alongside Tanya Agathocleous, Sheila Levrant de Bretteville, Elizabeth Dillon, Laura Frost, Amy Hungerford, Nancy Kuhl, Vera Kutzinski, Amy Kurtz Lansing, Sanda Lwin, Joseph Roach, and Michael Trask. As chairs of the English department, Ruth Yeazell and Langdon Hammer were always encouraging and supportive. Wai Chee Dimock deserves a special measure of gratitude for her collegiality, her insightful commentary, and the remarkable example of her work. Jennifer Baker has read every page of this book—many of them more than once—and I hope this tradition will continue. Since joining the English department at Michigan State University, it has been a real pleasure to come to know a new set of colleagues. Stephen Arch, Patrick O'Donnell, Judith Stoddart, and Edward Watts were kind enough to read this work. Pat and Steve have been model chairs of the English department. Zarena Aslami, Aimé Ellis, Jennifer Fay, Scott Juengel, Lynn Makau, Justus Nieland, and Jennifer Williams brightened Morrill Hall. I have also learned a great deal from conversations with a wider circle of colleagues that includes Renée Bergland, Jeannine DeLombard, Michael Drexler, Gordon Hutner, Jeffrey Insko, Gillian Johns, Barbara Ladd, Rodney Mader, Donald Pease, Ezra Tawil, and Lara Vapnek. Michelle Massé made me realize that I wanted to do this work in the first place. Deirdre David, Rachel Blau DuPlessis, and Alan Singer confirmed that realization. Jerry Singerman has been an ideal editor and advocate. The readers for the University of Pennsylvania Press, Jennifer Fleissner and Trish Loughran, were outstanding. I profited immensely from their careful attention to my manuscript.

The kind friendship of Melissa Chmelar, Jonathan Griffith, the Lahiri family, Rita Myers, Brett Vapnek, and Michael Wade has meant more to me than I can say. Charlotte Kastner, Tom Kastner, Susan Pollack, Eric Schoonover, and Christine Treanor made New England a family home. Patricia Villalobos Echeverría and I have been friends since both of us were much younger. I am pleased that when we are together I still feel that young. Having Ada Pratt Boutchard for a sister makes me happy. Our parents, Joe and Sue Pratt, taught us that it was possible—and necessary—to do the things we cared about most. Karl Schoonover is everything and more. This book would not have been written without him, but that is the very least of it.

CPSIA information can be obtained at www.ICGtesting.com
Printed in the USA
BVOW08s1115280716

R7225700001B/R72257PG456195BVX1B/1/P